Thirty Years of Change in Puerto Rico

PRAEGER SPECIAL STUDIES IN
INTERNATIONAL ECONOMICS AND DEVELOPMENT

Thirty Years of Change in Puerto Rico

A CASE STUDY OF TEN SELECTED RURAL AREAS

Dorothy Dulles Bourne and James R. Bourne

FREDERICK A. PRAEGER, Publishers
New York · Washington · London

The purpose of the Praeger Special Studies is to make specialized research monographs in U.S. and international economics and politics available to the academic, business, and government communities. For further information, write to the Special Projects Division, Frederick A. Praeger, Publishers, 111 Fourth Avenue, New York, N.Y. 10003.

FREDERICK A. PRAEGER, PUBLISHERS
111 Fourth Avenue, New York, N.Y. 10003, U.S.A.
77-79 Charlotte Street, London W.1, England

Published in the United States of America in 1966
by Frederick A. Praeger, Inc., Publishers

Library of Congress Catalog Card Number: 66-26558

Printed in the United States of America

DEDICATION

To Luis Muñoz Marín

In recognition of his vital role in the imaginative
creation of new and realistic forms through which
material development becomes the seed for the growth
of the dignity and freedom of the human spirit.

FOREWORD

During the three decades covered by this study, the economy of Puerto Rico has greatly expanded, at first rather slowly and unsteadily but, since 1948, without interruption and at a very rapid pace. Per capita net income, expressed in constant prices, approximately doubled between the early 1930's and the early 1950's and had doubled again by the mid-1960's.

Were it quantitatively measurable, it seems likely that cultural change would be found to have been even greater. Added to the changed patterns of living implicit in the urbanization of an agrarian society and the development of a competitive industrial economy has been the direct cultural interchange resulting from an unprecedented movement of people. A great wave of emigration to the United States started in the mid-1940's and had developed by 1960 into a two-way flow of departures and returns in very large but nearly balancing numbers. Virtually every family in Puerto Rico has relatives and neighbors who have lived for a time in the United States and have become familiar with a society as highly developed and complex as can anywhere be found. Radio and television are omnipresent and bring into even the most remote barrios daily exposure to a culture that has now become more familiar than alien.

Puerto Rico has a jealously guarded Latin heritage and, in spite of many visible changes in manners and custom, its more inward culture remains distinctively Puerto Rican. But even within this, there is now a disposition to welcome and even to seek changes leading to better ways of living. In the traditional societies of most underdeveloped countries and especially in their rural areas, there is little hope for betterment and no such search for change--nor was there in rural Puerto Rico thirty years ago.

Rural Latin America resembles this earlier-day Puerto Rico. The Bournes have described and, in part, measured the results of a planned, peaceful revolution from the traditional toward the modern in ten rural communities in Puerto Rico. They make no claim of universality for the Puerto Rican model but their findings, both positive and negative, are suggestive of possibilities and pitfalls that may be encountered in any such development process.

The first part of their study outlines the central government apparatus of the Commonwealth, with emphasis on agencies and programs most concerned with rural affairs. The second part describes the ten communities under study, internal institutions aimed at improving rural life, especially the Second Unit Schools, and the resulting changes in socio-economic conditions and in personal attitudes.

The study shows that the ten communities have made progress, some more and some less than others. It also makes it quite evident that this progress has come from a combination of internally generated attitudes and efforts plus external assistance from the central government. The same warm humanism with which the Bournes have infused their own report was the solvent that blended all these efforts into service of a common purpose.

In all likelihood no one but the Bournes could have conceived and carried out this study. Puerto Rico is so preoccupied with its future that it pays scant attention to its past--nor would it have occurred to most of us that this model from our past might be relevant to present-day Latin America. The study benefits from the vantage point of time and disenvolvement from which it was carried out, yet it gains even more by reflecting the love of Puerto Rico and respect for Puerto Ricans that marked the devoted efforts of the Bournes in the 1930's. They have been the understanding and inspiring friends that effect the true bonding of any alliance for progress.

H. C. Barton, Jr.
Economic Advisor to the
Legislature of Puerto Rico

San Juan, P. R.

PREFACE

Many studies have been made in Puerto Rico.
The unique contribution of this project lies in the
fact that the directors can look back to Puerto Rico
after a period of thirty years and see many changes
by direct observation. Data collection, interviews,
and information on government programs were used as
checks on these observations. The method used was
in Redfield's sense: "not merely the technique of
observation and analysis, but also the conceptions
which allow us to characterize and compare."[1]

From simple observation and comparison we would
state hypothetically that planned change has been
good for Puerto Rico. This requires a definition of
"good." Any definition of "the good" may be considered
a value judgment, but we believe that, in Einstein's
words, "Every system has its special time and place
values. A time or space judgment has sense only if
we know the system with reference to which the judgment was made."[2]

We, therefore, maintain that what has been accomplished in Puerto Rico in these thirty years can
be considered good in terms of the response of Puerto
Rican society to the demands of the present and the
foreseeable future; the practical and ethical adaptation of means to ends which are recognizable and
acceptable by standards of physical betterment, material gains, the self-respect and growth of individuals and their ability to function in personal and
community situations as members of a democratic society. These are the concepts which have directed
and limited our conclusions, which have formed the
basis of our judgment of Puerto Rico as it is, with
reference to what it was thirty years ago. Where
bias appears, as it must, it is due to our involvement at certain points where significant changes occurred and by an empathy created by long and close

ix

contacts with Puerto Rico and Puerto Ricans. We can
only hope that any disadvantages will be offset by
the advantages of a unique opportunity for observation.

To make adequate acknowledgment of the help
given to us in this study is an impossible task.
Official liaison with the heads of government agencies established by Governor Luis Muñoz Marín, old
friendships of our own and new contacts have all
contributed richly. Factual material was made available for our use and, beyond that, the enthusiasm,
which is so characteristic of Puerto Rican leadership, was shared with us. We want especially to mention the Honorable Teodoro Moscoso, then head of the
Alliance for Progress, for his interest and help in
directing us to the proper officials in AID to consider this study and his later evaluation of it and
recommendation for its use. The cooperation of
Jaime Benitez, Chancellor of the University of Puerto
Rico, and of many members of the University faculty
were of great help.

We pay tribute to the memory of Dr. José Padin,
who was Commissioner of Education when the 1932 study
was made and to whom we turned for encouragement and
counsel. His integrity, wisdom, and wit never failed
us. We honor him as a great man. We also want to
remember Dr. José Osuna, Dean of the College of Education, University of Puerto Rico. His high standards and his vision made possible the creation of
social-work training in Puerto Rico.

Our Assistant Director, Mercedes Velez de Perez,
was one of the social workers who worked on the early
study. Her own distinguished record in the field of
social work since then gave a background from which
we benefited greatly. More than that, her interest
in the material of our project, her insight, her
skills, her sympathy with its purpose and the warmth
of her cooperation have been invaluable to us. She
is the author of the chapter on the Second Unit
Schools.

Maria Pons, our secretary during our stay in
Puerto Rico, was far more than a secretary. Her
efficiency and organizing ability made possible much
of what we were able to do and, as she became familiar with the project, she contributed to both form and
content. For the part of our work done in the United
States our secretary, Mrs. Henry Wheeler, gave us
the benefit of her intelligence and efficiency with
genuine interest.

Belen Serra, of the faculty of the School of Social Work of the University of Puerto Rico, was responsible for the compilation of all statistical
material on objective interviews and her interest
and good judgment were invaluable to us. Angelina C.
de Roca, Research Associate of the Social Science
Research Center, trained our field staff and compiled
all material on the depth interviews with a combination of accuracy and enthusiasm which contributed to
the spirit as well as the content of the study.

Raul Muñoz, Chief of the Section of Planning,
Evaluation and Research, Department of Health, not
only gave valuable advice himself, but made available to us from his staff the efficient and delight-
ful services of Herminia Soegard de Gaztambide and
Carmen Torrech in organizing research materials.

Dr. Howard Stanton, Director of the Social
Science Program in the Department of Health, helped
through his experience, particularly in setting up
our sampling of the ten communities.

The social workers who began their careers in
the Second Unit Schools in the 1930's made very important contributions to this study. Their contributions varied in kind and in quantity, but they shared
the conviction that the creative experience of their
work thirty years ago was a dynamic element in change,
both for themselves--in their professional careers--
and for the country people who experienced the meaning of community.

To our field staff--Elba Iris Rivera Calero,
Victoriano Rivera Cepeda, Miguel J. Fernandez Bjerg,

Esperanza C. de Kwitchoff, and Sonia Mejías, we owe
our thanks for their conscientious work, their interest in the task of interviewing and their understanding of its essential relationship to the plan and
purpose of the study.

The principals and many members of the teaching
staff of the ten Second Unit Schools gave great help
to us and to our field staff. We are greatly indebt-
ed to them for their hospitality and cooperation.

We owe much to all our consultants and to the
many persons in government agencies who gave so
freely of their time. Our special thanks go to
Pablo Roca, who was the statistician of the Department of Education when the 1932 study was made and
later Assistant Chief of the Division of Education
of the Pan-American Union; Pablo B. Vazquez Cal-
cerrado, Professor of Sociology and Cooperativism
at the University of Puerto Rico; Harris Bunker,
Associate Professor of Education, University of
Puerto Rico; José Martinez Almodóvar, Director of
the regional office of the Department of Education
in Humacao; and Helen V. Tooker, journalist and
author, who did the major part of the preparation
of the bibliography. And to Hugh Barton, Director,
Office of Economic Counsel, Puerto Rico House of
Representatives, for his continued interest, encouragement, and counsel.

At the end of our interviewing we talked with
the heads of departments of the government to ask
one question: "What is your dream for the future
of your agency?" All the answers combined high
hopes made practical by actual programs, recognition of weaknesses and problems, an impression of
personal dedication to defined purpose.

Finally, our thanks to the Department of
Anthropology of Cornell University, who made this
study possible by its inclusion in their Studies
of Cultural Change under contract with the Agency
for International Development; to Professor Allan
Holmberg and Dr. Henry F. Dobyns for their interest

and help; and to Mrs. Kay Hanna, Assistant, for her
patience and kindness.

Rhinebeck, N.Y.   James Russell Bourne
                                    and
                             Dorothy Dulles Bourne

Notes to Preface

1. Robert Redfield, <u>The Little Community</u> (Chicago: University of Chicago Press, 1955), p. 1.

2. Max Wertheimer, <u>Productive Thinking</u> (New
York: Harper Brothers, 1963), p. 27.

CONTENTS

Chapter   Page

LIST OF TABLES

LIST OF MAPS, CHARTS, AND FIGURES

Page

Maps

Charts

Figures

GLOSSARY

Achiote	A seed primarily used for coloring.
Agregado	Farm worker living and working on the property of a landlord.
Almuerzo	Midday meal.
Ama de Llave	Housekeeper--who directs the servants.
Anafre	Portable iron charcoal-burning stove.
Arroz Blanco	Milled rice--white rice.
Barrio	Subdivision of municipio-- smallest subdivision (political) of towns or cities--urban or rural.
Batey	Front or back yard--locale for reading the paper to illiter- ates and for holding informal political discussions.
Bohio	A rural hut made of wood, palm leaves or flattened kerosene cans, usually with thatched roof.
Calabaza	Squash or pumpkin.
Carretera	Main highway.
Caserio	Public-housing complex.
Central	Sugar mill.
Commisario	Local political leader.

Consolidated School	A school conveniently located for attendance of children from isolated one- and two-room rural schools--offering instruction in grades 4, 5, 6, and 7--the precursor of the Second Unit Schools.
CRUV	Urban Renewal and Housing Corporation.
Cuadro	Plot of land less than 3,000 square meters.
Cuerda	Approximately 4,800 square meters, or 97 per cent of an acre.
Desayuno	Breakfast.
ELA	Free Associated State--Puerto Rico's political status.
FERA	Federal Emergency Relief Administration.
Fiesta	Festival.
Fiestas Patronales	Celebrations in honor of the day of the patron saint.
Fogon	Stove made of concrete platform with holes to contain charcoal.
Fomento	Economic Development Administration.
Goose	A flatiron heated from an internal charcoal chamber.
Guineo	Banana.
Habichuelas Colorados	Red or kidney beans.

Independentistas	Independence Party.
Jibaro	Puerto Rican term for rural peasant.
Kilometer	Six-tenths of a mile.
Mayordomo	General foreman.
Municipio	A division similar to a township in the U.S.; a city or village within this geographical area is the actual seat of government and gives its name to the whole municipio.
Pan	Bread.
Parcela	Piece of land used for both housing and services in a housing development.
Parva	Light breakfast.
Peso	Coinage before dollar was introduced in 1900.
Pimiento	Pepper.
Plantain	Banana-like fruit which has to be cooked.
Poblado	Small settlement.
Porto Rico	When we took over Puerto Rico in the Spanish-American War Congress changed the name to Porto Rico. Some time later it was changed back.
PPD	Popular Democratic Party.
PRERA	Puerto Rican Emergency Relief Administration.

PRIDCO   Puerto Rican Industrial
                          Development Corporation.

PRRA   Puerto Rican Rehabilitation
                          Administration.

Programas Sociales   The program for parcelas,
                          mutual-aid housing, etc.

Publìco   Cars used for public trans-
                          portation as distinguished
                          from buses.

REA   Rural Electrification
                          Administration--U.S.

Ropero Escolar   Stock of clothing to dis-
                          tribute to needy pupils
                          established in Second Unit
                          Schools.

Rosario   Rosary service.

Tomate   Tomato.

Usufruct   Permanent use of the land
                          under the mutual-aid housing
                          program.

Velorio   Wake.

WPA   Works Progress Administration.

Yautia   Potato-like root vegetable.

Zafra   Sugar cane harvest.

Zapato Escolar   Collection of shoes for chil-
                          dren without them in the
                          Second Unit Schools.

Thirty Years of Change in Puerto Rico

CHAPTER **1** BACKGROUND,
PURPOSE,
AND METHOD

In 1932, a study was made in the areas served
by ten Second Unit Schools of the Department of
Education of the Insular Government of Puerto Rico
and published by the Puerto Rican Department of
Education. A comparison between the findings of
that study and the present situation in these ten
communities forms the basis for the present study.
In 1932, when the original study was made, economic conditions in Puerto Rico were so bad that most
people appeared to feel that the situation was hope-
less. There was the usual pattern of a few wealthy
landowners and businessmen; a relatively small middle class of small-business owners, teachers, professional men, and government employees. The vast
majority of the population was desperately poor,
with all the concomitants of poverty.

Wages were low for the men, and were supplemented in some sections by even lower wages paid to
women for doing needlework. Cut garments were sent
down from the United States to be embroidered or
hemmed--they went through contractors and sub-
contractors and finally to the women who did the
work in their homes. There were no wage controls
and the women were exploited to the hilt. In some
sections of the island one could also see jobless
men embroidering handkerchiefs. There were a few
shops in urban areas where this work was done and
better wages paid, but the majority of it was sub-
contracted rural homework.

Since sugar was by all odds the biggest agricultural activity on the island and was only a six-
month operation, there was necessarily high unemployment for half the year. Even though a tropical

1

country, Puerto Rico's other crops--tobacco, fruit,
coffee, cotton--were somewhat seasonal also.

At that time there were a few farsighted people
who thought Puerto Rico could be industrialized, but
no one seemed to know where to start. There were
practically no raw materials, and freight rates, due
to the coastwise shipping laws, were high.[1] There
was a lack of know-how and the only real asset was
the large number of people willing and anxious to
work--people with a high potential of skill, given
proper training.

Another handicap to industrial development, except in the large cities, was the lack of roads,
electricity, and water. No one wanted to encourage
people to move into the cities, which were already
surrounded by squatters in dreadful slums.

Much as the enlightened people in the government wanted to help, they were held back by lack of
funds. There was an income-tax law, but no enforced
penalties, so the tax was difficult or impossible to
collect. Other sources of taxes and income for the
government were inadequate and the total resources
were insufficient to do even the minimum that was
necessary. At that time, also, relatively little
federal aid was given. How Puerto Rico put its own
house in order and a brighter picture emerged are
part of this study.

Another serious problem for the population was
health. Sanitation in small towns and rural areas
was almost nonexistent, water supplies were pol-
luted; malaria, tuberculosis, gastritis-enteritis
and other diseases were endemic and often epidemic.
The resulting mortality rate was very high and life
expectancy very low. Due to lack of roads, sick
people were carried down the mountain paths on ham-
mocks to the nearest highway, then to be taken to the
municipal hospital, itself not very sanitary. Often
there was no doctor available when the patient ar-
rived, or for some time afterward. There were few
latrines in the rural areas, with a resultant very
high incidence of hookworm.

Overpopulation was a strong contributing cause to the health situation. Parents simply could not feed or care properly for their large numbers of children.

Malnutrition was an important factor in the death rate, not so much from starvation as by lowering resistance to disease. Poor and unsanitary housing was also instrumental in fostering disease and disability. Many of these troubles were due to ignorance. Even though the government spent an unusually high percentage of its income on education, less than half (46.5 per cent) of the children had an opportunity to go to school, and for a majority of these, this meant only third-grade education. Neither could they learn the essentials of healthy living at home, since there were no social workers or welfare services until 1930, and only inadequate ones for some years more.

In 1929, Theodore Roosevelt, Jr., then Governor of Puerto Rico, brought to the island a commission of the American Child Health Association headed by Dr. Samuel J. Crumbine, a pioneer in public health, to study health conditions and make recommendations to him. One of this group, Miss Amy Tapping, was a social worker of experience and imagination. The commission worked in close cooperation with the Department of Health, the School of Tropical Medicine,[2] and other government agencies. Miss Tapping learned that the Department of Education had placed social workers in its Second Unit rural vocational schools. Where extreme poverty is the rule and not the exception, where undernourishment and actual illness are widespread, interest in and understanding of individuals and their circumstances must be the basis for the development of program and work. Fortunately, these goals were a part of the atmosphere of the Second Unit Schools and made possible the use of the social workers as a dynamic factor in their growth and value.

In the year 1930-31, a simple community survey of the families living within the geographic area of each school was made. Ideas flourished and with them

a program was developed. During the summer school
of that year, which all social workers were required
to attend, the program of the 1930-31 school year
was the raw material for further training, which was
directed by the supervisor with the encouragement
and help of Dr. José Osuna, Dean of the College of
Education. General principles of generic social
work were taught, and a critical process of comparison between principles and practice resulted in an
analysis of the past year's work and the creative
development of a program for the ensuing year.

The training was continued in the next summer
school, and the community program in operation the
preceding year was used as the basis for academic
study and new planning for the succeeding year.
The community survey of each locality that had been
made during the first year was studied, and certain
areas of the island were selected, based on the
chief agricultural crop in each--sugar, tobacco,
coffee, fruit, minor crops--for special study. This
study was designed to show actual standards of living and the proportion of income for selected budget
items.[3] Existing problems, though generally known
to exist, were for the first time revealed through
the measurement of stark poverty and specific need.

Fifteen families were studied in each community,
five high, five medium, and five low income levels,
plus three in each community--high, medium, and low--
chosen for special study. The levels were determined
by the social workers who had worked in the communities for two years and were familiar with all families who had children in school. Although the base
of the study was economic, the resulting symptoms
were the specific health problems--tuberculosis,
hookworm, ascaris, and diseases resulting from malnutrition; extreme inadequacies in housing, clothing,
general hygiene and cleanliness; a depressed psychological acceptance of poverty, with related family
and community problems. The illustration of the relationship between certain family patterns and these
problems was clear: The resources for solution were
meager, but respect for the members of these communities was a key to the program. Existing forms of

mutual help, elements of cooperation, appreciation
of the hospitality of the people, of their self-
respect and desire for education, of their work and
of their gaiety and humor were the factors used to
motivate change. (A number of other studies were
made somewhat later which were measurements of the
effect of the program and pointed to future possibilities.)

The work was designed to discover the situation
of the individual school and to differentiate the
program according to local needs; to evaluate and
use all existing resources, through the Insular Departments of Agriculture, Health, Education, and
local organizations where they existed (i.e., municipal doctors, hospitals, etc.); to interpret the
educational program to the local communities on the
existing level of health, economics, and recreation.
No formal welfare agencies existed, poverty was universal, and health was a primary problem in almost
every home.

Even in the early days these schools produced
certain effects in the community which were an au-
gury of what would be done on a far larger scale in
the future. The lack of resources meant that the
effects lay largely in the sphere of social change
as distinguished from economic and in different attitudes. Little could be done to raise permanently
the economic level; only a limited amount could be
done to improve health, nutrition, and a way of life.
What was done, however, did have great significance.

The functions of the workers were outlined in
the Introduction of the 1932 study as follows:

> In such an economic situation as rural Puerto
> Rico presents, a social worker has two func-
> tions, we believe. The first is to make in-
> dividual adjustments and to solve particular
> problems under existing conditions. This
> means an effort on the part of the social
> worker to improve the standards of living
> which are based on the accepted norms of the
> community. We find individual variations in

any community which show that one family
lives better than another one having the
same income.   To understand these variations
and to incorporate the higher standard into
community life, it is necessary to know something of existing norms. The second function of the social worker, as we see it, is,
by research and the data furnished by her
community contacts and case records, to provide material that may in time help in the
solution of fundamental problems. For example, we believe that certain facts in regard to income which this study shows are a
clear indication of serious faults in the
economic order of rural Puerto Rico. Unless
a social worker sees the importance of this
second function, she is to a large extent
the servant of the status quo; if she uses
the present and the particular to guide her
to the future and to general problems she
may help to bring about valuable changes.
We believe that the facts revealed by this
study will be useful in pointing out the discrepancies between the present conditions and
a standard of living that would be acceptable
in any modern civilized community.[4]

If we look back at this 1932 study, the intan-
gibles are difficult to trace but they contributed
to the changing spirit and attitudes of people who
began to realize, however, indistinctly, that their
poverty and their problems--their education, their
health, their standard of living--were of concern to
the body politic.

With new information and understanding of the
present situation--change, growth, and development
since 1930--it becomes clear that we were doing something unique and important at that time; that the
program then instituted has had values for Puerto
Rico beyond its immediate impact on the communities
in which the Second Unit Schools (rural-vocational)
of those days operated.

The idea for the present study grew out of a

desire to see how the great changes which have come
to Puerto Rico have affected the ten communities of
the 1932 study; to see what had happened in thirty
years of change.

In thinking of the possibility of a project in
Puerto Rico as it is now, we saw the study more and
more as something that might be useful as an illustration of planned change and its effect on the
general--emphasizing the rural--society, and the consideration of the applicability to other countries
of the methods and program used in Puerto Rico. A
study of this kind must inevitably include some examination of the general political and economic
changes in Puerto Rico since the 1930's and their
effects on attitudes and class structure, personality types, and group characteristics. Puerto Rico's
Operation Bootstrap has been used as a demonstration
for representatives of the Point Four Program, but
this study deals with the effect of change and the
meaning of such change in actual programs which
might be applied to underdeveloped countries, especially where rural conditions--economic, educational,
political, and social--prevail for a large proportion
of the people. Official policies may fail to reach
down to these levels and have in too many cases shown
a lack of understanding of the deep effect of poverty
and lack of opportunity, with their inevitable social
and political consequences in outlook, social structure, and initiative. Where broad governmental planning touches people where and as they live--as we
believe it does in Puerto Rico--the changes, although
not always subject to satisfying quantitative measurement or predictability, seem to be the essential dynamic element--hope made real, visible, specific, and
applicable.

That certain simple methods of training and
program making were successfully used in Puerto Rico
thirty years ago is significant, as it was the means
of preparation of the people in those communities
for the changes that were to come, as well as providing a technique for training in similar situations
where resources for help to people in need are close

to nonexistent and where individual initiative, resourcefulness, and understanding are therefore at a
premium.

The beginning of change in Puerto Rico may be
variously placed in time according to the age, experience, and point of view of the informant. There
seems to be some relationship between attitudes and
the length of time a program has been in operation,
e.g., the pioneer spirit inevitably diminishes as
the program becomes accepted and routinized. This
may be interpreted as loss or as gain but it does
raise a question general to the problem of social
change: Can there be a dynamism in social planning
which remains constant and where the ongoing process
of constructive change is itself the renewed motivation? If this is possible, it must include both the
integration of research with government structure
and the continuing renewal of the excitement and
creative spirit of those who work on the programs.

The present study is designed to show (1) the
organization and function of planning; (2) government programs which affect the whole island; (3)
the application of these programs in each of the
ten selected areas; (4) the effect of such programs
on individual families, discovered through two types
of questionnaires (one largely objective, the other
interview in depth); (5) the comparison of standards
of living in 1962 with those in 1932; and (6) the
over-all influence of planned changes on the way of
life and the attitudes of the people living in the
ten communities.

Comparison among the communities will be related to the operation of government programs in
each and an evaluation of the effects, selectively
and as a whole.

That there must be chosen priorities for the
development of government plans is obvious, both
because of financial limitations and because judgment must be exercised on which programs are most
suitable for general growth. Therefore, in any
communities which one might select, one must expect

to find an uneven application of programs for
sons other than those directed to over-all pl

PURPOSE AND METHOD

Our purpose in this study is, therefore, first,
to assess the changes which have come to ten selected rural communities in Puerto Rico, studied thirty
years ago, as a result of programs planned and exe-
cuted, or in the process of execution, by the government of Puerto Rico. The difficulty of differ-
entiating between these planned changes and those
which, without planning, are affecting all societies
is recognized. Urbanization, industrialization, new
communications, and greater mobility are touching
more and more societies today. One can only say
that to make provision for the effects of these factors should soften the shock which comes from external influences and should help in the process of
adaptation. We make the assumption that planning
is desirable and proceed first to examine the quality and quantity of general planning in Puerto Rico
and then its local effects as observed in the ten
communities. Second, we attempt to interpret changes
in attitudes and values, in the communities and among
individuals as reflected in their responses to the
questionnaires. Our further hope is that by making
these observations and conclusions available, we can
supply useful illustrations of the effects of induced social changes in a rapidly developing society
characterized by the quality and quantity of directed
plans.

The method used for the collection and analysis
of material and data we divide into three parts.

1. The effects of over-all plans as they touch
the ten communities; the number and degree of application of government programs to each locality.

2. Changes in the ten communities recorded in
(a) descriptions of the communities in 1964 with some
comparisons with 1932; (b) questionnaires to 245 individual residents; (c) 67 individual interviews in
depth.

3. Through analysis of material from 1 and 2, and by free observation, to determine the meaning of observed and recorded change--both material and attitudinal--and to discover whether there is a further process in operation by which observed and recorded changes are transformed into new cultural values, possibly symbolic in nature. Any conclusions of this kind will not be subject to quantitative measurement but may yield answers to questions on "world view," on community and individual demonstrations of self-respect and pride, on levels of aspiration and hope for the future.

No attempt is made in this study to compare urban with rural residents, as Tumin, et al. have done in their study of social class and social change in Puerto Rico, but the importance of their analysis is recognized as an essential part of the background for any study which limits itself to rural communities. "Modern sociological writing is replete with the assumption that the urban environment, compared with the rural, is oriented to change."[5] Evidence of this is clear and pertinent in the quantitative growth of the new middle and lower-middle class which has taken place in the urban areas, and the drawing power of such areas is important in many of its effects on rural communities. Nevertheless, the strength of history and customs of rural living in Puerto Rico have strong counteracting emotional elements. The result for the planners of the future of Puerto Rico is the need to find a viable balance between urban and rural socio-economic factors.

Because the present study takes as its geographical communities the areas served by the Second Unit Schools, we give special attention to changes taking place in the philosophy and the program of the Department of Education in regard to rural education. In their plans the Department recognizes its dual responsibility: the education and development of the rural population and its preparation for modern agriculture and new ways of life which go with it; the educational (vocational)

needs of the young people who will gravitate toward
the growing industrial development--the factories
in small communities as well as in urban sections.

These changes in educational direction and
organization are in the building stage. We agree
with Tumin that the result may affect the "self-
conceptions and self-evaluations and . . . the ways
in which our respondents view questions of equality
and inequality."[6]

The 1932 study was not undertaken as research
primarily, but as a practical way of presenting a
real picture of the socio-economic situation of the
1930's in the ten rural communities for the development of a teaching and organizational program. True
comparisons between the 1932 and 1962 studies are
limited. But beyond these comparisons lies the whole
area of development since the planning programs were
inaugurated. The quality and quantity of change extend out beyond the 1932-62 comparisons and represent the most significant areas of new growth--a different political and social philosophy.

In the preliminary work done in 1962 (three
months in Puerto Rico with a grant from the Department of Education), one of the significant parts
was the revisit by six of the ten social workers--
and several of the home economics teachers--to the
communities where, in the 1930's, they had worked in
the Second Unit Schools. Some material from their
reports will be incorporated into this study.

When, in November, 1963, we returned to Puerto
Rico under the auspices of the Department of Anthropology of Cornell University, our plan for work on
data assembling was twofold: (1) to learn, through
interviews and the collection and assembling of
material, the planning, organization, and financing
of governmental agencies; (2) field investigation of
families in the ten communities--adjusting in three
of the ten communities to population changes, increasing proportionately the 150 families of the
original study. The population of Mediania Alta,
in the municipality of Loiza, and Lapa, in the

municipality of Salinas, had doubled, and in Hato
Tejas, in the municipality of Bayamón, had quad-
rupled.[7]

The work on interviewing and information material was done by the codirectors and the assistant
director.

For the field work a staff of five was selected.
The decision was made that they would work as a group
with a leader for each community, moving from one
community to another according to schedule. Three
were young university graduates, two of whom had had
some previous experience, one in teaching and the
other one in public welfare and business. The study
of group interaction and interpersonal relationships
in the field staff would make a study in itself.
The result was good--not only in variety of points
of view but in the development of group thinking.

The composition of the field staff, and the
fact that only one of them had had actual experience
in rural living, led to certain naive responses to
the contacts with rural life. Impressions of poverty made concrete by few rooms in the houses, scarcity of furniture, primitive sanitary arrangements,
were striking to them in the first communities visited. Although this must be to some extent dis-
counted, it has importance because it was a true
first view of poverty. It is interesting that they
were, simultaneously, impressed by positive qualities in the people who lived in these conditions.

The training and pretesting was done by a member of the staff of the Social Science Research
Center at the University of Puerto Rico. Meetings
were held with her and the field staff, and the codirectors and the assistant director, providing
background and direction. During their work in the
field, meetings with codirectors and assistant were
held on the completion of work in each community.

The preparation of questionnaires began in 1962
in the preliminary study and was carried on to its

final form in January, 1964. Before going to Puerto
Rico in November, 1963, the directors prepared a
rough draft. This was submitted in November and December to a group of the 1932 social workers on the
study of that year with a few additions. Their suggestions and those of several other selected persons, whose standing in the research field in Puerto
Rico is unquestionable, were incorporated into the
final form.

Before the field staff went into the communities, letters were sent by the Department of Education to principals of all Second Unit Schools involved in the study, asking for their cooperation.
This was followed by a visit by the directors to
each community to discuss the project with the
principal. The cooperation received by both the
directors and the field staff was warm, interested,
and most helpful. Each principal contributed from
his knowledge and understanding of the community.

One member of the field staff interviewed representatives of government agencies in each community to determine the extent and degree to which programs have been applied to the particular locality.

The sampling plan was worked out with the Social Research Program of the Department of Health
and carried out by a member of its staff. The description follows:

> Method Used in Sampling for Studying
> Thirty Years of Change in Ten Select-
> ed Areas of Rural Puerto Rico (Done
> by Howard Stanton and Frank Hernandez,
> assisted by Rita Rodriquez.)

The sampling for the study was done by
random selection of the cases. The procedure
employed consists of the following steps:
  1. The universe for each community is
defined in terms of the geographical area
served by the Second Unit School. The boundaries are tentatively established on the
basis of the school census figures provided

by the principal of the school. This information is verified with the help of the community residents when making the housing
survey. There is the possibility that the
school area has been enlarged with the addition of places from which they are now getting children and, likewise, there may be
places which formerly used the school services but are no longer sending children to
it.

2. A housing survey is made and each
housing unit is shown in a community map.
The term "housing unit" only includes inhabited houses or those which, although vacant,
give evidence of having been inhabited recently. Stores, bars, and other business
structures are counted as housing units if
part of the building is used as a dwelling
place. In such cases store clerks or other
employees are asked if there is someone living in the place. When the business structure is closed the presence of domestic
equipment in back of the structure, such as
television sets or external dishwashing cab-
inets or laundry lines, will be taken as
evidence that people live in the house.
There may be cases in which it is specially
difficult to establish this fact.

3. The universe is subdivided among
the different neighborhoods or social sectors as they are known in the community.
The number of cases to be studied will be
distributed proportionately among these
neighborhoods and sectors. Then the numbers are drawn at random and marked in the
community map.

4. Each housing unit selected is then
visited, identified and marked on the map.
The family is advised that within a few days
somebody will visit them for the purpose of
the study.

From two to four cases are selected, in
addition to the sample, to which all the
study instruments are applied. This is done
for control purposes. These cases represent

> extreme situations among the high- and low-
> income groups. This selection is made by
> the field staff following the advice of
> the local residents and in accordance with
> their own observation.

In addition to comparisons between 1932 and
1962 among our ten communities, some generaliza-
tions will be made from our data which conspicu-
ously affect human living in any society. These
are employment and satisfaction in work; health,
with life expectancy, infant mortality, and health
facilities as indexes; comfort in living, illustrated by water, electricity, sanitation, and housing; finally, the freedom of the individual--his
mobility, his education, his recreation, and cultural opportunities, and the effects of all the
preceding categories as they contribute to the individual in his society.

Notes to Chapter 1

1. The coastwise shipping law requires that
all persons and goods moving between two United
States ports be carried on U.S. flag vessels or
planes. Since U.S. shipping wages are higher than
those of other countries, freight costs are necessarily higher. This creates a hardship on Puerto
Rico and the Insular Government has been trying,
without success, to get a change in the law which
will alleviate the situation.

2. Then staffed by Puerto Rican doctors under
the University of Puerto Rico and doctors from the
staff of the College of Physicians and Surgeons of
Columbia University.

3. Luz M. Ramos and Dorothy D. Bourne, Standards of Living in Rural Puerto Rico, San Juan,
Department of Education Bulletin, No. 1, no date.

4. Ibid., p. 5.

5. Melvin M. Tumin with Arnold S. Feldman, _Social Class and Social Change in Puerto Rico_ (Princeton, N.J.: Princeton University Press, 1961), p. 44. Henceforth: Tumin, _Social Class_.

6. _Ibid_., p. 47.

7. U.S. Census 1930 and 1960.

CHAPTER **2** PUERTO RICO:

A CHANGING SOCIETY

One of the phenomena of our times is that the development of nationalism and the loyalty to local or national cultural patterns is so strong in a period of history when all parts of the world are drawn together and face common problems. These problems are the result, as we know, of multiple causes: new contacts brought about by the war; growing trade and interdependence in both natural resources and in manufactures; enormous increase in technological knowledge and skills; new forms of communication; opportunities for physical mobility and recognition of consequent interdependence; the growth of industrialization and the trend toward urbanization; and the developments in agriculture which make these tendencies logical and possible by the increase in agricultural production and the simultaneous decrease in number of farmers needed and the consequent availability of labor for other occupations.

The apparent contradiction between the idea of "one world" and the defense of separate nationalities and cultures can only be reconciled by a psychological interpretation analogous to the need of the individual to know himself, at least to the degree which makes possible a satisfactory and constructive adaptation to his society and his contribution to group thinking and action. Puerto Rico exhibits an essentially nationalistic position in its desire for self-government and in its pride and conscious devotion to its own cultural patterns. But, Puerto Rico is part of the United States, not only politically, not only through financial and economic ties, but also because of the impact of

United States culture on the culture of Puerto Rico.
This is reflected not only in practical involvement
in interests outside its own boundaries, but in a
complex cultural pattern. This impact is sometimes
clearly recognized, accepted and internalized, sometimes felt and unconsciously accepted, sometimes rejected politically and intellectually, but always
present. Because of Puerto Rico's history and its
unique political status it becomes a special case in
the world situation which we now face. It has been
involved for some time in the adjustment of a nationalistic society to a larger entity. Its special
character makes it impossible to consider it a model
for other countries; its particular development cannot be superimposed in toto on any other geographical
or political entity. Nevertheless, many of the factors of change which have been purposefully directed
in Puerto Rico exist in other places and the philosophy behind this direction and many of its practical
applications are adaptable to the needs of other
parts of the world. Each country, each locality,
differs, of course, from every other, but the very
fact that so many problems are shared by all, both
in developed and developing countries, demands an
effort to discover how successful programs in one
place can be adapted and applied in other places.
The culture of each country will shape the mold.
Ruth Benedict quoted an old Indian as saying, "In
the beginning, God gave to every people a cup and
from this cup they drink their life." Old cups may
be broken and new ones must be made, but we still
share the water of life.

    The more obvious examples of change and the cre-
ation of new patterns in Puerto Rico appear at first
sight in the urban communities, where enormous housing developments, superhighways, supermarkets, traffic, industrialization, and commercial activities are
immediately apparent. Such changes, from a predominantly rural society with only two large cities
(Ponce and San Juan) and several small cities (Arecibo, Mayaguez, Aguadilla) to a society which illustrates in such striking form present-day industrialization and urbanization, inevitably affect the rural

areas through population movement from country to
city, and increased communication and transportation.
These new interrelationships are important in both
their direct and indirect effects on the rural parts
of the island. This study will deal with the
changes which have come directly to the ten rural
communities through better access roads, electrification, water, health, agricultural programs, and
education; and those which have come indirectly
with the general effects of industrialization and
mechanization, actual or potential, threat or promise. These inevitably have brought greater mobility,
both toward the cities and between city and country,
increased knowledge of the world outside the community, changes in class structure and consequently,
as a cumulative result, new values and a different
world view. Such a change cannot move with smooth
consistency but

> interaction between individual personality
> and social setting, under these common com-
> pulsions, produces a remarkable array of
> regularities on such apparently diverse
> matters as mobility, media exposure, media
> approval, empathy, news range, opinion
> range, self-confidence (personal potency)
> and happiness. . . . Unhappiness is dis-
> tributed in close proximity to the sense
> of impotency and the lack of empathy.[1]

In any evaluation of a rapidly changing society
one must avoid the danger of a judgment which would
identify the change itself as a social good. No
philosopher, from Plato to the writers of the United
States Constitution, has been able to offer us abso-
lute values for changing societies. What they have
been able to give us is the idea of their own goals,
which we can always use by analogy to show the necessity of an ideal or a dream. Lewis Mumford has said
that "every civilization lives within its dream."
To see an ideal is essential. It gives direction,
motivation, and it makes judgment possible. The actual present goal is a "flying goal"--dynamic, not
static--its end cannot be seen, for it moves on

ahead of each accomplishment. Nevertheless, purpose
must be conceptually defined, for it not only determines direction but also forms the basis for decisions on pragmatic compromise and response to pres-
sures. Progress can be measured only as the process
of change moves in the general direction of the defined purpose.

When, for example, one asks whether or not family patterns and structure have changed in Puerto
Rico in the last thirty years, there must be a reason for the question and an evaluation of changes,
if they have occurred, in relation to goals--a relationship to be measured periodically as progress
toward a goal ideally defined. In the case of Puerto
Rico there is no question that the planners have
such an ideal goal. There is also no question that
the need to change short-term goals is recognized
and immediate attainments influence future defini-
tions. Measurements must therefore be used to mark
progress toward presently defined and articulated
purposes; at the same time it must be recognized
that changes may become the material for future
modification of means and redefinition of ends as
they can be seen at a given time. That there is an
ideal concept for any society alone is unchanged.
It creates the continuum of past, present, and future. Its form is always determined by the multiple
causes which exist in the contemporary scene often
bringing unforeseeable effects on programs; new
forms are determined not only by the thinkers and
planners but by conscious and unconscious reactions
of individuals, groups, classes, by the power structure, by changes external to the particular society,
by political actions and interaction among these
factors.

When interaction loses balance, when one or
more factors have dominant influence, direction may
be changed. In the last analysis revolution may occur which can either reinforce or destroy the ideal.
Practically, decisions affecting the socio-economic
situation of Puerto Rico are constantly subject to
these influences of thought, action, and reaction.

It is conceivable that the balance could be destroyed, as the balance of nature can be destroyed.

Muñoz Marin has said, "Men of conscience who
now have the technological tools to defeat extreme
poverty also have a moral obligation to devise means
to do so." Such a "moral obligation" is recognized
in one way by the Communist-oriented societies, in
another by those which relate their means to democratic principles: freedom of choice and opportunity; a government responsible to the will of the
people. The moral obligation therefore requires decisions as to means which will not violate the ideal
--a consistent relationship between means and ends;
adaptability which guarantees creation, not destruc-
tion.

There is a distinct relationship between social
structure and the development of a planned society
as it exists in Puerto Rico. Questions of social
philosophy become involved when one asks whether
or not a society predominantly composed of an uneducated and economically deprived lower class can be
organized along democratic lines. The situation in
Puerto Rico thirty years ago, when the Second Unit
Schools were established, was certainly one of de-
privation and of a low level of education in the rural zone. One of the purposes of these schools was
to encourage the growth of a sense of community as a
step toward group action, toward a new relationship
of neighbor to neighbor, based on common needs and
interests. Although formal education already enjoyed a high prestige value, this was a form of
education new to the rural communities of Puerto
Rico. It was a step away from complete dependence
on the landlord and therefore the forerunner of a
genuine social change.

As we reexamine the ten communities in this
study, we find that the direction of movement in all
communities is from the traditional to the modern
society; the distance covered varies in each and
shows the irregularities of this progress with the
corresponding satisfactions and discontents of a
people in transition. Individual reactions condition

the process and rate of adaptation. But there is no
doubt that the intervention of the government
through planned programs has touched all parts of
the island--even those which show the least differences in measurable material gains.

The rural communities show no such striking
growth of the middle class as is evident in the
cities, but the tendency is there, and where such
a movement as the Department of Agriculture Programas Sociales is in operation, the physical evidence is noticeable in the parcelas. These small,
neat, concrete houses, close together, individually owned (special conditions of ownership are described later), are a conspicuous change from the
bohios (thatched huts) or huts of wood and zinc
scattered over the mountains.

The latter are still the predominant type of
housing in many areas but they stand in marked contrast to the growing number of parcelas and to the
public-housing developments in many towns in the rural sections. The huts of the old order were very
seldom owned by the residents and even in cases
where there was individual ownership of the house
but not the land, the owner could be evicted at the
pleasure of the landowner.

These are important factors in change from traditional to modern society--symbols both physical
and psychological. But changes in occupation and
education may be even more important; they may be
the most important factor in a new power structure.
Tumin in discussing class says:

> There is, on one hand, the traditional so-
> ciety with its emphasis on land and property
> ownership, resulting in a clear-cut two-
> class society, the wealthy few and the many
> poor. In this society, men can feel worth-
> while regardless of sharp material differ-
> ences between themselves and others . . .
> but side by side with this traditional
> orientation runs another orientation, which
> begins to emerge in Puerto Rico with greater

clarity. It is one in which land ownership
is no longer the overwhelmingly dominant
claim to status. Now new men come to the
fore, with power given to them by new political processes, by advanced skills secured in formal educational institutions,
by ownership of industrial means of production and favored positions in service industries.[2]

Implicit in such new orientations are many difficult transitions but it should be pointed out that
the changes are taking place through growth rather
than revolution; no violent overturn of the class
structure has occurred. To a limited extent the
change began in 1898, when Puerto Rico was forced
to make some adaptations to the capitalistic system
of the United States. New directions, new functions,
and the growth of resources have provided the forms
for the prestige and power structure, at the same
time changing the proportions of the upper and lower
classes--both in numbers and in influence--through
the enormous growth of the middle class.

Changes in class structure can be deliberately
influenced through economic planning but always will
move from an original structure resulting from tradition and culture. But, when the idea of change, the
incentive of improvement, and the catalyst of hope
are introduced through the concept of planning, class
structure ceases to be static. The resulting movement can never be wholly directed even by the best-
defined goals and the wisest planning. A dynamic
situation is, by its very composition, creative.
Dominant middle class values may be affected by new
movement from below, as well as from above.

Some of the changes that arise in relation to
a planned economy concern the type and quality of
leadership and the degree to which individual and local group participation can be initiated and stimulated as a test of the democratic quality of both
the leadership and the planning programs.

In the case of Puerto Rico, political leadership is, and was, from the beginning of the recent changes (1940's with the growth of the Popular Party), of an exceptionally high order. This carries with it certain dangers as well as great advantages. The desire and ability to envision a goal and to take the necessary steps toward that goal are a temptation to do things _for_ people. To educate for genuine participation is a slow and difficult process, but the organization of planning in Puerto Rico provides the machinery which can be used with increasing efficiency and understanding. Some of the evidence, showing both participation and lack of adequate participation, will appear in analysis of the data, but the connection from barrio to high-level planning is there. Greater development of individual participation and local leadership must come and new forms for its exercise must be developed, especially in rural communities. It is a long way from the days of the dependence of the worker on the landlord, but the psychological effects of this change are not yet fully recognized or assimilated. Although many government services are taken for granted now, either as an accepted fact or as a right to be attained, earning a living depends more than ever before on individual initiative. In politics, primaries are no longer perfunctory; every candidate who has been in office for two years must face a contest. This is a new opportunity for individual political action and a new demand for political skills and personal motivation. The fact that over one-quarter of the total budget goes to education and that the program of the Department of Education is increasingly focused on the development of responsible citizenship and its ability to adjust to a changing economy is evidence of concern with the growth of democracy.

It should also be pointed out that Muñoz Marín, in the period when he was building up the Popular Party, first of all established a living relationship with the poor and uneducated; his appeal to them was to use their votes for a program of socio-economic reform and his election was their endorsement of a platform. That he was also able to build

up a group of able and devoted leaders, whose combined intelligence and ability made Operation Bootstrap possible, was a marked achievement. The group
was comparable in spirit and action to the days of
the New Deal, but exhibited more organization and
unity. This was partly due to other movements which
had preceded the coming to power of the Popular Party; the efforts of the United States Government, of
Governor Theodore Roosevelt, of the Departments of
Health, and of Education, the PRERA, and the PRRA,
and, in an outstanding way, of Governor Tugwell.
All these efforts, in each case carried out with
imagination and strong motivation, led most naturally to the concept of planning, and of planning for a
democratic society. Tugwell in The Place of Planning in Society wrote:

> How does it comport with representative gov-
> ernment? It is in fact, the only agency of
> government--or ever suggested for government
> --whose only purpose is to discover and im-
> plement the public interest. And since rep-
> resentative institutions are founded on the
> principle that sovereignty resides in the
> people, it is profoundly necessary for de-
> mocracy. Unless democracy is to be confused
> with permission for some to exploit others--
> which actually is a denial of equality--then
> some implementation of the principle of pub-
> lic interest is necessary.[3]

Planned change characterizes present-day Puerto
Rican society; political status and economic ties
connect it with a larger society. Its nationalistic
aspirations are strong--conscious and unconscious,
sometimes with strong political overtones, sometimes
satisfied by an effort to preserve and create a distinct Puerto Rican culture. How much Puerto Rico
can contribute to the solution of the national-
international problem of our times cannot be fore-
seen but the thrust of its effort cannot be ignored
by those who recognize the problem and are involved
in experiments seeking its resolution.

Notes to Chapter 2

1. Daniel Lerner, <u>The Passing of Traditional Society: Modernizing the Middle East</u> (Glencoe, Ill.: The Free Press, 1958), p. 103.

2. Tumin, <u>Social Class</u>, p. 182.

3. Rexford G. Tugwell, <u>The Place of Planning in Society</u>, Technical Paper 7 (San Juan: Puerto Rico Planning Board, 1958), p. 38.

CHAPTER **3** PLANNING IN PUERTO RICO[1]

Planning is defined and described by Rafael Pico, first president of the Puerto Rican Planning Board: "It is a rational way of projecting the future from the experience of the past and the present."[2] As Pico points out, planning is of ancient origin, and among the Spaniards, was copied from the Romans. A drawing exists of the plan for San Juan, dated September 12, 1519. In 1932, James R. Beverley, Governor of Puerto Rico, brought to the island the architect Harland Bartholomew, who pointed out the need for zoning in San Juan and for a regional plan for the island. The work done by the Puerto Rico Relief Administration (PRERA), 1933-36, which carried out thousands of projects in the island, was limited in its planning by the emergency character of its program but attempted to relate its work to basic as well as temporary needs.

In May, 1942, the first law establishing planning was passed. The act established a planning board to work toward these goals. Its powers and duties were laid out in a master plan approved May 12, 1942.

> The board shall prepare and adopt a Master
> Plan, which shall show, with any accompany-
> ing maps, charts and explanatory matter, its
> recommendations for the development of Puerto
> Rico and may include the general location,
> character and extent of the land, minerals,
> water, vegetation and animal life and their
> present and possible future utilization for
> mining, power, irrigation, flood control,
> navigation, draining, domestic and industrial

27

uses of water, fishing, recreation and the
general welfare; and of residential, commercial, recreational, manufacturing, transportation, institutional, governmental and public utility facilities and operations by
whatever desirable categories, and the possible future utilization and development for
these or other purposes and for the general
welfare.

The Board shall include in the Master
Plan the urban, suburban and rural parts of
the island, but the Master Plan of Puerto
Rico need not include minor resources, uses
or facilities which are of a strictly local
character. The Board may adopt the Master
Plan as a whole or in parts, and may amend,
add to, or itemize it or any part thereof.
The Board may in its discretion prepare a
separate master plan for the possible and
advisable development of any municipality or
its urban area, which may include resources,
uses or facilities not included in the Master
Plan of the island.[3]

These statements make clear the scope and purpose of planning in Puerto Rico. The act of 1942
was made possible by the vision and wisdom of a
group of men of unusual devotion and ability. The
leadership of Governor Muñoz Marín, then president
of the Senate, was essential to the changes that had
taken place. This legislation had many roots in the
past and reflected the influence of many personalities, but without this expressed ideal and its practical organization, Puerto Rico would have been
largely at the mercy of haphazard socio-economic
forces.

This project is designed to show that the
changes which have taken place are good, that they
represent measurable progress toward the goals set
up in the General Purpose and that the organization
of the Planning Board, with its coordinating functions, is competent to continue this progress in
the future.

Although the approach of the Planning Board and its predecessors was concerned primarily with the economic situation of the island they were, sometimes unconsciously, also dealing with the cultural and human problems of developing societies: the changes from traditional to modern ways of life and the difficulties of the transition involved.

The first work of the Planning Board included: a division of engineering, a division of finances for the preparation of the Economic Program, a division of insular industries and services, and a division of urbanization.

Much work was necessary to overcome public opposition and to make clear what the real meaning of planning is and how it protects the individual in the exercise of his rights; it was also necessary to meet objections from some of the government departments which saw in the Planning Board a threat to the development of their respective programs.

In 1950, the Planning Board was assigned to the Governor's office. The Governor would coordinate its work with that of the Office of the Budget and Personnel. The Board would also be advisory to the Legislature and would maintain relations with the municipalities on local matters--revising and approving permanent projects in their relationship to over-all plans.

The work of the Board includes, of necessity, planning for cooperative action between the public and private sectors of the Commonwealth. This has become one of the keys to planned change in Puerto Rico. Both the incentives to private capital and the control of its development characterize the industrial and commercial planning. The establishment of government corporations, financed by the sale of bonds on the open market, demonstrates the possibility of combining patterns of capitalistic and government financing. This has made it possible to finance the initial costs of electrification, water, and other programs, each operating as an entity

within the over-all plan and making available to
communities and individuals improvement in living
standards, sanitation, etc. through the sale of
these commodities combined with the resources of
the Puerto Rican Government.

The Government Development Bank is the agency
responsible for long-term intermediate and short-
term financing through a central system of marketing
bonds. The bank serves public corporations, such as
the Water Resources Authority and the Industrial Development Company, the municipalities and the Free
Associated State of Puerto Rico, represented by the
Treasury Department. The largest proportion of this
financing goes to the public corporations.

Recognition must also be given to the part
played by the Federal Government and private investment from the United States in the economy of Puerto
Rico. Heilbroner has said in his book The Great
Ascent that in developing countries "the necessary
germinal core of industrial capital must be obtained
from abroad."[4] This can come through "trade, investment or aid." In the case of Puerto Rico, all
three are involved, with the replacement of aid by
federal programs applied to Puerto Rico in the form
of matching appropriations and federal financial
programs.

Although Puerto Rico receives far more financial advantage from its political status as part of
the United States than any Latin American country
through a U S. aid program, nevertheless there is
some basis for theoretical comparison. Planning in
Puerto Rico has been based from its beginning on the
analysis and use of all available resources. It
recognized the necessity first to put its own house
in order. This meant consideration of such obvious
requirements as modifying the tax structure and tax
collection and other revolutionary changes in land
tenure and industrial development.

Economic and social planning rest fundamentally
on the natural and human resources of the island.

The understanding of these resources comes first,
and then their use for development. The budget must
represent in fiscal terms the decisions on proportions, priorities, and specific allocations. This
is done by the preparation of a yearly model budget
and its relation to a six-year plan. (In the Department of Health, planning is done through 1975.)
It becomes the blueprint for present and future
organization and growth.

The original budget of the Planning Board was
$100,800 but it has grown with added responsibili-
ties.

According to the plan, the Planning Board stimulates and coordinates the programs of the government departments. A major function is related to
public works--their regulation, coordination and
progress. Through the Governor, legislation is proposed and promoted. The coordinated plan for communities is the basis for decisions on electric
lines, aqueducts, industries (both government-
organized and private), housing projects, parks,
etc. The process of carrying out public-works projects must be in accord with the Economic Program.
Recommendations of the Planning Board are presented
to the Executive and to the Legislature; they must
receive legislative authorization and appropriation;
the Department of Public Works receives detailed
plans, consults the Planning Board, adjusts to the
budget and then submits its proposals to the Planning Board for final authorization. In 1957-58
more than 1,000 projects were submitted to the
Planning Board, of which 950 were approved at a
cost of $46,000,000. The rejection of public-works
projects which do not conform to the over-all plan
is as important a function of the Board as approval.

Coordination with municipal government is carried out through local planning commissions made up
of nine members, including the mayor, the president
of the municipal assembly, three others appointed
by the mayor, and four appointed by the president

of the Planning Board. Minority parties are represented on these commissions.

A division of the Planning Board coordinates
the work of the Economic and Industrial Development
Company, the Departments of Agriculture, Commerce,
Government Development Bank, Port Authority, Urban
Renewal, Authorities for Electrification, Water,
etc. One example of the value of such cooperation
is given in a quotation from Candido Oliveras,
when President of the Planning Board (1961):

> In 1957 there was imported $74,000,000 worth
> of wheat, flour, cattle feed, grains, fer-
> tilizer, refrigerated meat, meat products,
> milk products, flour products and eggs.
> These imports were for the direct consump-
> tion of the people. Some of these, refrig-
> erated products, milk, meat, etc. were sold
> direct to the consumer. In other cases it
> went to the consumer by way of shops for
> bread and other flour products. In other
> areas such as that of cattle feed and fer-
> tilizer, it was used for the production of
> cattle and poultry. We see that these im-
> ports--$74,000,000 represent consumption of
> $129,000,000. We calculate that in the year
> 1974, we can reduce imports to $15,000,000
> due to local production and can increase
> consumption and exports of these products
> to $250,000,000.[5]

A second illustration of the coordinating function was shown when the Department of Education
planned the construction of schools in a part of the
island where the Planning Board schedule had a projected hydroelectric project which would require
flooding the area. The result of cooperation between Planning Board and the Department of Education
led to a change in the location of the proposed
schools to a place which could be used by the inhabitants of the valley when they were moved to a
new site.

Roads must be constructed with a view to industrial growth and to the balance in urban-rural
planning; they must also be coordinated with the
program and financial aid provided by the Federal
Government. It is clearly difficult to separate
urban and rural planning because of their interdependence.

As in all modern societies, the pull of the
cities is felt in Puerto Rico with the corollary
that, as mechanization and the application of
present-day knowledge in agricultural production
become more effective, fewer workers in agriculture will be needed. Although in our opinion planning in and for the rural areas in Puerto Rico is
rapidly catching up with urban and industrial planning qualitatively, much still remains to be done
in working out a balance between urban and rural
communities and their economic interdependence.
The fact that the effort has been made, and is continuing, to bring industries to the rural areas
shows great foresight on the part of Puerto Rican
planners. Throughout the world, as societies mod-
ernize, the trend tends to be to migrate from country to city. If, in Puerto Rico, there can be wise
decisions on where the balance lies in regional
planning it will be a contribution of real dimen-
sions.

The functioning of the Planning Board combines
the ideal and the practical. The need to bring
ideas into conformity with the budgetary resources
makes its actions realistic. The process of pre-
sentation of plans from the government agencies,
the time schedule set up for preparation for legislative action (eleven months), the provision for
public hearings and regard for criticism by the
press, consultations with the Governor, the Secretary of State, the Secretary of the Treasury, and
the Director of the Bureau of the Budget--all these
are the parts of a process that is thoughtful and
orderly and that follows a democratic method.

To decide priorities in planning and in the
long run for proportions in appropriations is the

function of the Planning Board and the Governor.
This is recognized. For decisions preliminary to
the final action for the over-all plans, however,
the heads of government agencies have responsibility not only for practical plans for their own agencies but for value judgments in such planning.
Without this the dream would be lost, the inspiration would die. That the parts must be fitted into
a whole is accepted with the idea of planning, and
growth must come for the organism as a whole. Thus,
education cannot exist as an end in itself but must
be geared to the needs of the society; some areas
of agriculture must be curtailed where it is no
longer profitable, no longer able to absorb the number of workers who formerly lived, however inade-
quately, on the land; schedules for health programs
must be selective because they must combine, in the
proportions which are practicable, public health and
individual care; public works must be used to serve
other agencies according to the general plan but
must also be a source of jobs in an economy where
there is unemployment.

    Therefore, in passing any judgment on planning,
these considerations are all parts of the whole.
General welfare is the purpose, changing as the various parts of the economy move, revised in the plans
devised for the periods ahead. Not everything can
be predicted, outside forces may influence rates of
change.

        It is the destiny of the planning agency to
        accept, from those who define the general
        aspirations, their definition of what ought
        to be, to make this definition precise and
        practical, to show how much of it is feasi-
        ble and how that much can be attained--in
        alternate ways if there are such--and to
        pass this precis on to the decision-makers
        with recommendations, taking it back with
        such modifications, wise or unwise, as the
        people's representatives suggest or demand
        and putting it together again as commanded.
        . . . The planning agency is a coagulator,

a putter-together, a conjoiner which brings
hope into focus and promises into possibility, a protector of reason among competing
imaginative conceptions, a reducer of vague
expectations to measured charts, tables and
maps, a filler-out of strategies with the
stuff of tactical reality. It is sometimes
a killjoy; but sometimes a fulfiller of
dreams.[6]

To imagine, to coordinate, and to make decisions on
priorities--this combines creativity with order and
judgment. This process lies at the heart of Puerto
Rico's progress; it is a symbol of the dream becoming reality. The fact that mistakes are recognized
and changes made, that balance is kept among the
many parts, that no goal is regarded as static, make
up the ingredients of a remarkable performance. It
is, of course, easy--and perhaps sometimes right--
that the interested observer finds things to crit-
icize; no doubt one can see areas apparently neglected, individuals who do not benefit directly
from the programs now in operation, questions on
the priorities selected. But no one can look at the
accomplishments without a recognition of the wisdom,
the dedication, and the effectiveness of the planners in Puerto Rico.

Looking back over the last thirty years in
Puerto Rico, we find great forces at work which are
responsible for both the visible and the invisible
changes which have taken place.

Certain accomplishments of the planning program
in relation to both short-term and long-term goals
can be noted. The following show progress toward
goals:

1. Increased employment at higher wages, more
security, and greater satisfaction in work.

2. Increased life expectancy and health.

3. Increased comfort in living, through new facilities in electricity, water and housing.

4. New forms of economic development through cooperatives, incentives for both industry and agriculture.

5. Greater freedom for the individual through new kinds of mobility, higher income, education, recreation.

Another category could be set up illustrating programs for temporary or experimental purposes. Illustrations would be:

1. Public welfare for employables (pending the increase of employment opportunities); shoes for school children, school lunches, distribution of surplus commodities--all for the improvement of health and physical well-being.

2. The program of Fomento, with its special incentives to industries.

3. Experimental programs such as the coffee program and certain housing programs.

It was such programs as these, undertaken by Operation Bootstrap, which were concerned primarily with essential means for health and economic improvement. Muñoz Marín, using the expression "Operation Serenity," gives the new purpose for the future: "An attempt to give to economic effort and political freedom objectives that can commend themselves to the spirit of man in its function as leader of, rather that of servant to, the economic processes."[7]

It should be noted that the optimistic view of Puerto Rico's future is not universally accepted. Gordon K. Lewis in Puerto Rico, Freedom and Power in the Caribbean, points out the growth of conflicting economic interests, the development of pressure groups--American style--and

> the old cleavage, to take a final example, between the landed gentry and the city commercial interests promises to be replaced,

> as new class lines harden, with a new al-
> liance between land owners and the urban
> business groups. . . . Industrial society,
> as Durkheim has pointed out in a well-
> known analysis, is unique in that it re-
> leases in its members voracious and essen-
> tially limitless appetites for material
> goods and satisfactions.[8]

Perhaps this astringent criticism is a useful
counteraction to any complacency about current performance and could help to give content to the idea
of Operation Serenidad.

We have said little about the political changes
which have been so important to the new life of
Puerto Rico. This study will not take a position on
the question of Puerto Rico's political status vis-
à-vis the United States, which is now being studied
by a committee over a two-year period before making
recommendations to the Congress of the United States
and the people of Puerto Rico. But the great inspiration which Commonwealth status brought about is
essential to an understanding of the motivation for
change. The preamble to the Constitution of Puerto
Rico declares:

> The democratic system is fundamental to the
> life of the Puerto Rican community;
> We understand that the democratic sys-
> tem of government is one in which the will
> of the people is the source of public power,
> the political order is subordinate to the
> rights of man, and the free participation
> of the citizen in collective decisions is
> assured;
> We consider as determining factors in
> our life our citizenship of the United
> States of America and our aspiration con-
> tinually to enrich our democratic heritage
> in the individual and collective enjoyment
> of its rights and privileges; our loyalty
> to the principles of the Federal Constitu-
> tion; the co-existence in Puerto Rico of

the two great cultures of the American Hemi-
sphere; our fervor for education; our faith
in justice; our devotion to the courageous,
industrious, and peaceful way of life; our
fidelity to individual human values above
and beyond social position, racial differences and economic interests; and our hope
for a better world based on these principles.

The Popular Democratic Party's program, adopted
in 1960, contains a series of commitments which required legislation of a budgetary nature. Among
others, the following would be enumerated:

    I. <u>Education</u>
        Construction of 2,000 classrooms dur-
        ing the next four years.

   II. <u>Health</u>
        To provide 1,800 hospital beds during
        the period 1960 to 1964; and provide
        pure water to the thousands of fami-
        lies who are still without this ser-
        vice in the rural zone.

  III. <u>Housing</u>
        1. Property tax exemption up to
              $15,000 for owner-occupied dwell-
              ings.
        2. Sale of apartments in public hous-
              ing projects.
        3. Face the problem of the excessive
              increases in land values.

  IV. <u>Labor</u>
        Introduce social measures to alleviate
        the problems resulting from mechanized
        agriculture.

   V. <u>Agriculture</u>
        1. Provide subsidies for farmers en-
              gaged in tobacco cultivation.
        2. Establish credit facilities for
              small agricultural businesses.
        3. Continuation of subsidies to the
              sugar cane growers.

VI. Transportation and Communication

Construction of 600 kilometers of
highways and the improvement of 500
additional kilometers.

The budgetary procedure is outlined as
follows:

We try to determine in the first instance the minimum sum that would be required to maintain the level of development
that has been obtained. In general terms
we make this determination in the following
manner:

a. Examining the situation in the immediate
past year and for the current fiscal period, and including the following:
1. Funds available during each of the
two respective years (those left
over from previous years and new allocations).
2. Expenditures during the year (work
completed or in the process of construction).
3. Estimated surplus at the close of
the year.[9]

GROUPING OF THE MUNICIPALITIES OF PUERTO
RICO FOR PROCESSES OF PLANNING

Puerto Rico has had extraordinary success in
its effort to raise the standard of living. Without
doubt, this development, which has to some extent
reached all municipalities on the island, has not
been carried out with the same vigor and effectiveness in all, and efforts to equalize advantages are
the purpose of the long-term regional plan. Certain
municipalities, especially those of the metropolitan
area of San Juan, have absorbed the greater part of
the development, although others have also made
great gains. Imbalance occurs in the net increase
of income among the municipalities; opportunity for
employment varies greatly; concentration of population, particularly in the San Juan area, intensifies
differences in the economic level between it and

smaller municipalities. The uneven development
among municipalities is illustrated by the influx
into Bayamón (part of the San Juan metropolitan
area) which showed (1950-60) a 341.9 per cent increase in population. The municipality of Arroyo,
on the other hand, showed 14.1 per cent while the
increase for the whole island was 129.5 per cent.
Others actually showed a decrease. Uneven employment opportunity was, of course, the chief reason--
San Juan alone providing 19,203 new jobs.

It is natural that private investment should
establish new industries, businesses, and services
in those areas where development is easiest. It is
necessary for industry to share common services and
therefore to establish its location with regard to
facilities and the availability of labor. But the
metropolitan areas face special problems because
the resources for the development of good living
are not equal to the rapid increase of population.
To offset the disadvantages, the Development Company
works on a principle of decentralization of industry
to relieve this pressure.

The Planning Board, beginning in 1957, has been
studying and formulating plans for regional development in order to orient the growth in such a way as
to give to the whole island the benefits which ac-
crue from employment and the services which the government can provide as a result of increasing prosperity. The following outline gives the points considered for development:

1. The underlying purpose of the government
has been to minimize the socio-economic differences
which exist among the municipalities in Puerto Rico.

2. In order to establish a pattern for the location of business, industry and services, the accessibility of the principal ports was the first consideration. This was decided for three basic reasons:

a. The island imports a high percentage of articles
    for local consumption.

b. Puerto Rico, because of the limitations of its
    own size, does not constitute a market adequate
    to absorb its industrial products, and there-
    fore, depends on exterior markets, especially
    the United States.

c. The type of industry which has been established
    and has the greatest potentiality of growth in
    Puerto Rico imports all, or nearly all, its raw
    materials.

Therefore, based on these criteria, the three
chief regions for the island have been established
as the cities of San Juan, Ponce, and Mayaguez,
where the main ports are located.[10]

The setting up of these regions represented,
first, the need to formulate plans for the growth of
these as urban centers--for social and economic development according to a major urban plan. Following this came the study of possibilities for making
certain municipalities in each of the regions surrounding these cities accessible for the other municipalities within the regions--a grouping based on
topography, roads, transportation, and the accompanying changes from traditional to modern ways of life.

The subcenters, though showing orientation toward the center, manifest vast differences and become important in the regional grouping as areas for
development, as well as in their relation to the
main center of the region. For example, one group
of municipalities in the Ponce area already has a
high degree of industrialization. Here are located
the large oil refineries, and other commercial and
industrial development, with resulting higher economic levels. The other sector of the Ponce region
reaches into the most remote mountains with scattered agricultural population (one of the municipalities in this section is Adjuntas, where one of our
study communities is located), and the towns of
Jayuya and Adjuntas as centers. The development of
two such disparate sections requires entirely different types of planning. Similarly, in the San

Juan area, there are isolated municipalities--
Orocovis and Barranquitas. Here, agricultural workers represent 46 per cent of the population and the
standard of living is among the lowest in the island.

Obviously, then, the plan is not based on homo-
geneity within these regions, but rather on the functional interaction among the several municipalities
within each region and their direction toward the
center. As one index of this, the movement of workers from one municipality to another was analyzed:
among the residents, those who were employed elsewhere and where they worked; among the nonresident
workers, the places where they were employed. The
transportation facilities and use were also studied
and it was found that the three regions were the
logical centers from this standpoint; the most distant places were no more than ninety minutes from
one of the centers and were near enough to a subcenter of the region to make each regional division
practical as a plan for development.

The following factors are considered significant in the establishment of the three regions:

1.   Availability of ports
2.   Existing metropolitan areas
3.   Political organization
4.   Concentration of population
5.   Distribution of industrial employment
6.   Commercial sales and services per capita
7.   Economic levels
8.   Number of nonresident employees

Taking these factors as a point of departure,
the area of influence of each of these metropolitan
areas was determined. The most important was the
evaluation of the degree of dependence of the municipalities on the center or subcenter and the accessibility of these centers for further development.

The characteristics analyzed were the following:

1. Administrative divisions used by the different government agencies and corporations. These
divisions of regions and subregions of the Planning
Board cross other established regional divisions of
government agencies already in operation. These remain as practical administrative units. The Planning Board must, of course, take into consideration
in over-all planning the practical requirements of
these agencies in carrying out their respective programs.

2. The movement of employees--i.e., the analysis of the relation between residents and place of
work of the workers in each municipality in Puerto
Rico.

3. The availability of transportation and the
distance in time of each municipality from the center.

4. The geographic location of the municipalities with respect to the urban centers (this included analysis of physical conditions, topography,
and whether these limited or furthered the accessibility of each municipality).

The first requirement in the area studies was
the specific possibility for maximum development of
potentialities, minimizing of isolation in the distant municipalities, and the amelioration of the
limitations which interfere with progress.

In setting up subregions, the most prosperous
areas were selected on the grounds that these formed
the centers within the region. Clearly, the index
of prosperity can only be used in a relative sense
and is not universally applicable to all municipalities within a region, but each of the subregions
has as its center the most prosperous municipality.

One of the tests in analysis of the three centers was the number of residents from other municipalities who travel daily to work in these cities.
In 1960, a total of 25,964 workers were employed in

San Juan who were not residents of this municipality; and in Ponce there was a registration of 2,892
such persons; in Mayaguez--a total of 2,712.

The comparison of the figures for the three
main urban zones, with statistics for the rest of
the municipalities of the island, show effectively
that San Juan, Ponce, and Mayaguez are the principal sources of employment in Puerto Rico.

REGIONS AND SUBREGIONS

```
San Juan Region I
        Sub Bayamón      - Hato Lejas
         "  Caguas       - Juncos - Mangó
         "  Loiza        - Rio Grande - Medianía Alta
         "  Cayey        - Cidra - Bayamón
         "  Arecibo      - Sabana Hoyos
Ponce Region II
        Sub Adjuntas     - Yahuecas
         "  Juana Dias   - Collores
         "  Salinas      - Lapa
Mayaguez Region III
        Sub Moca         - Voladores
         "  Aguadilla    - San Antonio
```

As an illustration of the separate jurisdic-
tions of individual government agencies, the plans
of both the Department of Health and the Department
of Education may be cited. In each case, the regional plans now considered in these departments represent fresh research, reexamination of old divisions
of organization, and a program of decentralization.
This shows that the opportunity exists, within the
over-all programs of the Planning Board, for the
flexibility recognized as a necessary ingredient in
the best adaptation of departmental organization to
special needs of the population. Decentralization
would mean that the regions would become autonomous
in certain respects but it would involve also--and
more importantly--the coordination of services within each region. As far as the development of new
methods of the democratic process within a complex

Planning Regions and Sub-regions as Defined by Planning Board as of 1962

LEGEND

———————— Region Boundary

- - - - - - - - Subregion Boundary

———————— Municipality Boundary

A Subregion Fajardo

society are concerned, these new forms of organization are striking examples of the ability and the
confidence of Puerto Ricans to experiment, to test,
and to create.[11]

The description of the Department of Health experiment, using Bayamón as the experimental region,
includes too much detail for this report, but the
general aim was to "assure a higher quality of
health services by providing better opportunities
for professional growth to medical and allied personnel and by allowing the utilization of their
professional skills at the highest possible degree
of efficiency." This required new forms of communication, the integration of clinical services,
physicians from (formerly) municipal hospitals becoming members of the staff of the base hospital,
and chiefs of clinical services in the regional base
hospital carrying consultative and supervisory responsibilities for local functioning of health centers. In certain fields of medicine, where use of
laboratories and specialists are most necessary, the
regional hospital, in the case of the Bayamón region, affiliated with the University of Puerto Rico
medical school. The base hospital has special resources to offer but the flow of patients, of education, and of services is a two-way one between local
and regional centers. The full organization and administration of the regional idea includes changes
in nursing services along lines of community health
service, nutrition, etc.; public health, including
environmental sanitation, the training of inspec-
tors, control of communicable diseases; health education.

If this program is found good and extended to
other regions, it will change completely the present
form of administration which is described in the following quotation:

> In the present centralized organization and
> administration of the Department of Health
> of the Commonwealth of Puerto Rico (see sec-
> tion on reorganization of the Department of
> Health) all major and important decisions

are made at the central departmental office,
by the Secretary himself or by division or
bureau chiefs by virtue of authority dele-
gated to them. Personnel working on intermediate or local echelons of the organization have very little, if any, participation
in program planning activities conducted at
the level of the offices of the Secretary
of Health. A two-way communication system
is missing. Thus, the central level issues
orders and the intermediate local levels
follow orders.

This organizational and operational
setup is responsible outside the Bayamon region, and still to some extent inside the
region, for the uncoordinated, unrelated operation of health and welfare institutions
throughout the island of Puerto Rico. Thus,
in municipalities, public health units, public welfare units, and hospital units the
services are geographically integrated in
a health center, but professionally operate
in a vacuum. Although these units serve the
same clientele, the by-products of this organizational setup is a situation in which
there are overlappings of programs on the
one hand, and gaps in programs on the other.

At the regional or district level general hospitals operate as separate organizational units of service. Their only relationship with local health and welfare
centers is along one-way avenues of communication by which service is given to patients
from these centers on a referral basis.
There are no professional relationships between the technical staffs of the health
and welfare centers and those of the general
district hospitals.[12]

There are five proposed regions for health services. In the Bayamón region Health and Welfare
will be integrated; in the others welfare services
will continue their own programs and all welfare activities will be under the direction of a Deputy

Secretary of Health. The general health care program will be directed by a Deputy Secretary of
Health. Both deputy directors will be responsible
for the coordination of the two programs.[13]

SUBURBAN PLANNING

A special program for planning suburban development has been started. In these plans it is recognized that closer cooperation is needed between
agricultural and urban planning; in this CRUV (Urban Renewal and Housing) must be more concerned as
suburban communities grow and the separation between urban and rural becomes less distinct. The
Planning Board envisages a "green belt" as part of
this new suburban development and sees also the
changing distinctions among urban, semirural, and
suburban. It has the hope that communities may develop, or be developed, in which there will be a
mixture of classes in which public housing may be
included and where there will be increased opportunity for upward mobility. From an economic standpoint, municipal services--electricity, water, sewage, etc.--can be better provided where population
density is greater and adjustments to this need can
be made. Those communities or areas which remain
truly rural do not at present come within this
category.

POPULATION

The problem of population control cannot be
adequately dealt with in this study, but neither can
it be completely ignored. Its bearing on economic
and social improvement is no greater and no less
than in other parts of the world; in other words,
the danger exists that population increase can offset the advantages of economic growth.

> The implications of the present patterns of
> fertility and mortality for future popula-
> tions have great significance, particularly
> in view of the national aspirations of the

less developed areas for improving levels
of living. To achieve higher levels of
living, income per capita must, of course,
be increased. Planners must, therefore,
be aware of what the prospects are for future population to be able to set desired
economic goals and lay plans for their
achievement.

By the end of the century, Latin America will have the most rapidly growing population, more than trebling to reach a total of 650 million from a level of about
200 million.[14]

This quotation serves as preface to what must
be said about the effect of population on the future
of Puerto Rico. In the 1930's Puerto Rico was a
heavily overpopulated island. The actual increase
and the rate were both among the highest in the
world.

The Planning Board has prepared an elaborate
Analisis de Población (Informo Preliminar), 1940-80.
This analysis deals with both quantitative and qualitative factors of the population question and gives
the following points of view for its report:

1. We know that population is a field
of both quantitative and qualitative data.
These data answer for us the when and the
where of population In this phase we are
interested in the growth, in the vital statistics, in the quality, composition and
distribution of the population.
2. We know that population is a dynamic field of human behavior which requires sociological interpretation. It is
in this phase that we are interested in
knowing how cultural changes are affected
by population and the social interaction
with population trends.
3. We know that population is a field
of social action and here we ask the following question: What is the significance of

the data? What ought to be done and what
can be done?
        4. The primary purpose of planning is
to provide adequate satisfaction for the
physical, social, economic and cultural
needs of a given population. This makes it
evident that the study and understanding of
the growth, distribution and composition of
this same population is an indispensable
element in planning.[15]

    Table 1 shows population increase and rate in
three cycles--from 1775 to 1960.[16] During the first
cycle--1775 to 1881--the decrease is attributed to
the high rate of infant mortality.

TABLE 1

Population Increase

	Year	Pop. in Thousands	Table of Annual Increase
First Cycle	1775	70	4.61
	1800	155	3.20
	1815	221	2.34
	1832	330	2.42
	1846	448	2.17
	1860	583	1.92
	1877	732	1.32
	1887	799	0.87
Second Cycle	1899	953	1.50
	1910	1,118	1.54
	1920	1,300	1.56
	1930	1,544	1.69
	1935	1,724	1.95
	1940	1,869	1.89
Third Cycle	1950	2,210	1.69
	1960	2,349	.62

Estimates since 1960 have been affected by a marked change in the emigration predictions. It may well be that the trend of return to Puerto Rico from the continental United States will actually increase in numbers, bringing the problem of population increase to a critical point and accentuating the difficulties of housing and employment.

Table 2 illustrates the estimate of the employment situation based on a figure of zero emigration, showing a possible rise in unemployment from 13.3 per cent in 1960 to 31 per cent in 1980.[17]

TABLE 2

Civilian Noninstitutional Population, the Labor Force, Employment and Unemployment, with an Assumption of Zero Migration, Puerto Rico, 1960-80

Year	Civilian Population (noninst.)	Labor Force	Per cent of Partic- ipation	Employed	Per cent of Unem- ployed
1960	1,379.0	625.3	45.0	542.0	13.3
1962	1,454.0	670.0	46.1	585.3	12.6
1970	1,911.0	916.0	47.9	689.4	24.7
1975	2,189.3	1,082.2	49.4	752.6	30.5
1980	2,526.3	1,250.1	49.5	862.3	31.0

The birth rate has been decreasing and it may be hoped that this trend will continue. Raw data on reproduction projected for 1960 give a rate of 2.13 and for 1970 of 2.04.

The report of the Planning Board concludes with a series of recommendations dealing with such questions as decentralization as a means of spreading

the opportunities for work and the space for living,
and recognizes the general tendency toward a lower
birth rate where more urban ways of living prevail,
with higher levels of education and occupational
opportunities.

The remedies suggested for overpopulation are
of a socio-economic nature and there is no doubt
that these are of very great importance in population control. However, the specific subject of
birth control also deserves most serious attention
in Puerto Rico, as in other parts of the world. Its
history in Puerto Rico has been an erratic one since
its inception, as part of the program of the PRERA.
For a full program to be undertaken would require a
change in the position of the Catholic Church. If
such a change occurs the facilities of Puerto Rico
could very quickly put a program into operation due
to the groundwork which is already there. The value
of such a program is, we believe, of great importance in the lives of individuals as well as in its
impact on the population problem.

Certain accomplishments of the planning program
in relation to both short-term and long-term goals
can be noted. The following show progress toward
goals.

1. Increased employment at higher wages, more
security, and greater satisfaction in work.

2. Increased life expectancy and health.

3. Increased comfort in living, through new facilities in electricity, water, and housing.

4. New forms of economic development through
cooperatives, incentives for both industry and agriculture.

5. Greater freedom for the individual through
new kinds of mobility, higher income, education,
recreation.

EL DOLAR PRESUPUESTARIO DE 1965
THE 1965 BUDGET DOLLAR

PROCEDENCIA – *WHERE IT COMES FROM*

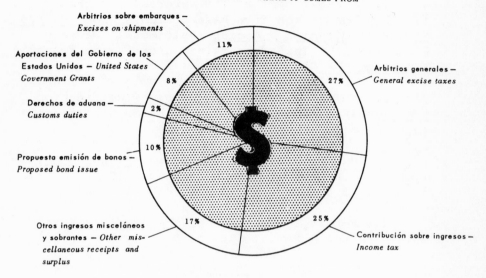

Arbitrios sobre embarques — *Excises on shipments*

Aportaciones del Gobierno de los Estados Unidos — *United States Government Grants*

Derechos de aduana — *Customs duties*

Propuesta emisión de bonos — *Proposed bond issue*

Otros ingresos misceláneos y sobrantes — *Other miscellaneous receipts and surplus*

Arbitrios generales — *General excise taxes*

Contribución sobre ingresos — *Income tax*

11% · 8% · 2% · 10% · 27% · 17% · 25%

DISTRIBUCION – *WHERE IT GOES*

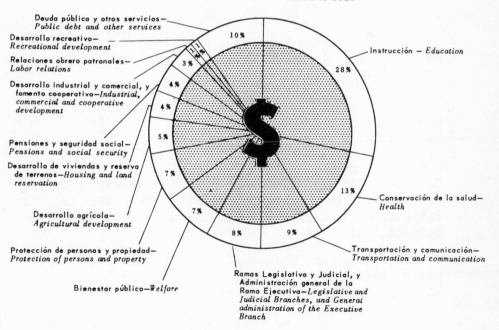

Deuda pública y otros servicios — *Public debt and other services*

Desarrollo recreativo — *Recreational development*

Relaciones obrero patronales — *Labor relations*

Desarrollo industrial y comercial, y fomento cooperativo — *Industrial, commercial and cooperative development*

Pensiones y seguridad social — *Pensions and social security*

Desarrollo de viviendas y reserva de terrenos — *Housing and land reservation*

Desarrollo agrícola — *Agricultural development*

Protección de personas y propiedad — *Protection of persons and property*

Bienestar público — *Welfare*

Instrucción — *Education*

Conservación de la salud — *Health*

Transportación y comunicación — *Transportation and communication*

Ramas Legislativa y Judicial, y Administración general de la Rama Ejecutiva — *Legislative and Judicial Branches, and General administration of the Executive Branch*

10% · 3% · 4% · 4% · 5% · 7% · 7% · 8% · 9% · 13% · 28%

Notes to Chapter 3

1. A great part of the material for this sec-
tion has been taken from Rafael Pico's book Puerto
Rico Planificación y Acción (Baltimore: Waverly
Press, 1961). The other main source is the Economic
Report to the Governor, 1963.

2. Rafael Pico, Puerto Rico: Planificación
y Acción (Pamphlet), (San Juan: Banco Gobernamental
de Fomento para Puerto Rico, 1962).

3. Puerto Rico Planning Board, Planning Act
(rev. ed.; Santurce: Planning Board, 1962), Section
3, pp. 2, 3-4. (Act No. 213 of May 12, 1942.)

4. Robert L. Heilbroner, The Great Ascent (New
York: Harper & Row, 1963), p. 83.

5. Pico (1961), op. cit., p. 26.

6. Tugwell, op. cit., p. 38.

7. From remarks by the Honorable Luis Muñoz
Marín, Governor of Puerto Rico, at Harvard University, June 16, 1955.

8. Gordon K. Lewis, Puerto Rico, Freedom and
Power in the Carribean (New York: M.R. Press, 1963),
pp. 256-57.

9. Commonwealth of Puerto Rico, Office of the
Governor, Puerto Rico Planning Board, Eduardo Rivera
Rivera, Director Bureau of Public Works, Methods and
Procedures in the Preparation of the Four-Year Fi-
nancial Plan, July, 1963, pp. 10-11.

10. Junta de Planificación, Estudio para deter-
minar la Agrupación de los Municipios de Puerto Rico
para Propósitos de Planificación.

11. It should be inserted parenthetically that
this comment comes from one of the directors of the
present study as a result of her experience in the

1930's when the Department of Education was only
beginning to free itself from the influence of the
continental United States' methods in education.
The establishment of the Second Unit Schools and
various adaptations to Puerto Rican needs began
then under the leadership of the Commissioner of
Education, Dr. José Padín.

        12.   Puerto Rico Department of Health, Region-
alization of Health and Welfare Services in Puerto,
Progress Report, July 1, 1958-December 31, 1959
(Rio Piedras: The Commonwealth of Puerto Rico),
p. 47.

        13.   Ibid., p. 59.

        14.   Philip Hauser, "Man and More Men: The
Population Prospects," Bulletin of Atomic Scientists,
June, 1964, p. 7.

        15.   Puerto Rico Planning Board, Office of the
Governor, Analisis de Poblacion, translated from
Chapter XIV.

        16.   A. J. Jaffe, People, Jobs and Economic
Development (New York: Columbia University Press,
1959).

        17.   Puerto Rico Planning Board, Analisis de
Poblacion, Table XXXV, p. 106.

CHAPTER **4** GOVERNMENT
AGENCY
PROGRAMS

This chapter describes the programs of government agencies which we deem to have specific pertinence to this study. The proportions given to the several programs are not to be construed as judgment on their importance. Our purpose is to give a general view of the planning and execution of programs of the Commonwealth Government which will throw light on the reasons for and effects of change in the ten communities of this study. They thus become samples of the local effects of large scale planning as described in Chapter 3.

Material for this section has been drawn from interviews with heads of agencies or persons in charge of particular programs, from the official reports of the departments or other agencies, and from general observation.

DEPARTMENT OF EDUCATION

This section is taken from our interview with the Secretary of Education, Candido Oliveras, on April 8, 1964, supplemented by material from an interview with Dr. Martinez Almodóvar and Rafael Bonilla, of Rural Education.

Since the advent of the American Administration in Puerto Rico, efforts have been made to apply the principle of universal education. During this century, or the part of the century that has already elapsed, attempts have been made to provide enough teachers and schoolrooms so that no child should stay out of school because of lack of opportunity.

However, in spite of all efforts, because of the
rapid increase in population, the improvement of
living conditions in Puerto Rico, and especially
improvement of health conditions, a larger number
of children are surviving and thus the number of
clients increasing, demanding more rooms and educational opportunities. In spite of these efforts,
in 1940, for example, only about 50 per cent of the
children of school age were in school. In 1952,
the Governor and the Legislature of Puerto Rico established, as part of planning, for the first time
attendance goals to be fulfilled during the balance
of the decade. These attendance goals were the
following: 91 per cent of school children between
six and twelve years of age should be in school in
1960, 75 per cent of the school children thirteen
to fifteen years, and 41 per cent of school children
sixteen to eighteen years of age. These age brack-
ets correspond to ages of children in elementary,
intermediate, and high school. By 1957, the three
goals had been surpassed. At present, more than
80 per cent of the children between six and eighteen are already attending school. In other words,
some kind of education has at least been provided
for every child who reaches school age and is physically and mentally fit to go into school.

Wrestling with increasing numbers, trying to
meet the quantity goals in some instances meant some
kind of deterioration in regard to quality of instruction. For example, when there were not sufficient teachers, the so-called double enrollment or
two-shift plan (three hours with 31 per cent of
elementary pupils in 1962) was adopted. No problem of this kind existed in secondary and high
schools. Where there were teachers and no rooms,
the interlocking system (five continuous hours of
school in one room for one group of children during
the morning under one teacher--24 per cent in 1962)
was used. A second group was then taught in the
same room under a different teacher in the afternoon (56 per cent got less than six hours).

Another factor that contributed to the weakening of instruction in Puerto Rico was the adoption

of the mass-promotion system, which meant that children without the necessary skills and knowledge had to be promoted to the next grade in order to make room for the ones coming behind. It meant also putting in service teachers without the necessary training, having to use materials in insufficient quantities and of a lower quality in the schoolroom, and several other measures which had the result of weakening instruction.

In recent years, because of the high priority given to education by the Government of Puerto Rico and because of the rapid economic growth that has occurred in Puerto Rico, increasing resources have been devoted to education (28 per cent of the total budget). These increased resources have permitted subsequently more attention to the quality of instruction. Double enrollment in the urban zones of Puerto Rico beyond the third grade has recently been successfully eliminated.

In the rural zone, however, the reduction has not been substantial, but new schemes to improve the quality of education are being employed. The first of these is a new program known as the Rural Education Program, which depends mainly on better supervision in the rural zones of Puerto Rico.

Ciales, which is being developed as a model for rural education, was typical of problems in 1961. The supervisor oversaw up to 58 teachers. The schools suffered from lack of equipment, etc. Now there are 56 itinerant teachers, but 150 are needed with constant evaluation of achievement.

Itinerant principals were selected carefully so that each of the isolated schools could be visited once every two weeks instead of once or twice during the year as formerly. These itinerant principals are submitted to an intensive training period, to better assist rural teachers solve day-to-day educational problems. Together with better supervision, more and better books and better school services (transportation, scholarships, and economic assistance of other types) have been provided.

There has been a change in the philosophy of
rural education. An example of the need for such
change is evident from a sample of 700 students
where it was found that only 2 per cent or 3 per
cent were going into agriculture, and 60 per cent
went on to high school from the rural schools. The
need for new programs both for agriculture and new
industry is apparent. The Departments of Education,
Labor, and Agriculture are cooperating, with the
help of federal funds, on retraining in the development of a "human resources" program. An effort is
made to encourage individual decision so that those
who are suited to life in the rural zone can stay;
those who wish to move will be able to (trained with
emphasis on English for those who wish to go to the
continental U.S. and agree to go). Specialized local education in the rural zone is being developed,
i.e., poultry in Aibonito, tractors in Bayamón, cattle in Ciales.

A second experimental measure is instruction
through television directed especially at the improvement of teaching in the rural isolated schools.
An English course for the first and second grades
marks the first attempt. It is difficult to get good
models for the teaching of English, not only in the
rural schools, but everywhere in Puerto Rico.
Through TV, teachers with the right pronunciation
serve as reasonably good models. Settings and situations in which English is used are also available.
The programs were begun with only those two courses,
but by 1964 there were twenty-two different direct-
instruction programs on the air. In 1964, only
about 300 TV sets were in use, but in the 1965 budget
Commonwealth funds were earmarked for the purchase
of 1,000 sets. By 1967, it is hoped there will be
TV sets in all schools of Puerto Rico (one set for
every three or four rooms in the urban zone).

A new idea is now being tried in a few schools
in the interior of the island. Since it is not possible to organize isolated schools under the so-
called interlocking system, because children might
not be able to arrive at the required early morning
hours or leave at the late evening hours required

under this plan, a special teacher to teach one subject (English, social studies, or mathematics) to
students of all elementary grades will be used.   The
regular teacher would teach all other subjects, thus
increasing the teaching time to four hours daily.

Discriminatory practices connected with appoint-
ments of teachers and distribution of materials to
the rural schools are being eliminated.   In time,
all rural communities will have complete elementary
schools, instead of the present one- or two-room
schools up to the third or fourth grade.   In the
larger rural-population nuclei, second rural units
or intermediate schools will continually be established.   In all instances, free transportation will
be provided so that rural children may be able to
continue their studies in urban secondary schools.

The 1961 budget for free transportation of children amounted to $670,000.   In 1965, the appropria-
tion for this purpose was $2,500,000.   About 60,000
children are receiving free transportation from
their places of residence to a rural school or to
an urban school.

Another new measure that has been applied to
improve the quality of education is the organization
of exemplary or model schools.   The idea behind
these schools is as follows: The Department of Education wants to demonstrate in practice that it is
able to organize the necessary factors to provide
the kind of education that the parents want for
their children; to show that they have the know-
how; that they are able to perform the right kind
of educational job if the necessary resources are
provided.

There are more than twenty elementary and two
model high schools already operating as such or in
the process of being organized as such.   These model
schools provide a full curriculum including home
economics, manual arts, music, art, physical educa-
tion--subjects which are not always provided in all
schools.   There is a library and a librarian.   These
schools are organized under the single-enrollment

plan. Children are grouped according to their level
of achievement or academic potentiality into groups
of retarded, gifted, and normal children. The best
possible school principals are selected in every
case, a very important factor in the effort to improve the quality of education. Emphasis is given
to reasoning rather than rote or memory in the
teaching-learning process. A very strong community-
relations program has been instituted in all model
schools.

Parents seem to be satisfied with the results
of these efforts. For instance, in 1964, three out
of every four students who graduated from the Juan
J. Osuna High School (in Rio Piedras) passed the
University entrance examination. Everyone who applied for admission to the College of Agriculture
and Mechanical Arts passed the examination. These
results are comparable to those of the best private
schools in Puerto Rico. Of course, Juan J. Osuna
School serves a neighborhood of middle-income or
high-income families which represent the economic
strata that feed the enrollment of private schools.

Another effort to enhance the quality of instruction is the Special High School Program, being
developed with the economic support of the Ford
Foundation. Its main features are the following:

Subjects are taught with a higher degree of
interrelationship, using either languages or social
studies as the linking subject. In other words,
when the unit of early Roman history is being taught
in social studies, students in English and Spanish
will read literature of the same period. Children
are grouped to receive direct instruction or lec-
tures from the most competent teachers in the subject. Then, they are distributed for discussion to
their rooms. Discussion in the room is conducted to
allow broader participation by all children. Emphasis, again, is on reasoning rather than on ac-
cumulation of knowledge. This high school program
is being developed jointly with the University of
Puerto Rico to provide an opportunity for the training of teachers within the same atmosphere.

Education students are appointed as teacher aids within this program. They are paid a small fee of $80, so that they may devote additional time to practice during this stage instead of the one semester of practice. In this program, they have two years of practice in the schoolroom under competent master teachers.

Audio-visual aids are being more frequently and effectively used in the schoolroom. The program has been organized so that the teachers may have films, projectors, TV sets and other media to strengthen and enrich the process of teaching at all levels.

The Vocational Education Programs are being expanded and enriched. Also, additional regular vocational schools have been planned and are being built; vocational shops are being provided in smaller towns. The program is also being expanded so that vocational training will be provided to youths who do not meet regular academic requirements. More than 1,000 of these youths are already attending special courses provided for them.

These are some of the efforts that have been made in order to improve the quality of education. There is reason to believe that there has already been noticeable progress. Of course, there are problems that cannot be solved immediately. It is hoped that in the near future teachers' salaries will reach a higher level, thereby attracting the best talent in Puerto Rico. The Department of Education believes teaching to be one of the key professions in any society and sees no reason why a person with the necessary intelligence should go into another profession because the teaching field may not offer the necessary level of compensation. Together with the improvement of salaries, other improvements are hoped for. These include the quality of teachers' training through better selection, improvement of the curriculum of the College of Education, and the elimination of the Normal Diploma--that is, raising the requirements to four years as basic for the preparation of teachers. Also, a better balance between content and methodology is anticipated.

The present fiscal and economic limitations
that hamper teachers' work, and the production of
teaching materials that respond better to the specific conditions and realities of Puerto Rico (materials specifically prepared for use in Puerto Rico
instead of the mere adaptation of material produced
elsewhere) are two more areas for improvement.

Of course, in fields such as mathematics and
science the material produced for use in other
places may be as good for use in Puerto Rico, but
in connection with other subjects such as arts and
social studies, the situation is different. Impres-
sive progress toward this end has been made by the
Department's Printing Press and Editorial.

Together with the expansion of the regular
school system, eventually there will be regional
colleges in most parts of Puerto Rico. Some of
these regional colleges will result as an outgrowth
of present high schools or technical institutes. It
is hoped that in time a system will be provided
which will afford education sufficient in quantity
and adequate in quality to comply with the consti-
tional principles that "Every person has the right
to an education which shall be directed to the full
development of the human personality and to the
strengthening of respect for human rights and fundamental freedoms."

The changes in the Department of Education from
1932 to the present are marked also by significant
organizational and philosophical differences. Thirty years ago the structure of the department was
highly centralized and hierarchical, although, during the incumbency of Dr. José Padín, modifications
were beginning to appear. These were due, however,
to the ability of Dr. Padín to recognize new needs
and to give opportunity for the development of new
ideas and new plans, rather than to a change in the
structure of the department itself. Now the value
of a large degree of decentralization is recognized.
This is due not only to the connection with over-all
planning for the island, with its programs for re-
gionalization, but also is a recognition of the

enrichment which comes from the full use of individual initiative and imagination. There is no question, in our opinion, that this change will engender a spirit of experimentation, as well as encourage the incorporation of ideas now present but capable of great growth.

When Rafael Pico in 1945 withdrew his name as candidate for the position of Commissioner of Education he did so because of the controversial question of the teaching of English, which he felt was "not a subject for political interference, but should rightfully be reserved for educators and experts on the methods of acquiring a second language." But, more importantly for the present, he went on to add:

> Puerto Rico needs a new educational
> policy, not only in the question of
> English but throughout the curriculum,
> so that our educational system will
> really serve the best interests of the
> community, which is engaged in a far-
> reaching program of social and economic
> reform. What I or any other self-
> respecting educator must insist on is
> freedom to develop the educational pro-
> gram required by our conditions, with-
> out political interference from any
> source, without strings attached to the
> position and with ample advice from ex-
> perienced technicians.[1]

This freedom came only when, instead of a commissioner appointed by the President of the United States, the Secretary of Education was appointed by the Governor and enjoyed new power in the ELA in 1952. This means that such freedom has been possible for less than fifteen years--a short time to establish an education system which will "serve the best interests of the community." That there is new vision and fresh inspiration behind the recently inaugurated or revised programs is no small accomplishment for such a period.

In view of the ferment today in the whole field of education, we see in all of these changes in the Department of Education great potentialities for a flowering of ideas and their application in Puerto Rico. We are, in view of the direction of this study, particularly interested in the attention now being given to education in the rural zone where, we believe, many latent possibilities are stored.

The chapter on the Second Unit Schools illustrates the new view of the Department of Education on education for the rural zone. It is of central importance to this study. The history of these schools over the thirty-year period illuminates the effect of other changes on the rural society: the cultural transition from traditional to modern patterns of living and the new aspirations and needs of a transitional period; the new goals which must be articulated and a corresponding balance between agriculture and industry.

UNIVERSITY OF PUERTO RICO

Chancellor Jaime Benitez said in his annual report (1964):

> Since May 1955 we have doubled our student body, our faculty, our graduate class, our resources and our problems.
> . . . During the past thirty years enrollment has doubled every ten years.
> . . . Unless there should be a catastrophe in the life of Puerto Rico there is no possibility of checking the rate of increase in the numbers seeking higher education.[2]

Such swelling numbers indicate the need and the demand for varied personnel in the expanding economy of the island. We believe that it also reflects the prestige which education holds in Puerto Rico and in many cases the intellectual curiosity and the love of learning which represent the highest ideals of any educational system. That the impact of such

numbers, an anticipated enrollment of 45,000 to
50,000 in 1974-75, creates innumerable problems is
inescapable. Of this increase it is estimated that
only about 30 per cent will be absorbed by the
growth of private colleges and universities, leaving
the heaviest burden on the University of Puerto Rico.

    To fulfill the accepted obligation for higher
education in Puerto Rico, the Chancellor made the
following report:

    1. It (the University) should in-
    sist that the concept of regional col-
    leges, so successfully initiated at
    Humacao, be extended to other sections
    of Puerto Rico.
    2. It should provide for the bulk
    of the enrollment in the first two years
    in these regional colleges.
    3. It should keep the educational
    offering of the regional colleges at
    the highest level, link it closely with
    both secondary and higher education,
    and guard against regional ambitions to
    convert these colleges into little uni-
    versities. Similarly it should not per-
    mit their transformation into vocational
    schools. Terminal and short courses
    should be offered. But their central
    responsibility should be the preparation
    of the youth who are preparing to enter
    their third year of study at Rio Piedras
    or Mayaguez. It should be remembered
    that according to the plan which has
    been sketched here the regional colleges
    will be caring for 60 per cent of all
    the students of the first and second
    years at the University of Puerto Rico.
    4. It should so evolve that both
    the Rio Piedras and the Mayaguez cam-
    puses become each day more vigorous cen-
    ters of higher education where the dom-
    inant tone is set by professional,
    graduate, research and creative programs.

    5.   The growth of the Rio Piedras campus should take place exclusively at the level of this third year and above. . . .

    6.   It is calculated that the enrollment on the Mayaguez campus should increase at a much more rapid rate than that at Rio Piedras. It should almost triple in eleven years. Furthermore its growth should be along academic and professional lines corresponding to its present development, its potentialities for future excellence and the general requirements of Puerto Rican life. . . .

    7.   The cultural extension programs of Rio Piedras and Mayaguez should continue and expand. The programs of extramural instruction should be taken over by the regional colleges.

    8.   The expected tripling of the programs in Medicine, Dentistry, Health Sciences and Nursing can be met as soon as the necessary buildings are constructed. . . .[3]

The total proposed budget for 1964-65 was $30,309,546.

The University of Puerto Rico gives the M.A. degree in the following fields: the Department of Spanish Studies, Public Administration, Social Work, Public Health, Public Health Education, Science; the Doctor of Philosophy in Science, Medicine, Dental Medicine; the Bachelor of Laws degree through its School of Law; and Doctor of Medicine from the School of Medicine--School of Tropical Medicine.

The demands on the higher-education system are enormous and controversy is bound to arise as to the best way to use financial resources. What should be the proportions allocated to general liberal arts education, special training for teachers, technical training, and graduate professional education? The University now offers six types of bachelor's degrees:

Education, Liberal Arts, Business Administration,
Engineering, Agriculture, and Health Sciences--in-
cluding Pharmacy.

Decisions on priorities and educational policies are among the most crucial for Puerto Rico's
future. They involve not only questions of finance
but of organization and emphasis. How can the quality of teacher education be geared to the changing
needs of the Department of Education? What is the
responsibility of the University for training to
meet the growth of automation in industry? How far
should the University go in providing graduate work
or should its bachelors go to the continental United
States or to foreign countries for further professional education?

Some of these questions are also applicable to
the recruitment of faculty, which now numbers 1,932
--five times its number twenty-two years ago. During this time, quality, in terms of preparation, has
shown a marked improvement--27.7 per cent now holding
the doctorate and 50.5 per cent the master's degree.

The scholarships offered by the government
through the public schools should be mentioned because of their unique importance to a democratic
system of education. They ensure opportunity for
able students to receive higher education, satisfy the desire of many parents for an education
for their children which they are not financially
able to provide, and give promise for the quality
of future leadership as well as an educational level
commensurate with anticipated economic and social
development.

DEGREES AND DIPLOMAS CONFERRED BY THE UNIVERSITY OF PUERTO RICO
1941-42 TO 1962-63

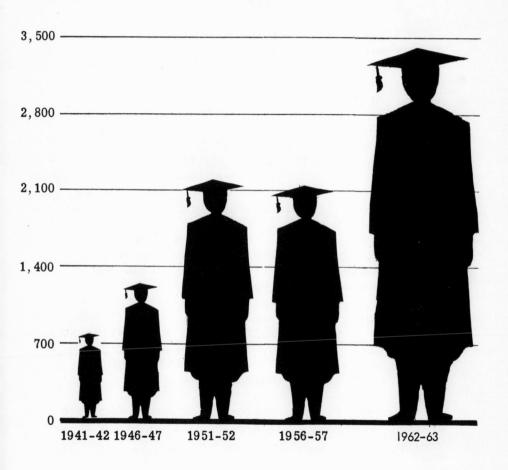

COMMUNITY EDUCATION

One of the most unusual contributions to Puerto
Rican development has come from Community Education.
This is a division of the Department of Education
created by an act of the Legislature in 1949. The
preamble to the law reads as follows:

> The goal of community education is to
> impart basic teaching on the nature of
> man, his history, his life, his way of
> working and of self-governing in the
> world and in Puerto Rico. Such teach-
> ing, addressed to the citizens meeting
> in rural and urban communities, will be
> imparted through motion pictures, radio,
> books, pamphlets, posters and group
> discussions.
>   The object is to provide the good
> hand of our popular culture with the
> tool of a basic education.
>   In practice this will mean giving
> to the community the wish, the tendency
> and the way of making use of its own
> aptitudes for the solution of many of
> its own problems of health, education,
> cooperation, social life through the
> action of the community itself.
>   The community should not be civi-
> cally unemployed.
>   The community can be constantly and
> usefully employed in its own service,
> in terms of pride and satisfaction for
> the members thereof.

The description following is taken from the program of community development carried on by this division.[4]

> From the start we interpreted the law
> that created us to mean that we were
> given the opportunity to help the neigh-
> bors of the rural and urban communities
> of Puerto Rico in their analysis of what

it means to think and behave democratically and to make this the foundation
upon which to "re-construct" their lives
as individuals, as members of a family
and as neighbors within their community.
We believed that this was the way, the
only way we knew, to establish and keep
alive an equalitarian society.

Objectives

1. To help the families of a community to have faith in themselves and
in their neighbors and to discover with
them the ways to express this faith.
2. To help the neighbors understand that it is their right and responsibility to know and to participate in
all matters affecting their communal
welfare and that knowing this they can
find the way to create a dynamic community supported by their own efforts
and contributions.
3. To help the neighbors develop
the process of group discussion in meetings where democratic participation is
assured and where consensus, reached by
agreement based on thorough analysis,
takes the place of voting.
4. To help them see that no planning and action by a community can be
democratic in its nature unless it is
based on scientific study.
5. To help the neighbors examine
the old patterns of cultural control,
the patterns of influence and power in
the society they know, in order that
through this examination they may find
the way to enjoy fully the freedoms
guaranteed to them constitutionally.
6. To help them learn through
practical experience that freedom from
dependence does not mean the substitu-
tion of an independence that rejects
all outside contact; that, on the

contrary, the opposite of the enslaved
condition of dependence is one of interdependence where all educational,
technical and scientific help inside
and outside the community is sought
and shared.

7.   To help the people of a community (including their leaders) study,
through a living experience, the purpose and role of democratic leadership.

8.   To help them come to action,
to the solution of a problem as the result of these concerns so that any physical expression of their labors shall
be understood not as the end product
but as a natural contribution in the
democratic order of things.

9.   And when the day comes for
celebrating the solution of a problem,
to help them see clearly that just as
the planning and action was theirs, so
the speech-making, the laughter and
the praising must be theirs. For who
can better dedicate a new road or a new
school than those who with their heads,
hands and hearts helped to build it?
In this way, in the words of Walt Whit-
man, they will understand the nature of
past struggles; "that it is proved in
the essence of things that from any
fruition of success, no matter what,
shall come forth something to make a
greater struggle necessary."

CRITERIA FOR THE SELECTION
OF COMMUNITY LEADERS

1.   Was he a man of the people? A
man whose aim is to build self-confidence
in the individual, must first believe
in that individual. We wanted a man of
quiet dignity, who spoke of his neighbors as a man like himself. We did not
want a man who thought in the "we-they"
pattern. We preferred him to live in

the country and if he did, to do so by
choice rather than by chance. However,
where he lived was not as important as
how he felt about himself and his fellow man.

2. Could he work in his own community? Contrary to what some might
consider good personnel practice, we
believed there were no advantages to
be gained by uprooting a man from his
environment and sending him to a strange
community. If for some reason a worker
possesses qualities which make it difficult for him to relate himself to his
own neighborhood, they would undoubtedly be the same ones which would make it
hard for him to work elsewhere. The
man we hoped to find was one who enjoyed working with his own people and
would be accepted by them.

3. Was he a happy man at home?
We foresaw that the demands of the job
were so great that as far as his family
went, the only man who could serve with
security was one who, being a good husband and father, had the full support
of his wife and children.

4. What concerns had he shown for
the problems of his community? We wanted a man who had seen himself related
to the other members of his community
and had been involved in programs of
planning and action. However, we were
most interested in the way he had been
active.

5. What were his attitudes toward
authoritarian behavior? Toward the
"poor man's" right to participate? Toward the concept that more land, more
education, and more influence is the accepted criteria for leadership? The
candidate who showed disdain or lack of
faith in the people's ability and right
to think for themselves could hardly be

successful at the task of stimulating
all people, regardless of their station
to work together for the common welfare.

6. Was he a secure person? When
challenged, did he rationalize, go on
the defensive, or discuss the problem
with intelligence and freedom? We
needed a man of stability. The depth
of our interviews, the walks we took
with him and the observations we made
as he entered new situations gave us
some evaluation of his security. However, we had to depend upon the three
months of training to bring out a greater measure of this concern.

7. Did he have a set of moral values which he used on all situations and
all people indiscriminately? Or was he
a person capable of analyzing beyond
the single act into the deeper motiva-
tions of human behavior? We believed
there was no place in our program for
the superficial moralist.

8. What was his attitude toward
the opinions of others? Was he a man
of intolerant partisan views in such
areas as politics, labor, or religion?
If so he would not be our man, for we
were looking for one who would permit
self-expression in others; a man free
to work with all.

9. Was he a static personality
or did he possess the capacity for
growth? This was a basic concern. If
he had this potential for growth and
was not threatened by critical evaluation, he could reach high levels.

Training is an interrelated part
of a program which puts as much importance on selection and supervision as
on training. The same district supervisor and central office staff member
who began the initial hunt for the man
and who sat in the selection interviews,
will later be present at the training

session and then continue with supervision in the field. . . . If a man
has the basic personal equipment for
the job, he will find that each moment
of stress is a door to new understanding.

Training Objectives

1. To help the individual come to
a clear understanding and acceptance of
the principles of democratic life in a
community. This is the paramount objective and becomes the guiding star
around which other aims revolve. He
will get this understanding by study
and through personal experience, not by
being told.

2. To examine at depth in the
Puerto Rican society the cultural patterns of behavior that have a direct
relationship to democratic community
life. We will help him dig into the
roots of the attitudes of the people.
He must come to an analytical, balanced
approach to the people and their culture, at the same time keeping the
warmth and understanding which make
him one of them.

3. To look into himself and his
own conduct with enough freedom and
flexibility to be able to put a mirror
to his actions, reflecting for his scru-
tiny everything from the way he talks
to his children to the way he approaches
a farm laborer as compared with the way
he presents himself at the home of the
land owner. Only to the degree that he
is able to do this can he be objective
in looking at others and thus get to a
deeper sense of democratic principles--
principles which otherwise would remain
at an entirely theoretical level.

4. To create in him, as a result
of continuous self-examination, a

positive desire for personal growth
based on an honest understanding of
himself, his convictions and his moti-
vations in relation to the aims of his
work.

5.   To help him through his own
reasoning to understand his role as an
educator. There are intensive discussions of what it means to help a person
come to his own conclusions rather than
to be led to conclusions pre-determined
for him. The details of the process of
reasoning and the process used in helping a person come to his own conclusions
are thoroughly discussed. Extensive
use is made of role playing. At this
stage, however, we put much more emphasis on the validity of the educational
process than on the methods and techniques of the educator. These he will
discover as he begins to work in the
community and during later in-service
training. It is better that the discovery of techniques and methods is
postponed, for then he will be free to
examine them and accept or reject them
in the light of his experience. A firm
foundation of beliefs is essential to
prevent a man from falling into for-
mulas.

6.   To help the group organizer
understand the structure of leadership
within a democratic framework, learning
to recognize the elements present in his
culture which can contribute positively
to the development of sound leadership
and to identify the forces at work
against it.

Because of the nature of his past
experiences in a culture where the roots
of leadership are authoritarian, the
trainee will need not only his initial
orientation period, but years of practice and many in-service training periods before he can come to full grips

with this problem. A few weeks of training with a democratic group-discussion
leader can easily be put aside as theoretical when confronted with the stress
of on-the-job decisions. A considerable
amount of role playing is undertaken,
with the aim of helping him evaluate his
own concepts. In this healthy learning
device, he gets many new slants on himself.

He may discover, for example, that
he is so irritated at having sinned as
a do-all in his own community, that he
acts now toward such a leader by ignor-
ing him or by pounding on him hard. He
may find he is so deeply moved by his
new awareness of the evils of dependency that he wants to choke this knowledge
down the throats of neighbors who do not
seem to care.

7. To help the trainee understand
the meaning of group discussion. Of
all the subjects brought to training,
this is perhaps the only one where all
the members of the group become involved in a totally new endeavor. Previous experience in this area has not
provided them with a background upon
which to make sound conclusions.

The analysis of this subject is
left purposely for the end of training. By then the group has achieved
some measure of cohesion, and each man
is convinced of the value of good group-
discussion techniques from the struggle
each has experienced rather than from
text-book theories. The trainees are
then able to analyze the behavior patterns they will gradually shed. They
look back with new awareness at the man
who has blocked the progress of the
group by forcing acceptance of his ideas
without discussion; at the man who, appearing to listen, is really waiting for

a pause to plunge in himself; at the
man who hears the truth but argues
against it because it is more comfortable emotionally to misunderstand.
And in these men, each sees himself.
He can now laugh at his earlier com-
pulsion to spotlight himself by a beautiful but meaningless speech. And he
is amused when he remembers how angry
he became when the group rejected one
of his brilliant ideas.

        In fact, it often happens that by
the end of training, both supervisor
and group organizer have become so sen-
sitive to democratic procedures in
group discussion that during the initial
field experience, his fear of acting un-
democratically produces passivity when
he could and should be more dynamic.

        But we think it better to take this
risk, for it is easier to develop conscious techniques with a man who begins
with this kind of sensitivity than with
one who ignores the implications of
autocratic action.

        8. To help the field worker orga-
nize a program of work, keep adequate
records, and have a positive attitude
toward supervision. This is not introduced until the end of training and is
presented then in such a way as to leave
the worker free to contribute to its
formation. When a plan of work is finally developed it is the result of
group thinking. The records the group
organizer agrees to keep are those which
he and his fellow workers decide are
essential to the task. The supervisory
relationship is evolved from many periods of discussion in which he contributes
his share of the thinking. In this way,
the organization of his job comes about,
not arbitrarily, but in a spirit of
analysis and study. The careful planning by the group organizer of each day's

activity; his weekly schedule based on
a three-month program of work; his
well-kept, functional records, many of
them reading like diaries; the high
level of supervision that prevails
throughout the program, all attest to
the fact that this approach is the most
successful one.

In spite of the fact that this program requires
time because of its special forms of community education and training of leaders, it shows (at the end of
1963) technical help given for the continuation of
71 aqueducts, 62 roads, community centers, and school
construction. In 162 communities, 15,000 families
had benefited from the program; 159 projects had
been carried out at a cost of $2,813,000, of which
$1,440,000 came from government general funds. ELA
contributed $939,000 toward the $1,898,000 cost of
an additional 117 projects. Thirty-nine projects
were in process. In the 1964-65 budget, $700,000
was appropriated for work in 70 communities.

COMMISSION FOR IMPROVEMENT
OF ISOLATED COMMUNITIES

The work of this commission grew out of an experiment started five years ago by Professor Lydia J.
Roberts, in charge of Special Programs, Department
of Home Economics, University of Puerto Rico.

A pilot project was set up in the isolated community of Dona Elena located in the mountains, eight
or ten miles from the main road. An examination was
made of the residents of this community which revealed serious nutritional lacks. To meet the needs,
of which this was evidence, a three-point program was
established: (a) three meals a day for children,
(b) education of children and parents in the essentials of nutrition, and (c) work with families to
increase home production of food. Success in this
experiment and the interest of the Governor led to
the establishment of the commission, consisting of
seven members appointed by the Governor and including

heads of the Departments of Health, Public Works,
Agriculture, and the Planning Board. During the
first year, a home economist and an agronomist were
employed to live and work in each of five isolated
communities. With additional appropriations there
were, by 1964, twenty-one communities carrying on
this program with fourteen more to be added.

The project has now become a cooperative one
with the United States Army Tropical Research Medical Laboratory, under the direction of Dr. Irwin C.
Plough, Colonel, U.S. Army. This has made available
the necessary services of physicians, biochemists,
technicians, and dietitians, as well as food transportation and equipment for workers.

In addition to the scientific value of the nutritional studies and of the program specifically
directed toward the needs revealed, some of the results have been the building of roads, provision of
latrines, parasite control, housing improvement,
better gardens, and better breeds of chickens raised.
All of this has created a desire for improvement
in living conditions and has raised standards of
living.[5]

DEPARTMENT OF HEALTH

Probably the most striking figures showing the
effects of the new programs as they apply to human
life come from the Department of Health.

Dr. Juan Pons, former Secretary of Health, in
an address[6] to the Convention for Social Orientation,
May, 1962, describes the "peaceful revolution" which
has taken place in the field of health. Much of his
address is incorporated in this report on health.

The decade of the 1930's added three calamities
to the existing poverty and high mortality and morbidity of the island. These were the hurricane of
1928, the world-wide depression, with its strong
impact on Puerto Rico, and the hurricane of 1932.

But this same decade saw the birth of a new concept
of the function of a democratic government in the
field of health. "Although all the civilized world
showed an accelerating decrease in mortality rates,
the progress of Puerto Rico in public health has no
parallel in any other country." From 1930-60, life
expectancy rose from 40.65 years to 69.56; mortality
rates decreased from 19.7 per 100,000 (1930-39) to
6.7 in 1960; deaths from diarrhea and enteritis from
409.5 (1930-39) to 39.5 in 1960; tuberculosis from
212.5 to 29.3; malaria 54.1 to 0; infant mortality,
88.3 to 43.7.

Before the decade of the 1930's four events of
significance had occurred: "the establishment of
the tuberculosis hospital at Rio Piedras, the organization of the first Public Health Unit, the creation of the School of Tropical Medicine and the
institution of two small district hospitals, one in
San Juan, the other in Ponce."

In 1933, with the coming of the PRERA, and federal relief funds, much was done to promote health
programs. But, as Dr. Pons says, these programs
were not immediately incorporated in the regular
health institutions of the Insular Government but
became a base for later expansion and coordination.

The war years, because of the difficulty in
importing drugs and the slowdown in professional
training, brought deleterious effects in one direction but, on the other hand, advantageous changes
through the improved understanding of personal and
home hygiene on the part of men returning from military service.

As Puerto Rico moved into its period of greatest change--1945 to the present--it has shown great
acceleration in every aspect of the health program:
organization, facilities, use of new scientific resources, number of doctors and nurses (the number
of doctors has quintupled since the decade of the
1930's), provision of potable water for rural areas,
and general improvement in living conditions.

Many problems remain. Morbidity rates and infant mortality, chronic diseases, and others, must be reduced, but the emphasis given to health needs is reflected in the annual budget appropriations. In the recommendations for 1965, 13 per cent of the total budget is to be devoted to this use. In 1956, 19,399 persons received public assistance because of total or permanent incapacity. This points clearly to the relationship between health and welfare programs; it represents 88 per 100,000 of the population (New York State has a rate of 26 per 100,000). That many of these people could, by health and rehabilitation programs, be removed from the category of the unemployable is highly probable. Dr. Pons also emphasizes the relation of rapid socio-economic change to mental and psychosomatic health problems and, as everywhere the life span has increased, to the problems of old age.

Dr. Pons ends his paper by pointing out the need for more preventive work and more rehabilitation. This is certainly the greatest challenge of our age in the field of health and its aim is to give that greater vitality and well-being which frees the individual for maximum development.

This was corroborated in an interview with Dr. Guillermo Arbona, Secretary of Health, who said that the present emphasis is on rehabilitation-- physical and mental. The work of the Division of Public Welfare adds, through its work with the disabled, aged, etc., to the improvement of health and the plans of this division for more rehabilitation should bring great improvement to general well- being.

It should be pointed out that services other than those under the Department of Health have made marked contributions to the health of the Puerto Rican community: nutritional services, milk stations, school lunches, breakfasts for preschool children, surplus-food distribution. In regard to hookworm, he said that the effects are largely offset by improved nutrition; the latrine problem is

largely solved and there is an increasing number of
toilets and septic tanks being installed. Infant
mortality has been reduced to 40 per 1,000 but should
come down to 20. (It has come down from its highest
index of 120 per 1,000.) The TB test at its highest
incidence showed 86 per cent, now it shows 3 per
cent. Better water is needed in isolated regions.
Polio vaccine was given in one weekend to 96 per
cent of one-half million children under six years of
age. The same was done for the second injection,
using the schools.

In relation to the regions set up by the Planning Board, it has already been stated that boundaries vary according to the present needs of the various agencies. Through increasing coordination of
programs they may eventually coincide. The boundaries for the Department of Health are based on practical considerations--where people travel, where
they buy. Coverage comes through district hospitals,
health centers, public health centers, and Public
Welfare Units (see section on Welfare). Evening
clinics are now being established for working people.
This also means more efficient use of plant and personnel.

Five of the registered hospitals have nursing
schools with 200 to 300 graduates a year. The training is subsidized by the government, which requires
that work be given in return. This provides personnel for the rural zone.

Service is free in all the units of the Health
Department. Two-thirds to three-fourths of the population receive such services. The Secretary favors
a compulsory health plan (which is not approved by
the Medical Association) which would make payments
possible for the increasing number of persons able
to pay. Only 23 per cent of the population is covered by voluntary health plans (Blue Cross, Teachers'
Association).

In 1948, federal funds were made available to
provide enough beds for an integrated hospital system

according to the standards set up by the Federal Government. By 1962, the Insular Government had appropriated 19 million dollars for this purpose, 51.7 million came from the Federal Government, and municipal and private funds amounted to 18.5 million dollars.

TABLE 3

Health Program, 1962

	Existing	Needed	To Be Built
General Hospital Beds	6,171	10,782	4,611
TB Hospital Beds	1,773	2,688	915
Psychiatric Hospital Beds	2,769	11,980	7,211
Chronic Hospital Beds	321	4,792	4,471
Health Center Beds	397	7,188	6,791
Public Health Units	51	80	29
Diagnosis & Treatment Centers	122	240	118
Rehabilitation Facilities	2	32	30

The government planned in 1963 to finish all started work, providing 740 additional beds. They also plan to start new projects for 588 more beds.

Publicity has made people conscious of their need and the possibility of using hospitals, health

centers and health units. This has brought significant changes in expectations and consequent demand
for health services. Some 82 per cent of all
births now occur in hospitals.

Where thirty years ago, the sick were carried--
often down mountain trails--all the way to the municipal hospital or the doctor, now the ambulance can
be called and gives good service. Of course, there
are still isolated communities with poor access
roads but good roads are closer to all communities
and new access roads are constantly under construction. The number and quality of health services is
immeasurably greater than it was in the 1930's; the
despair associated with illness has become hope.
The ambulance, to dwellers in the rural zone, has become a symbol.

TABLE 4

Life Expectancy at Birth, in Years

1903	1910	1920	1930	1940	1950	1960
36.66	38.17	38.46	40.65	46.01	60.85	69.56

TABLE 5

Deaths and Death Rates, by Decades from 1930 to 1959, and for
1960 from All Causes and by Diarrhea and Enteritis,
Tuberculosis, Malaria, and Infant Mortality

	Deaths				Death Rates			
	1930-39	1940-49	1950-59	1960	1930-39	1940-49	1950-59	1960
General Mortality[a]	33,426	29,262	18,045	15,841	19.7	14.5	8.1	6.7
Diarrhea and Enteritis[b]	7,034	5,552	2,059	934	409.5	226.0	92.5	39.6
Tuberculosis[b]	4,880	4,287	1,322	692	287.6	212.5	59.3	29.3
Malaria[b]	2,946	880	22	0	145.6	54.1	1.0	0
Infant[c]	7,597	7,558	(1950-54) 4,654	3,325	125.5	88.3	(1950-54) 58.6	43.7

[a] per 1,000 population   [b] per 100,000 population   [c] per 1,000 live births

BASIC HEALTH AND WELFARE DISTRICTS, 1962

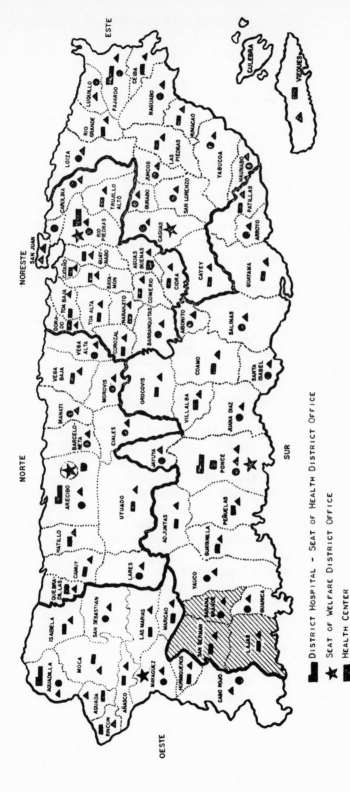

Prepared by:
Organization and Methods Section
Drawn by:
Division of Health Education
Department of Health of Puerto Rico
June 1962

DISTRICT HOSPITAL – SEAT OF HEALTH DISTRICT OFFICE

SEAT OF WELFARE DISTRICT OFFICE

HEALTH CENTER

PUBLIC WELFARE UNIT

PUBLIC HEALTH UNIT

FOR WELFARE PURPOSES THESE MUNICIPALITIES ARE
PART OF THE WEST DISTRICT

GENERAL HOSPITAL ADMINISTERED JOINTLY BY THE MUNICIPAL
GOVERNMENT AND THE DEPT. OF HEALTH

PUBLIC WELFARE

For the people of Puerto Rico, unemployment remains the chief economic problem, depending for its
solution on the further development of industry, agriculture, service, and professional occupations.
If the rate of economic growth, including capital
investment, construction, agricultural reforms, and
resulting consumer demand, continues according to
the planned schedule, present unemployment can become an asset--an adequate labor force, the necessary condition for future investment. At present it
is a liability because loss of income results in de-
privations the state is bound to relieve in some way.

> This conception of public responsibil-
> ity of the whole for the part used not
> to be a majority one; it was therefore
> not official. It is rapidly getting
> beyond argument. There is not quite
> yet universal acceptance of the prin-
> ciple, and there are recurrent efforts
> to relieve government of such responsi-
> bilities; but the main trend is evident
> to all who are not blind. Even reac-
> tionaries hardly ever, any more, suggest
> the abolition of minima: they do not
> suggest either that the support of gov-
> ernment may not be necessary at strate-
> gic points, for sagging sectors of the
> economy: and there is little objection
> to the principle of social services.
> The argument, nowadays, is mostly about
> their desirable extent.[7]

> Public welfare is not only committed
> by its very nature to the camp of democ-
> racy; it is also essential to its func-
> tioning as a social system by the rec-
> ognition of common humanity and basic
> dignity it extends to individuals at
> their point of greatest vulnerability.[8]

Because the function of public welfare has not
been sufficiently integrated with the planning process, there has been until recently evidence of a
lack of imagination in the program. This has been,
in our opinion, a failure on the part of the planners to see the constructive possibilities of a public welfare program which could do much more than
take up the slack, and a failure on the part of the
Public Welfare Division to see its role as an in-
tegral part of a great economic and social movement.
As in many parts of the United States, the recognition of the economic as well as social importance of
rehabilitation has been slow. Reasons are many and
understandable. The New Deal legislation which
brought the Federal Government fully into the field
of welfare (and gave the label of "Welfare State" to
both friends and enemies) dealt with the manifold
aspects of human need which were revealed by the depression crisis. In Puerto Rico, during the days of
the Puerto Rico Emergency Relief Administration,
there was an effort to see the "needy" cases, to
whom relief and work were given, in the context of
the whole economy. This involved the organization
of constructive work projects, through the recognition of the desire of Puerto Ricans to work for what
they received, the possibility--though too seldom
the realization--of preventive programs and the hope
for the incorporation of emergency action in plans
for future development. Relating this directly to
public welfare, a bill was introduced for the creation of an independent Department of Public Welfare
in the (then) Insular Government. This bill was not
passed and public welfare services have remained as
they were before, a division within the Department
of Health.

The close relationship between health and welfare is easily seen and many advantages have accrued
to the welfare program from its association with the
Department of Health, which is remarkable for its
achievements in public health and individual care,
for its experiments in organization, and its excellent research programs. The breadth of view may be
illustrated by some quotations from the Second Annual Report, Social Science Program of the Department

of Health, the grants for which have been given "for
the support of research in anthropology, sociology
and social psychology having planning implications
in social welfare and health. . . ."[9]

> The chosen line of work of the Program
> may be defined as the study of the de-
> terminants and consequents of given
> forms of social structure. Any given
> activity may be characterized by the
> channels in which its interactions are
> normatively concentrated. The pattern-
> ing of these channels is presumed to be
> understandable not only in the sense
> that interactions along it are predict-
> able, but also in the sense that such
> patterns come into existence as part of
> a sequence of circumstances and that
> once in existence they create predict-
> able limitations on the possibility of
> various kinds of further change. The
> analysis of structure leads, in many of
> our studies, to an examination of social
> categories and self-images as substan-
> tive forms in which structure is ex-
> pressed.[10]

The description of one study will illustrate
the value and practical applications to be drawn
from such work in developing programs for a period
of rapid social change:

> 1. WM "Family Life of Working Mothers"
> NIMH grant M-5870 (1/1/62-12/31/64:
> $89,573) Director: Howard R. Stanton.
> Assistant Director: Elia Hidalgo.
> Sponsoring institution: Commonwealth
> Department of Health Data collection
> phase.
>   A study of the effect of maternal
> employment in a rapidly industrializing
> society, based on participant observa-
> tion and interviewing in a sample of
> twenty neighborhoods including 3,000
> households. The research is designed

> to examine effects of maternal employ-
> ment on the child's personality, the
> marital relationship, and the mother's
> self-image. We are investigating the
> ways in which these effects depend upon
> the social context--in particular, the
> family and neighborhood structures.
> Since other studies to date have found
> relatively little effect, we will also
> be looking for adaptive mechanisms
> which may permit the family to absorb
> even major changes in time--use without
> consequent changes in patterns of re-
> lationships.[11]

The conclusions of this study can be applied to
situations new to Puerto Rican society where many
women are working, for the first time, outside their
homes. Such a study also has a bearing on the question of day care for children of working mothers,
for aspects of the current child welfare program.
It can at this point be only a pathbreaker but it
makes clear the value of research projects the conclusions of which can be tested in new situations as
the effect of industrialization spreads and touches
more and more the family relationships and the place
of the family in society.

A study such as the one briefly described would
seem to have a closer connection with welfare than
with health, but it shows that the Department of
Health is involved by interest as well as organization in questions of welfare. The question must be
raised, however, as to whether or not an independent
Department of Welfare would be in a better position
to establish similar and equally close ties with the
Department of Labor in view of the close connection
with employment; with Education through many mutual
concerns such as vocational education as an important factor in rehabilitation; with CRUV because
welfare and housing are closely interrelated.

> Public Welfare in Puerto Rico has
> achieved a degree of development which
> would well warrant its administration

in a separate department as in virtually all parts of the United States. Not
only does it involve a wholly different
discipline from that of public health
but its particular role in government
needs to be understood in its own unique
terms. Public welfare has its own place
in the total range of governmental functions and needs, in my opinion, to take
its place in its councils, joining its
voice and its experience to those of
the other branches of government service.[12]

Our present study is concerned with organization only
because of its importance to planning. It is our
opinion that more could have been done in the development of human resources--what has been done has
opened up many possibilities.

The following is an example:

A new program (April, 1964) for school subsidies to children of families receiving public welfare allowances is an illustration of the close connection between welfare and education. The program
is an ad hoc plan set up to make education possible
in the lowest-income families; it is a recognition
that education is essential to progress toward the
good society. It applies to children above kinder-
garten level and includes vocational education.

The primary purpose of the special program is
to make it possible for children of poor families to
stay in school to age eighteen and for those who
have left school, for economic reasons, before this
age, to return. It is hoped that, though the additional allowance is small, it will encourage parents
to keep their children in school. It will help to
provide incentive to the children and young people,
themselves.

Such a plan involves complicated budgetary
operations because it requires constant adjustment

to relief rolls but it is an important sample of the
effort of the Division of Public Welfare to provide
a series of social services which will lead to the
rehabilitation of recipients of economic aid and to
the prevention of dependence.

The most constructive, inclusive, and exciting
program of the Division of Public Welfare is the proposed ten-year plan, which presents practical recommendations for the rehabilitation of families with
annual incomes below $2,000.

Philosophically, this ten-year proposal represents revolutionary thinking of a kind which is beginning to permeate the social-work field everywhere.
It is revolutionary because it means that public assistance may truly become public welfare; because it
sees a new integration with the whole economy, the
whole culture. In the continental United States,
the process of change is slow, it meets with resistance from vested interests, from sentimental resid-
uum from a past of charity and philanthropy; from
the difficulties involved in the fundamental reorganization of agencies and new demands for cooperation.
Puerto Rico will face these same problems in greater
or less degree, but the new proposals represent
practical plans which have been worked out by a de-
liberate confrontation of the existing situation and
attention to the points at which new approaches can
be made, taking the presently possible steps in the
progress toward the goal. The way in which the question arose, which led to the ten-year plan, is
interesting.[13]

In 1961, the San Juan Star published an editorial calling attention to the paradoxical situation
in which 600,000 persons were receiving surplus food
from the Federal Government (U.S. Department of Agriculture) and, at the same time, there was an unemployment rate of 12 per cent despite an unmet demand
for agricultural laborers.

In response to this editorial, the Governor
asked that a study be made to throw light on this
situation and to analyze the problem which it

presented. The study was made by a committee on
which the Department of Labor, Public Welfare Division of the Department of Health, and the Planning
Board was represented. The function of the Department of Labor was to gather additional information
concerning families included in the statistics of
both employed and unemployed, checked according to
their receipt of public assistance or surplus food.
The Division of Public Welfare verified this information through all Public Welfare Units in the island. The final analysis was made by the Planning
Board and the Office of Statistics of Public Welfare.

Summary of the report follows:

   1. Of the 96,000 families receiving public assistance, 42,000 had no
members capable of working. They were
women caring for young children, the
disabled, or the aged.
   2. In those families receiving
public assistance, where there were
persons able to work, the persons employed were, for the most part, un-
skilled workers whose wages were lowest in the wage scale of the island.
   3. The percentage of unemployed
among members of the families receiving public assistance was higher than
that of the population as a whole.[14]

A few statistics regarding population figures
might be appropriate here: Size of families on relief is 5.7 members compared to 4.8 for the general
population. Some 11 per cent (10,560 families) have
ten members; 20,156 of the thirteen-to seventeen-
year age group are among relief families; between
the years eighteen to twenty-nine, there are 10,415
young people on relief. All could benefit from centers of work and study.

This study urges that a high priority be given
in socio-economic planning to its recommendations.

This would be essential if its premise were accepted:
"that the program of public assistance in Puerto
Rico be limited to those families which do not include employable persons." This is the desirable
goal which can only be attained by a gradual process,
because, to quote again from Elizabeth Wickenden:

> Economic planning in a democratic set-
> ting must take into account the total
> population, the total income available
> for its support, and the most equitable
> way to divide this income in order to
> meet the needs of all. Whether the
> struggling jibaro shares his pot of
> beans and rice with his own and his
> wife's aged parents, the orphaned child
> crying at the door, and his unemployed
> neighbor or whether the struggling gov-
> ernment finds the means to finance a
> public assistance program the charge
> against the economy is still there.[15]

The proposed program includes: orientation for
youth, community education and cultural activities,
religious orientation, subsidies to selected institutions; legal services for the protection of minors
and abandoned children, legal services to families;
work with school dropouts in connection with programs of the Department of Education; day care for
children of working parents, training programs, medical services, services to the blind through training
courses, scholarships and library facilities, courses
and recreation for the aged; services of care and
training for the mentally retarded. Special services
are also planned for drug addicts, mentally disturbed
children, and delinquents.

The present services of the Division of Public
Welfare and those proposed differ in purpose and emphasis rather than in actual subjects covered. The
proposals would require organizational changes and,
in some cases, new legislation. To make such a program effective will require a new orientation for
public welfare personnel and should draw them closer

to the problems of planning. This, in turn, will
require greater cooperation with other departments
of the government and greater understanding of economic factors. Public assistance can no longer be
looked upon as the caretaker for those left behind
in the socio-economic progress of Puerto Rico; it
must become, in a new sense, the adjuster of those
least able to adapt themselves to change, as the
discoverer of new potentials among the under-
privileged, as the searcher for causes of maladjust-
ment, as the agency best able to understand the deep
effects of poverty.

This brings us face to face with the most difficult problems of a planned society in a democratic
framework: the protection of the rights of the individual who must find his place in a period of
change and rapid industrialization, involving the
transformation of traditional to modern patterns;
the decision on priorities with the necessity for
understanding on the part of legislators and the
public. Should money be appropriated, and at what
point, for rehabilitation of the delinquent child
in order to make him a contributing member of society, or should it be spent for greater opportunities
for the normal and constructive members of society?
Should new factories be built as investment for increased employment opportunities or should the money
be spent on raising present welfare allowances? Economics, like individuals, must make those adjustments
which make existence possible.

In this plan the hope is expressed that with the
inauguration and establishment of the programs recommended, only the unemployables would receive relief and its suggestions are designed to put into
the labor force many who are now not only unemployed
but unemployable due to disabilities of various
kinds--physical incapacities, lack of training, in-
ability to adjust to new situations, old age, and
the general effects of a life of poverty. It is obvious that such a plan depends on job opportunities
and education and, in the long run, on some form of
population control. The connection with other programs as well as the rapid implementation of the

recommendation of the Welfare Division is, in our
opinion, one of the most important areas for governmental planning. It is such apparently Utopian goals
which have inspired in Puerto Rico the most practical
programs: to eliminate poverty, both physical and
spiritual, is one of the great dreams of our age.

In Puerto Rico the estimate of families with
incomes of $2,000 or less is 209,000; 23 per cent of
these (48,550) have less than $500 annual income.[16]
Because many of the rural areas present problems of
poverty, because many from the country move to the
cities in the hope of finding employment or a fuller
life, but often end up as slum creators and slum
dwellers, there is an urgency to deal with these
matters.

Again we see the difficulty for the planners in
making decisions on priorities and the complexity of
financing which is involved. Competent personnel is
essential. Much will depend on the enrichment of
the social-work training, on collaboration between
social work and the social sciences, on the effective uses of research projects carefully designed.
Those competent to do the constructive work required
must have opportunity to use imagination, must relate
techniques to ideas.

Under its regular program (through July, 1963)
the Public Welfare Division of the Department of
Health is responsible for the operation of all pro-
grams--federal and Commonwealth--in the welfare
field. This means that it meets all federal requirements for matching funds and additional funds from
the Commonwealth budget.

A program of direct economic assistance to families is shown in Table 6.

TABLE 6

Public Assistance

	Total	State	Federal
Administrative Costs	$2,560,346	$2,560,346	
Direct Aid with Matching Fund	17,195,000	8,020,000	$9,175,000
Direct Aid Without Matching Fund	200,000	200,000	
Emergency Aid	100,000	100,000	
Medical Services to the Aged	200,000		200,000

Child Welfare

This program is designed to provide services for the development of children in their own homes, health and psychiatric services, for institutional care, for foster homes and adoption, for orientation of children who leave institutions. Underlying these activities is the fundamental purpose: education of the community to prevent problems from arising or becoming acute, and to keep children in their own homes.

TABLE 7

Amounts Budgeted for Child Welfare, Services
to the Disabled, Institutions

	Total	State	Federal
Child Welfare			
Total Adminis-trative Costs	$871,054	$409.928	$461,126
Total Services	665,685	583,362	82,323
Total Budget for Child Welfare	1,536,739	993,290	543,449
Services to the Disabled	48,999		
Total--Public Welfare Budget (Exclusive of Institutions)	22,316,421	12,383,515	9,932,906
Institutions			
Children's Homes Total Budget	664,948	646,542	18,406
Industrial School	591,574	587,700	3,874
Juvenile Homes	204,054	196,305	7,749
Treatment Centers for Boys	84,817	84,817	
Boys' Camps	63,620	63,620	
Institute for Blind Children	105,265	105,265	
Home for Blind Adults	102,336	102,336	

Food Distribution

A program of the U.S. Department of Agriculture
for the distribution of food to recipients of public
assistance, to patients suffering from tuberculosis
or cancer, and patients in prenatal clinics, to
children recommended by Public Health Units, to institutions of public welfare and other nonprofit
institutions. The Commonwealth Government provides
funds for all costs of distribution, personnel, rent
of distribution centers, transportation and vitamin
enrichment. There are 78 distribution centers for
food, 218 milk stations. Pounds of food distributed
(1963) amounted to 96,592,289 to 688,820 persons, as
well as hospitals and other institutions, and 761,264
pounds of milk. This obviously supplements substan-
tially the allowances for public assistance.

A limited staff, until recently, could not do
an adequate job. The situation has been relieved by
new provisions (1962-63) of the Social Security Act
giving additional funds for the aged and lowering
the age limit, by increased incomes of families
(budget based for those truly eligible), special
policies based on real needs of the family. The
last of these is based on a division of the family
into two parts: the nuclear family; the extended
family (additional members of the household). By
estimating the two groups separately, deducting contributions of earnings by those employed, and then
combining, the total has been reduced by 10 per cent.
This is also a way of making accurate estimates of
the total number who make up the household.

In 1958, needs estimated at $80 per month per
family (5.7 members in welfare families as against
P.R. average of 4.8) were divided: 45 per cent for
adults, 33 per cent for children.

Before 1958--example
                Estimated need $80
                45 per cent of $80   36
                Less $20 for private
                    income   -20
                                           $16 paid

After 1958--example

Estimated need	$80
Less private income	-20
	$60
45 per cent of $60	$27 paid

The new formula gained $11.00. The study was repeated for the extended family. This may close 10 per cent of the cases and allow, on the same budget appropriation, $3,000,000 for other uses.

This means that some of the restrictions in services, which had been necessary because of budget deficits, can now be taken off. The Federal Government allows discretion in deducting the first $10 earned.

The new program for rehabilitation would make possible further reduction of relief costs. Labor departments and the Veterans' Administration cooperate on social-insurance agreements; there will be workshops by region and municipality with a coordinator to observe and report, and working projects under the Board of Vocational Rehabilitation cooperating with Public Welfare. Public Welfare now has liaison with Fomento and with Public Works; also programs with the Department of Education, Rehabilitation and Vocational Education for Public Welfare institutions and for children from welfare cases. The hope is also to work with adults.

Whether or not the ten-year plan of the "Bienestar Publico ante el Proposito de Puerto Rico" is completely put into effect organizationally, it is a clear indication of a changed point of view. The emphasis is already on rehabilitation. This appears in many reports and documents of the Division on its various current programs. This does not mean any diminishment in the importance of the individual but rather an enhancement of his value, seen in the context of his potential contribution to the economy and to the whole material cultural and spiritual growth of Puerto Rico.

TABLE 8

Persons Served by the Division of Public Welfare

(From the Statistical Office, February 19, 1963)

Public Welfare Programs	At End of Quarter Dec. 31, 1962	At End of Last Quarter Sept. 30, 1962	At End of Same Quarter Last Year Dec. 1, 1961
I. Public Assistance			
Cases	117,176	117,863	121,602
Persons	292,887	293,000	299,565
Adults	110,457	110,995	114,519
Children under 18	182,430	182,005	185,046
Average payment per case latest month	$11.47	$11.47	$11.48
Total spent in latest month	$1,347,284.75	$1,353,658.25	$1,391,996.00
Applications pending	2,733	3,513	3,745

II. Child Welfare

Families	6,161	6,066	5,899
Children under 21	14,455	13,029	10,195
Community	12,645	11,229	8,501
Foster homes	1,235	1,218	1,149
With "amas de llaves"	386	330	159
In public institutions	1,557	1,523	1,466
In private institutions	253	277	228
Children waiting to receive services	1,520	1,540	1,528

III. Other Services

Home for blind adults	96	93	97
Blind receiving instruction at home	146	147	136

TABLE 9

State of Employment of Civilian Population--
Exclusive of Institutions--Who Receive
Assistance or Who Do Not
Receive Assistance

	Total		Not Receiving Aid		Receiving Aid or Commodities	
	Number	Per Cent	Number	Per Cent	Number	Per Cent
Families	495,600	100%	376,100		119,500	
Persons	2,392,700	100%	1,713,700	100%	678,900	100%
Civilian population 14 years or more not in institutions	1,416,300		1,055,100		361,200	
Available workers	628,710	26.3%	506,300	29.5%	122,400	18.0%
Employed	539,200		442,300		96,800	
Unemployed	89,500		64,000		25,600	

Outside of labor force (housewives, disabled, etc.)	787,600	32.9%	548,800	32.1%	238,800	35.1%
Less than 14 years	976,400	40.8%	658,600	38.4%	317,800	46.8%
Percentage of unemployed	14.2%		12.6%		20.8%	
Rate of participation in labor force	44.0%		48.0%		34.0%	

Source: Division de Bienestar Público, Junta de Planificación, San Juan, P.R., Study of State of Employment of Families Who Receive Public Assistance or Federal Commodities in Puerto Rico, July 1961. September, 1962, p. 7.

TABLE 10

Division of Public Welfare Statistics, June, 1964

Receiving	Number of Families	Number of Recipients	Percentage of Population
Public Assistance	78,557	273,273	11.6
Child Welfare Services	7,141	18,830	0.8
Federal Commodities	117,235	674,586	28.7

(Population reported, Puerto Rico, 1960 Census = 2,349,544)

TABLE 11

Median Weekly Family Income, Type of Assistance, Urban and Rural, July, 1961

Type of Assistance	Total	Urban	Rural
Average of total population (families)	$17.99	$29.80	$11.78
Families in both programs	4.44	4.07	5.16
Families receiving public assistance	4.02	3.67	4.23
Families receiving only commodities	14.22	23.41	12.00
Families not receiving help	28.10	35.40	15.33

CHART 1

Division of Public Welfare, Department of Health

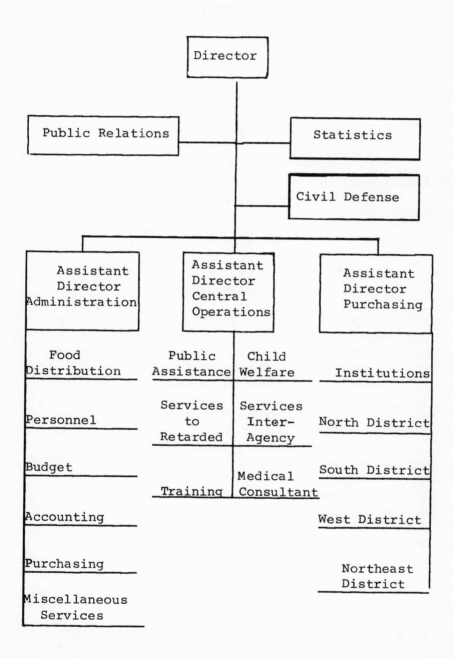

DEPARTMENT OF JUSTICE

Services in the court system are of great importance. Puerto Rico faces the same problems which characterize many present-day societies and has recognized the need for services both of prevention and rehabilitation in dealing with the whole question of crime--its causes and its treatment.

The following services are offered to the Superior Court:

Family Relations

This program was established to help unify the family through counseling--cases referred by courts or other agencies and by request of individuals for services.

During the year 1962-63, 5,142 cases were accepted.

Program for Minors

The function of this program is to provide social services to minors in collaboration with the Superior Court "to provide the orientation necessary to their welfare in harmony with the public interest." In 1962-63 this service was given to 5,719 cases.

Juvenile Probation

Over 4,161 cases received help and adjustment through probation officers.

Supplementary psychological and psychiatric services are offered and 357 psychiatric, 147 psychological, and 15 neurological evaluations were made.

DEPARTMENT OF LABOR

In an interview, Secretary of Labor Frank Zorrilla defined the goal of the Department of

Labor as "adequate income for everyone: the ideal;
that this income should come from work in which a
man or woman can take pride." This statement would
be endorsed by all the countries of the world today
where the need and the right to work are recognized.
It has a special meaning in those countries which
are facing a rapid industrialization without a long
period of gradual transition and where the social
effects often mean the transformation, at varying
rates, of an agrarian society into an urban industrialized society.

The problem of unemployment is the core of the
economic problem for Puerto Rico today. This fact
appears repeatedly in this report. It is at the center of all planning; it affects all decisions on
priorities; it has a special poignancy because its
effects on human beings are so clearly seen.

In countries already industrialized there is a
concentration on other questions: automation, the
psychological effects of monotony in work, the use
of leisure. In Puerto Rico it is understandable
that these questions are secondary, that attention
must first be given to the goal of jobs and the effect of wages on standards of living. To the laborer, the agregado, the cane worker, a factory job
brings the hope of many satisfactions. These satisfactions are actualities for thousands of workers
now. The effort of Fomento to place factories
throughout the island and to relate location to regional planning gives promise of a better balance
between the growth of cities and the development of
life in small towns and country. The Departments of
Education and of Health are conscious of their responsibilities to the new society in training and
facilities. The Department of Agriculture, through
the Programas Socialies, has been instrumental in
introducing the parcelas and small farms--a way of
life which already offers a transition for the agricultural workers of the past from their work as
"agregados" to factory workers or new types of agriculture. This means not only a new type of community (described elsewhere) but, with new facilities
for transportation, it also means an available labor

supply. Puerto Rico is, through such programs, planning for the future. Increasing mechanization in the sugar industry, growing industrialization, and mobility will be bringing new problems but they may be ameliorated by the foresight evident in current planning for the future. The changes which have already come have brought new freedoms to many --freedom to move from place to place, to select a job (though still limited by circumstances and financial necessity); better health, more leisure, less worry.

In 1936, the Department of Labor under Commissioner P. Rivera Martinez, published a report of over 600 pages on Social Legislation in Puerto Rico. This book describes forms of labor in Puerto Rico from its earliest colonization through the changing and growing sense of responsibility, expressed in laws dealing with labor, up through 1936. This again points to the fact that the roots for recent growth were well established in earlier times

Two forms of forced labor existed in colonial times:[17] One where workers were under agents, the other, African slaves. In 1503, the Spanish Crown authorized the use of Indians to work on construction, in mines and in agriculture, under Spanish overseers. The conditions of work, and the kind of work, to which the Indians were totally unaccustomed, led to rebellion on the part of the Indians, who were then declared slaves. "By the year 1542 the Indians had practically disappeared from Puerto Rico due to illness, exhaustion, death or emigration to neighboring islands."[18] The importation of Negro slaves was authorized in 1501.

In 1869 the new Spanish constitution extended to Puerto Rico freed slaves, guaranteed the right to assemble, freedom of speech, and other civil rights. Following this, the Civil Code, also extended to Puerto Rico, regulated contracts, specifying protective measures for workers.

This background, with both its positive and its negative connotations, is important. The class

system, growing out of slavery and a system of
forced labor, represents the negative aspect, as far
as the development of democratic society is concerned, but, on the other hand, we see in the latter
part of the nineteenth century and immediately preceding the change of sovereignty from Spain to the
United States a recognition of human rights which
went far in its promise of new freedom for labor.

No single subject could illustrate more clearly
than the field of labor what the change in sovereignty meant to Puerto Rico--socially, economically, and
politically. To follow the history of labor--legis-
lation, union organization, the culture of the work-
er--carrying on the work done by Vicente Geigel
Polanco, would provide new insights into the whole
process and meaning of change. It is important to
note that in 1936 laws on the books covered such subjects as a joint resolution to stimulate handwork
and native industries; the creation of a tobacco
institute; cooperation with the Federal Government
in housing construction; fixing of interest rates on
debts; creation of a vocational institute for the
blind; accident and occupational disease security;
pensions for government employees; a board of child
welfare; a reform school; establishment of the rights
of employers in case of strike; plan for the organization of the Labor Department.[19]

It is obvious that the Department of Labor has
had, from its inception, a broad conception of social responsibility. The poverty of the island in
the 1930's, the fact that this was before the New
Deal and that therefore the Federal Government made
no contribution, meant that many programs were extremely limited in their operation. Nevertheless,
the vision was there, the needs were recognized, the
legislative program was developed for Puerto Rico.
This represents in practical form an example of
adaptation to the introduction of modern capitalism
with its accompanying problems, and a psychological
and social preparation for what was to follow at the
time of the governorship of Tugwell and the establishment of the Commonwealth with the leadership of
Muñoz Marín.

The following quotations, taken from Fernando Sierra Berdecía,[20] throw further light on the goal and organization of the Department of Labor.

> The public labor policy of Puerto Rico embraces two fields of action; (1) governmental initiative through legislative action, or action taken by virtue of the law, fixing and enacting protective standards for labor; and (2) the initiative and action of the organized labor movement strengthening and extending governmental standards through collective bargaining.
>
> The effectiveness of any public policy must be evaluated in the light of the problems which arise from its establishment and introduction. In the development of the public labor policy in Puerto Rico we are faced with one fundamental problem: that of unemployment. Workers are divided into groups: those who are employed and the unemployed. While a worker is unemployed, he is not receiving direct benefit from the public labor policy, nor from governmental efforts, nor from collective action on the part of labor unions; and when his unemployment is permanent, due to lack of employment opportunities, his social need reduces and limits his enjoyment of his civil liberties and rights. The total absence of purchasing power in an unemployed worker affects the economy in general, and, in particular, the contractor of goods and services and the workers who for remunerative wages made the article or render the services.
>
> The Government of the Commonwealth of Puerto Rico has entrusted the introduction and development of its part in the public labor policy to agencies, namely: the Department of Labor and the Labor Relations Board, which operate

separately in their respective juris-
dictions.

The Labor Relations Act of Puerto
Rico and the Board which administers
this law are the instrumentalities
created by the Legislative power to
guarantee these collective rights to
workers. Because of the fact that the
National Labor Management Relations Act
of 1947 (Taft-Hartley Act) has jurisdiction in Puerto Rico, the range of
the Puerto Rico Labor Relations Board
and the Labor Relations Act is limited
to agriculture and Government instrumentalities that operate as private
enterprises. In Puerto Rico the Taft-
Hartley Act is being applied in the
same way as in the territories and the
District of Columbia, which involves
interstate commerce as well as commerce
within the Commonwealth. At present we
are trying to clarify the so-called "no
man's land"--those industries over which
the National Labor Relations Board has
no jurisdiction and in which our jurisdiction is doubtful.

The New Minimum Wage Act establishes that proceedings before the
Board and the Minimum Wage Committees
named by the Board be of a quasi-
legislative nature; and that the public hearings be conducted as public consultations, in which all interested
parties and persons have the opportunity to present their information and data
as well as their recommendations.

The Minimum Wage Act provides that
the Board shall revise the minimum wages
of all industries, including those which
produce articles for interstate commerce, at least once every two years.
The U.S. Fair Labor Standards Act of
1938, as amended, establishes that the
Federal Wage and Hour Division must

revise the minimum wages of all industries engaged in the production of
articles for interstate commerce at
least once a year.

The twenty-two mandatory decrees
in force when the new Minimum Wage Act
was approved, in June 1956, covered
around 280,000 workers, and had increased their income by approximately
thirty-three million dollars a year.
The new Minimum Wage Act of 1956 was
itself responsible for an increase in
the income of around 238,000 workers
(in the season of greatest industrial
activity) to the tune of fifteen million dollars a year. The nineteen decrees approved under the new act cover
around 110,000 workers, increasing
their income by nearly $12,000,000
yearly.

The Constitution fixes the regular
working day as of eight hours and provides that only through extra compensation, which will never be less than $1\frac{1}{2}$
times the normal wage rate, as specified
by law, may any work be done in excess
of this daily limit. Act No. 379 of
May 15, 1948, limits the working day to
eight hours in any period of twenty-
four consecutive hours, and the work
week to forty-eight hours.

The functions connected with the
enforcement of legislation on wages and
hours and working conditions; the act
providing for compensation in cases of
unjust discharge from employment; the
one providing for rest-periods at half
pay for maternity purposes before and
after childbirth for working mothers;
and those which regulate the employment
of women and children, are carried out
by the Department through the Bureau of
Labor Standards and the Bureau of Legal
Affairs.

There are in Puerto Rico several
programs of social security against
industrial hazards: (1) insurance
against work accidents; (2) the U.S.
Old Age and Survivors Insurance;
(3) insurance against illness or death
of chauffeurs working for pay; (4) unemployment compensation in the sugar
industry; (5) the Employment Security
Program, which will start benefit payments in January 1959, and which is at
present collecting employers' contributions. This program will cover over
200,000 workers in manufacturing and
service industries, excluding agriculture, domestic service and homework.
This program, within the economic limitations of Puerto Rico, follows the same
structure and philosophy of unemployment
security as in the United States. It is
a sister-plan to an employment service
which actively negotiates employment
for the unemployed.

The industrial expansion in Puerto
Rico can be determined through the following statistical data: In 1940, compulsory work-accident insurance administered by the State Insurance Fund
covered 9,000 employers with a payroll
of $75,000,000. Today, this same com-
pulsory insurance against work accidents
covers 37,000 employers with an insured
payroll of around $475,000,000. We
must also take into consideration that
the first minimum wage act was approved
in 1941 and that from that date on,
whether by the Puerto Rico Minimum Wage
Board, or the U.S. Wage and Hour Division, these wages have been revised very
frequently.

Technological progress is essential
to the economic development of a country
in order to increase its industrial pro-
ductivity, and to enable it to compete
legitimately with other manufacturing

areas. This increase in production is
indispensable to raising the standards
of living of all the citizens. The
introduction of technological improvements is, therefore, necessary for the
economical development and the welfare
of the people. . . . The increase in
production: (1) yields greater wealth;
(2) augments the necessary capital for
new investments and thus creates new
employment opportunities for the unemployed; (3) reduces noticeably the cost
of production, thereby permitting in-
creases in wages; and (4) makes price
reductions to the consumer possible, in
both goods and services.

Regardless of what has been said
previously, it is a fact that in its
initial period, technological advancements in businesses and industries already existing, produce unemployment
and suffering to the displaced workers
and their families. It is necessary to
reduce this suffering to a minimum, until the economic expansion produces its
result of direct benefit through the
increase in jobs and in wages for the
workers.

Puerto Rico presents an unusual
picture of economic development. The
industrialization program has created
thousands of new employment opportunities. The new industries which are
being established on the Island usually
start out with all the technological
improvements which science can provide.
In the case of these new industries,
technology or mechanization do not produce unemployment, since in each newly
established industry each occupation
which is created is an additional source
of employment to those already in existence on the Island. On the other hand,
the businesses which were in operation
before the industrialization program was

started, be they agricultural, manufacturing or service industries, have to become modernized. Only in this manner can greater production, lower production costs, higher salaries, and reasonable prices to the consumer, be attained. Besides, in no other manner can these industries compete legitimately with similar enterprises which produce for the same market. This modernization will inevitably cause technological unemployment. . . .

Employment security programs are necessary, and they have been created to guarantee to workers a minimum income and the continuation of their purchasing power when they become unemployed because of reasons beyond their control.

It is my belief that a public policy should be adopted to the effect that technological advancements be introduced in a planned system, so that they will not cause--as far as possible--abrupt changes, that may displace workers in great numbers. As far as is practical, these innovations should follow the normal rhythm of the economic expansion of the country.

It is my opinion that industry, organized labor, and the Government should work in mutual agreement, anticipating the introduction of these changes, so that the technological advancements, the plans for social compensation and the creation of new employment opportunities may be coordinated and developed simultaneously.

The government of Puerto Rico neither encourages nor discourages the migration of Puerto Rican workmen to the United States or any foreign country; but it considers it its duty to provide the proper guidance with respect to opportunities for employment and the problems of adjustment to environments which are ethnologically alien; and it is likewise its duty through such guidance of Puerto Rican workmen who migrate to the United States and other countries, to endeavor to reduce to a minimum the natural problems of adjustment arising out of any migratory movement of this nature.

The working conditions for migrant workers are specified before they leave the Island. After the workers leave Puerto Rico, the Migration Division's offices located in the United States keep a close watch on the progress of adjustment of the workers to their new jobs.

Puerto Ricans, as American citizens, enjoy complete freedom to move from one locality to another in the United States. Any Puerto Rican who wishes to leave the Island to go to the mainland, can do so whenever he wishes. Migrants who leave the Island on their own initiative are furnished information and guidance by the Employment Service as to any problem that may arise on their arrival, as well as to food, climate, clothing, etc.

The Department also arranges for the workers to pay the lowest possible rates for transportation, under the guarantees of comfort and security established by the government of the United States and Puerto Rico. It advises employers on the kind of food that Puerto Rican workers prefer, to make them feel more comfortable and adjust to their environment more easily.

Agricultural workers in the United States have never been covered by protective labor legislation, which has been limited to workers and employees in non-agricultural jobs. They have been specifically excluded from such legislation. The worker's contract

which is approved in Puerto Rico contains, as I have pointed out, the basic
principles of the social legislation
of Puerto Rico. The wage rate certi-
fied as the prevailing one at the time
the contract is signed by the workers,
actually becomes the minimum wage they
are to receive.

The Bureau of Labor Statistics of the Department of Labor is at present carrying on a study of
incomes and expenditures. A similar study was last
done in 1953.

DEPARTMENT OF AGRICULTURE

Natural Vegetation and Soils

Before the coming of the Europeans to Puerto
Rico, the island was totally covered with natural
vegetation. The Indians lived largely around the
coastal area and their food came from yucca and
corn, crabs, mollusks, and other seafood. As late as
the nineteenth century, 75 per cent of the island
was covered with woods. With the increase of population, this percentage was reduced to 20 per cent
by 1925.

There has been a great deal of exhaustion of
the soil and large areas of erosion. These changes
in the vegetation of Puerto Rico have diminished the
agricultural opportunities of the island.

In the early days of the Spanish occupation,
the extraction of minerals from the rivers was the
main occupation, but this period ended after a short
time, by the middle of the sixteenth century, and it
became necessary for the colonists to turn to agriculture for their subsistence.

Early in the period of colonization, sugar was
introduced into Puerto Rico from Santo Domingo. By
1815, sugar was being exported to the United States

and at the end of the century the value of sugar
products passed the 4-million-peso mark. Coffee
was introduced relatively late, in 1736 from Haiti,
but by the end of the Spanish period it was the
principal product, reaching, in 1897, 50 million
pounds with a value of more than 12 million pesos.
Tobacco is indigenous to the island. For many
years, it was raised on small plots for the local
cigar market. By 1897, the production had grown to
4 million pounds with a value of 1 million pesos
and became the third-ranking export from Puerto
Rico.[21]

Other than these crops, Puerto Rico raised only
minor crops of fruits and vegetables native to the
country. Sugar cane has remained, up to 1962, the
most important agricultural product not only in actual value but, in large measure, as the determinant
of land values.

Now the dairy industry equals in value the production of cane. This represents an extremely important change economically and a very real accomplishment in agricultural planning because it takes
a large amount of marginal land out of sugar production.

It has required scientific study of grasses
suitable for pasture, which can be raised on land
which had been used, in addition to sugar, for the
production of coffee and tobacco. It thus becomes
one of the major factors in a better balanced and
more productive agricultural program.

Although Puerto Rico has a diversity of minerals, relatively few have proved commercially profitable at this date. Among these that have been
developed are manganese--deposits found in Juana
Diaz (one of our ten communities). In Juana Diaz,
marble is quarried also. On the southeast coast
large quantities of salt are produced through evap-
oration of sea water and used for domestic consumption. Recent discoveries of minerals with sufficient content of nickel warrant further exploration
and probably development.

Studies made under the auspices of the Development Corporation indicate the possibility of the existence of oil. As Puerto Rico now imports very large amounts of oil (most of it refined in Puerto Rico), discovery of oil would give very great impetus to the Puerto Rican economy. Explorations, with more than a little hope of success, are being conducted near Utuado for copper.

Following is a statement from Guillermo Perez, United States Department of Agriculture, head of the sugar program, which gives an idea of what is being done in the agricultural field to stimulate both quantity and quality of cooperative production.

> The Federal Government, through the Department of Agriculture, has many services in Puerto Rico which benefit all communities. In the sugar industry, subsidies are given to the producers as a guarantee of proper minimum wages and proper payment to farmers. Under "Marketing" is the "School Lunch Program" which receives large sums of money and surplus food products. There is also distribution of the latter through Public Welfare.
> Another activity is the Rural Development Agency and Soil Conservation Program, which works to preserve the land from excess of erosion and other soil conservation practices. The Farmers' Home Administration subsidizes farm and land development and house building. The Bureau of Forestry cooperates with the Commonwealth Government in reforestation. The Federal Experimental Station in Mayaguez devotes its energies to the development of agricultural products and farm practices.
> The Agricultural Conservation Agency, formerly the AAA, administers subsidies to the sugar industry and works in cooperation with the Commonwealth Government, which makes a larger

proportional contribution to the program than does any state. Puerto Rico
has become a high-cost sugar-producing
country, which has caused the withdrawal
from sugar production of 84,000 acres
of marginal land. Also, greater efficiency in the mills has caused the closing down of possibly twelve mills in
the last ten years; probably ten more
will close down in the near future.
Mechanization is a burning question,
opposed by labor, but inevitable if the
sugar industry expects to compete in
the U.S. market. A great deal of experimentation is done in variety and
yields, as well as in mechanization of
the harvesting processes. The reduction of labor may be from 100,000 to
15,000 when these programs are completed.

The owners of 56,000 acres that
have been withdrawn from cane production
were questioned about their return to
cane growing if prices were better,
labor was available, and other advantages were provided by the government.
The owners, 36,000 of the 56,000, said
they would under no circumstances go
back into cane. The rest of the owners
of 20,000 acres said that they would or
might go back if certain conditions
were met. Sugar land that has been
eliminated from sugar production has
been distributed as follows: 60 per
cent or so in pasture or grass for dairy
production; a small percentage has been
used in building new roads and the remainder is either in housing developments or in the hands of owners who are
holding it for price speculation. A
very large majority of the land taken
out of sugar is in the northern part of
the island in the area between Arecibo
and Fajardo.

> In 1930 when sugar was by all odds
> the major crop and industry of Puerto
> Rico, land values were set on the basis
> of sugar property; now that has changed
> and the tremendous development of ur-
> banization has influenced the value of
> land out of proportion to its original
> value as agricultural land.

In an interview, Secretary Rivera Santos, of
the Department of Agriculture, stated that the
problems of the department come largely from the
outside, i.e., urbanization, competition with industry, and technological developments forcing other
new forms of competition. Before 1952, sugar was
profitable at $6.25 per 100 pounds. The island was
able to produce its quota without difficulty until
the hurricane of 1956 and the drought of 1957. Sugar is not as flexible as some other crops, and
changes take more time. These figures plus an es-
calator clause for wages have made subsidies necessary.

The sugar cane and dairy industries are now
about equal in money value and beef raising is being
developed rapidly, having doubled in the last ten
years. Meat consumption is also rising rapidly and
beef must still be imported.

Mechanization is coming slowly to the island,
the changeover having only been started fifteen
years ago as against seventy years ago in the
United States.

The laborers and the unions still fear the advent of mechanization and cannot forget the old days
of unemployment. The government is well aware of
the situation and is taking steps to see to it that
mechanization does not create large-scale unemployment.

One unfortunate event affecting the fruit industry was the fact that Florida publicized a story
stating that Puerto Rican fruit was infected by the

Mediterranean fruit fly, which caused the placing of
a quarantine on the island fruit.   This was not true
but it ruined the grapefruit industry and the production of grapefruit in Puerto Rico has practically
disappeared.   Incentives for bringing back the
orange and grapefruit are being paid primarily for
the purpose of raising these fruits for juice canning and freezing.

The department is working very hard to develop
the banana and plantain industry and is experiment-
ing on Jamaican types which are resistant to the
Panama disease.

For some years the development and modernizing
of agriculture was in part neglected due to the effort being put into manufacturing.   This is understandable because everyone realized fully that no
amount of modernization could enable Puerto Rico to
be self-supporting on agriculture alone.   It was
estimated in 1930 that, based on the number of acres
of tillable land needed to feed one person, Puerto
Rico could not raise food enough for more than
600,000 persons.   Sugar was so much more profitable
than any other crop that it was better to raise and
sell sugar and import basic foods rather than raise
them.   The PRERA tried an extensive pilot program of
raising rice, a high-consumption food on the island,
and it only served to confirm the hypothesis that it
was more profitable to raise sugar and buy rice.

When it was decided to put more emphasis on
agricultural production in order to balance the
economy and make the best use of the available land,
the following steps were taken.   (It is still true
that, except for the tremendous increase in dairy
production, agricultural efforts have been concentrated on export crops such as sugar, tobacco, coffee, etc.).

The Agricultural Credit Corporation was set up
to give credit to farmers who could not get the usual
commercial credit in order to carry out their work.
The money is loaned at 5 per cent interest for a

period up to eight years. The corporation has $2.5
million capital and $250,000 a year for expenses--
this is a revolving fund--and up to 1963 it has made
756 loans. This is for all types of farming.

Sugar

Beginning in 1963, funds became available
for credit to farmers to buy sugar cane equipment
and machinery and for the establishment of more machinery centers in strategic points throughout the
island.

In 1962, incentive payments were established to
restore land taken out of sugar, for the application
of lime to correct acidities, for the purchase of
new seed, and for combating pests and diseases in
the newly seeded areas.

In 1962, incentives of $50 per acre up to 50
acres per farmer were paid for replacing old plantings of sugar with new plantings of higher quality
and more variety. Up to 1962, 315,802 acres were
renewed and new seed was supplied for 212,416 acres.
During 1963, it was planned to renew 22,000 more.

In the period between 1952 and 1963, 72,000
acres were taken out of cane production. To re-
verse this tendency, incentives of $75 per acre up
to 50 acres were paid for the redemption of these
lands. During 1962, 742 farmers redeemed 5,494
acres and the outlook for 1963 was 5,300.

Incentive payments for purchase and use of lime
at a rate of $4 per ton are available to farmers.
In 1962, 89 farmers took advantage of this offer on
1,096 acres. In 1963, it was expected that 1,500
more acres would be treated.

In 1962, in the program that was initiated for
free insecticides to be furnished the farmer, with
the farmer to pay for the application, 334 farmers
made use of this offer on 5,400 acres. It is estimated that 17,700 acres were treated in 1963.

Coffee

The coffee program has been redirected toward a maximum production of 380,000 hundredweight. To this end many acres have been retired from production, lands which are too poor for a good yield and also the lands which are too steep to cultivate economically, and production in more fertile areas has been intensified. The whole program has been designed for high quality and quantity on a minimum number of acres which can produce the above-quoted crop, which is consistent with the market demand.

The lands retired from coffee will be used for bananas, citrus fruits and improved pastures according to the quality of the soil and the steepness of the hillsides. Up to 1962, 29,000 acres of coffee land had been improved, for which the farmers received $11 million in incentive payments.

The basic concepts of the coffee program are as follows:

1. Incentives for rebuilding plantations, retiring low-producing plantations, and dedicating them to other uses.

2. Free distribution of seeds of bananas and other fruits and planting them on land retired from coffee but suitable for these fruits.

3. Credit through the Agricultural Credit Corporation for rebuilding plantations for coffee, for seeds for other crops, and for cattle.

4. Insurance against hurricanes for bananas, plantains, and other fruits.

5. Coordination of the staffs of various agricultural agencies to judge the potential of the farmer for the program.

6. Continue improving the marketing system for crops whose planting is promoted.

For 1964, $900,000 for incentives and costs of operation was promulgated.

Tobacco

There are 13,000 tobacco growers in Puerto Rico. The crop does not lend itself to mechanization, nor does the topography of the land on which it is grown. It is still very dependent on hand labor.

The government has programs similar to the others for assisting tobacco growers, one of which is cultivating seedbeds to provide high-quality plants at minimum cost to growers, to improve production per acre, and also the quality. This is under the general direction of the Agricultural Experiment Station and the program was started in 1956.

Up to 1963, they had distributed 94 million seedlings, enough to plant 11,500 acres, benefiting 9,800 farmers. During 1963, 1,600 farmers got more than 16 million seedlings for 2,048 acres, and the plan is to continue this service at the same rate.

In the fiscal year 1959-60, a program was started to provide loans from $300 to $2,000, at no interest, to build, repair, and enlarge tobacco curing barns. Farmers were given from five to eight years to repay these loans. Through 1963, 1,400 loans had been made to build and repair buildings with a capacity for 18,000 hundredweight of tobacco.

The Department of Agriculture provides insurance on the curing barns against wind and fire for farmers who have loans. Against hurricanes, 50 per cent of the value is insured and 80 per cent against fire. If a loss occurs, the balance of the loan is collected and a new loan for replacement is issued. Through 1963, 819 barns were insured with no premium. This is a continuing program.

Fertilizer is also given to farmers. Six hundred pounds are allowed to farmers with a quota of

1,000 pounds of tobacco and 3,000 to those with a quota of 4,000 pounds or more. This has benefited 11,500 farmers.

Pasture

In 1953, a pasture-improvement program was initiated to encompass 250,000 acres. Incentive payments were established for the eradication of weeds in permanent pastures, for the establishment of new pastures, for cutting or pasturing, for the application of fertilizer, and the construction of fences around improved pastures.

A farmer can get incentive payments up to $1,500 for the construction of wells, silos, molasses tanks, stables, corrals for calves, and milking parlors. Up to 1963, 905 such structures were built.

Between 1953 and 1963, 175,400 acres were seeded. This was about 70 per cent of the established goal: Also accomplished was the improvement of 80,000 acres by weed eradication. About $5.5 million has been spent on this--$2.8 million from the United States Government and $2.6 million from the government of Puerto Rico. Plans called for 30,000 acres more in 1963 and also for provision for more dairy facilities.

Individual Farms Under the Social Program of the Department of Agriculture

These farms are on land which has been bought by the government and sold at auction to individual farmers, the purchase price to be paid back over a period of forty years at an interest rate of 3 per cent. The individual farmers can also borrow up to $500 to build a house, buy equipment, seeds, fertilizer, etc. The land mortgage and the loan are amortized together. By 1962, 1,350 of these farms had been purchased with a total acreage of 22,170, or about sixteen and one-half acres per farm. This is a continuing program.

Parcelas

Another social program authorized is that of
the parcelas. From 1942-48, the land authority
handled this activity, but in 1948, it was transferred to the Social Programs division of the Department of Agriculture. Land amounting to an area
of 300 square meters to three acres is given to
families in perpetual use. Families can then build
their own homes on the land in the mutual-aid program. The sites are determined by the topography
and value of the land, its actual use, accessibility
to work, schools, roads, and other essential public
services. From 1942-62, $9 million was spent for
35,743 acres in this program, and 58,320 families
were resettled in 334 communities. Moreover,
some 4,987 parcelas were reserved for public services. Previous to 1942, 12,337 families had
been resettled under PRERA, PRA, and Farm Security.

It is estimated that there are 32,000 families
who need and want parcelas. The plan was for 5,000
in 1963, and the remainder at the same rate, creating 241 more communities throughout the island.
The purpose of creating these communities is to
bring people together where services are available
instead of being more or less isolated in inacces-
sible sites.

Low-Cost Housing

This program, carried out by mutual aid, provides homes for the families resettled on the parcelas. These homes have been built already in 238
of the 334 communities. The government provides
money for materials and forms for poured concrete
houses--the loan to be paid back in ten years. The
labor is provided by the neighbors--helping each
other under the supervision of a competent góvern-
ment aide. This is a revolving fund. Up to 1955,
only 959 houses had been built in five years. The
rate has been stepped up to not less than 1,000
houses per year, and in 1963, 3,000 were built. Up
to 1962, 15,934 houses all told had been constructed

at an average cost to the owner of $425. The con-
centration of families in the parcela settlement
makes it possible for the government more economically to provide water, electricity, and other services. The people have the satisfaction of owning
their own homes and working for cash wages rather
than being agregados and paid often in scrip or
products.

A new program for constructing slightly larger
houses for small farmers has been started, with 184
units completed at a cost of $550 each.

Rural Telephones

The Communications Authority of the Insular
Government cooperates with the Puerto Rico Telephone
Company in installing and maintaining rural pay
telephones. The Puerto Rico Telephone Company does
the maintenance, preservation, and repairs to lines
in the area of its jurisdiction and assumes cost of
labor and materials up to $25 per year. The Author-
ity reimburses the Puerto Rico Telephone Company beyond that figure. Up to June, 1962, there were 378
public telephones on 266 lines extending for 1,410
kilometers (kms.) and requisitions for 185 more, using 928 kms. of lines. The establishment of telephones in the rural zone has been of great importance in bringing country communities into the communications system.

Occupational Development

In 1960, a program was established to join idle
hands and uncultivated lands. In other words, incentives were established to improve methods on the
land and to teach skills to people without land.
These latter techniques were taught by means of minor public works, the use and repair of machinery,
the use of insecticides, etc.

During 1963, employment was given to 22,700
laborers who earned over $1.5 million paid by the
Federal Government and $463,000 paid by farmers.

They gave training in the use, care, and management of agricultural machinery in twenty towns to about 544 workers during the year, with the hope that they could eventually train 25,000 people in this manner.

DEPARTMENT OF PUBLIC WORKS

In 1932 there was a reasonably good network of main highways, paved but narrow, running between the cities and towns on the island, but access and feeder roads into the rural areas were practically non-existent. Farmers had to bring their products to the main roads on horseback or in ox carts and it was equally difficult to get supplies from the main roads to the farms.

At that time there was a railroad running around the island along the coast which had in the past done quite a passenger business as well as freight handling. By 1932, the passenger business was practically gone and the principal business of the railroad was handling sugar cane from the fields to the mills. This railroad is now completely gone and all of this work is handled by tremendous trailer trucks carrying up to twenty-five tons per load.

Following is the story of what has happened since 1932 in road building, which has made a very great difference in the economy of the island and the ability of the poeple to handle freight both into and out of the rural areas. In the transportation field also, a short statement is included showing the tremendous increase in business handled by the ports and airfields.

In 1936, the first United States Government aid was offered for road construction in the form of a $750,000 appropriation that was to be matched by the Puerto Rican Government. Actually, for the primary and secondary roads, urban streets and bridges, the United States contributed 45 per cent of the total cost and the Puerto Rican Government 55 per cent.

In the 1948-49 fiscal year, the regular program began, contemplating the construction of 735 kms. of roads at a cost of $209 million: 195 kms. of primary roads at $70 million, 470 kms. of secondary roads at $59 million, and 70 kms. of urban roads at $80 million. Of the total, the United States Government agreed to pay $86 million, and the Puerto Rican Government $122 million.

Definitions

Primary roads are those connecting cities and regions of major importance which will, within twenty years, have 1,200 vehicles per day.

Secondary roads are those connecting small villages and communities directly or by interconnecting with primary roads, the estimated use of which will be less than 1,200 vehicles daily.

Urban roads are all the extensions of primary roads, intersections, and road connections within urban centers of more than 5,000.

Municipal roads are all roads giving service of a local character to facilitate transportation of agricultural products and connecting rural and urban zones.

Up to June, 1962, the government had completed 539 kms., had 49 under construction, and 46 pending with funds partially assigned.

Besides the regular program, there were in the past four other lesser roads of rather short mileages which were built by emergency funds or paid for by the United States Government alone. These amounted to about 185 kms. between 1941 and 1948 before starting the regular program. Altogether from 1941-62, 725 kms. of primary, secondary, and urban roads had been built at a total cost of $121 million.

The municipal-road program, the most important item for rural communities, was begun in 1943, with

a projection of 2,600 kms. at an estimated cost of
$130 million. In the period 1942-62, there had been
constructed 1,161 kms. at a total cost of $47 mil-
lion. The general outline for the road program is
as follows:

1. Complete roads already started and needing
less than $100,000 to finish.

2. Close, or work toward closing, circuits between two or more main highways where cost is less
than $100,000.

3. Establish access to population centers.

4. Establish connections with areas of great
economic potential.

5. Initiate construction where nothing has
been done.

6. Each stretch of road should have maximum
utility for the citizenry.

Ports and Airfields

A total of some $33 million has been appropri-
ated this year for the expansion of airfields and
port facilities.

Of this sum, $12 million is for airfields and
$21 million for ports. In 1932, there were approx-
imately 6,000 passengers by air per year; in 1962,
1,736,000 passengers. Port facilities in 1932 handled 1,915,000 tons of cargo. In 1962, the tonnage
had risen to 14,526,320. Improvements are being
made not only in San Juan, but also in Ponce,
Mayaguez, Vieques, and on the island some regional
airports and heliports.

A new series of docks and warehouses, freight
terminals and bulk-handling equipment is being built
across the harbor from San Juan and will eventually
be the main dock area. Tourist ships will continue

to land their passengers on the San Juan side, however.

Freight-handling buildings and equipment are
being enlarged rapidly at the International Airport
in anticipation of the increase in air express and
freight service.

ECONOMIC DEVELOPMENT ADMINISTRATION

In 1932, in an agricultural economy where there
was lack of land for the population, economic conditions were so bad that everyone realized the only
salvation for Puerto Rico was to develop industrial
activity. This was difficult because of the almost
complete lack of raw materials. The only available
asset for such development was the large number of
workers, both men and women, and the fact that they
had a demonstrated potential of skill and trainabil-
ity.

Under PRERA a little was done between 1933 and
1936. But the PRERA, due to the fact that it was
primarily a stopgap organization, could not make
capital investments, although it could and did make
various studies as to the feasibility of different
types of industries.

During the Second World War, this subject was
taken up in earnest by the government and in 1942,
the Puerto Rico Industrial Development Company was
organized and authorized to build plants for the
manufacture of various items for use on the island.
It was particularly pertinent at the time, due to
the great loss of shipping between the United States
and Puerto Rico, to manufacture items out of local
materials for local consumption. The company had a
capital of $500,000 to start this work and it was
charged with "discovering and developing to the
fullest possible extent the human and economic resources of the island."[22] The capital was soon increased to $20 million plus the acquisition of a
fully operating cement plant. The money for this

development came from rum taxes which were returned
to the government of Puerto Rico by the United
States Treasury, Internal Revenue Service, by Act of
Congress, and retained by the government of Puerto
Rico with no strings attached. The government pro-
ceeded to build cement, glass bottle, cardboard,
footwear, and sanitary-ware plants until 1947. The
raw materials for all of these items, with the exception of footwear, were found on the island.
Cardboard, for shipping containers, is made from
waste paper. It was necessary for the government to
do this and to operate these plants temporarily in
order to get the program started, but, in 1947, emphasis was put on the encouragement and growth of
private industrial enterprises.

In 1950, the Economic Development Administration
was set up to promote the establishment of manufacturing plants on the island and to interest mainland
manufacturers in going down there. Its functions
were to point out to industries the value of establishing branch plants in Puerto Rico, to accelerate
training programs with management development and
on-job-training, and to give technical assistance to
the new owners. The Puerto Rico Industrial Development Company, now a subsidiary of the Puerto Rico
Economic Development Company, still continues to
build and lease plants of standard or special design, and handles the financial aspects of the program, but the government no longer operates any of
the industrial enterprises. In 1953, there were
thirty-three municipalities without factories. Now
there are only two.

One of the prime features of the program is
that no "run-away" firms were encouraged to come,
and no incentives were given to firms contemplating
closing out their United States operations, which
would create unemployment in the United States, but
tax-exemption incentives are given to bona fide owners, graduated according to the location of the factories. These incentives run from twelve years' tax
exemption in and around San Juan and the other big
cities, up to seventeen years' in the outlying areas
--those areas which are less desirable from a

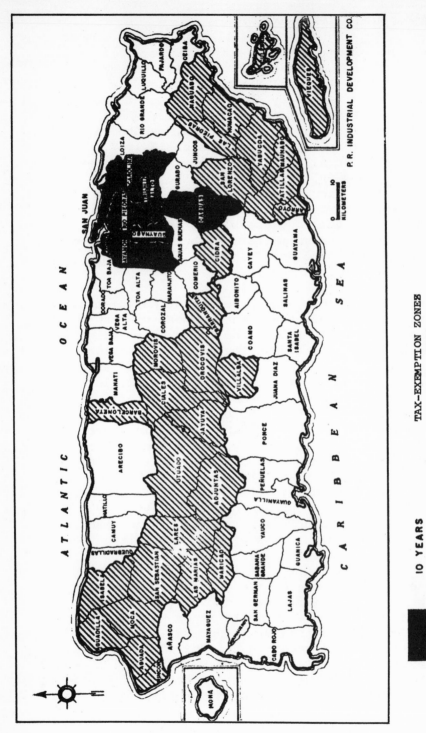

TAX-EXEMPTION ZONES
June, 1963

10 YEARS

12 YEARS

17 YEARS

P. R. INDUSTRIAL DEVELOPMENT CO.

INCENTIVES FOR FACTORY LOCATION

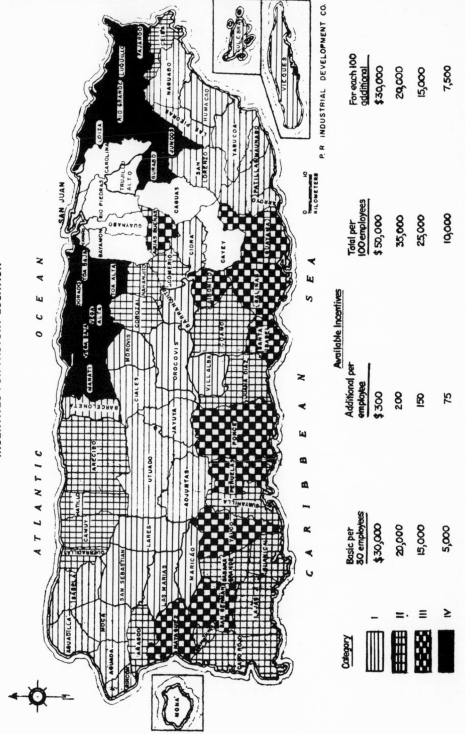

P. R. INDUSTRIAL DEVELOPMENT CO.

Available Incentives

Category	Basic per 30 employees	Additional per employee	Total per 100 employees	For each 100 additional
I	$30,000	$300	$50,000	$30,000
II	20,000	200	35,000	20,000
III	15,000	150	25,000	15,000
IV	5,000	75	10,000	7,500

manufacturing standpoint. These factories are not
only exempt from property taxes and municipal taxes,
but the profits on their operation are exempt from
Puerto Rican income tax. Dividends to local investors are also exempt from Puerto Rican income tax,
but those investors in Puerto Rican industry who
live in the United States or outside of the island
must pay income taxes like anyone else.

An effort is being made also to interest local
capital in the manufacturing expansion program and,
by 1963, one-third of the 1,000 plants were owned
and managed by Puerto Ricans or Continentals of long-
time residence, which bodes well for the future, and 10
per cent of the total investment also is locally provided.

Another feature of the program is that in order
to get tax exemption, the factory must produce either
an article not previously produced in Puerto Rico or
one of thirty-four articles designated by law.
PRIDCO also makes loans to new industry, the lowest
rates being for industrial zones which are underdeveloped.

One of the more risky investments which PRIDCO
made was in the tourist business, and a larger proportion of the total investment capital than normal
was provided to hotel builders and owners. This
has proven very profitable and the government is
underwriting a much smaller amount of the capital
to be invested than it did at first.

Another development in manufacturing has been
food- and feed-processing plants. In the case of
rice, as well as cattle and poultry feed, grain is
shipped in bulk and is milled and packaged on the
island, thus saving high freight rates and at the
same time making use of other products on the island
which might have gone to waste. An example of this
is the integration of feed mills and the tuna fish
canneries. The mills import soy beans in bulk,
press out the oil, using the pulp for feed. The oil
is sold to the tuna fish canneries, and tuna fish

scrap is in turn sold to the feed mills for use as
an ingredient in a balanced ration.

By December, 1962, incentives on 200 of the
1,000 new industries had run out and the factories
were paying local taxes just like any other enterprise.

This program has created 60,000 jobs in new
factories, and 60,000 to 80,000 in construction,
government, and related services. But 150,000 marginal jobs in home needlework, domestic service, and
agriculture have disappeared, leaving a net decrease
in the employed labor force of 10 per cent. Economic activity has increased 75 per cent and the employed labor force is increasing rapidly at the
present time. Since the above-mentioned marginal
jobs were very poorly paid, really starvation wages,
the net increase in income is much more than appears
from simple figures of the numbers employed. One
evidence of this is the fact that during the last
two years, the net emigration from Puerto Rico to
the United States has been zero. This, of course,
makes it imperative for the government to increase
its efforts to provide employment opportunities.

ELECTRIFICATION

(Water Resources Authority)

On Good Friday we drove to the country for the
night. Darkness came after the short tropical twi-
light and on the mountainsides lights appeared and
above the village of Comerio a lighted cross. Thirty
years ago the hillsides would have been dark and in
the town the lights would have been from small lamps
--picturesque but ineffectual.

So the symbolism of light appears--the dim sad
beauty of the past is gradually being lost in shadow.
Traditional society cannot offer to human beings the
instruments for living in a new age; where it remains even the old values tend to deteriorate.

Emotional disturbance may characterize much of the
transition but faces are set to the future. The
symbols of that future are new symbols with new emotional significance in which the spiritual must find
new meanings in material change. The lighted cross
may be a symbol of a new salvation.

The following quotations are taken from José
Mariano Ríos' speeches in a Seminar on Rural Electrification held in Puerto Rico, in 1959.

> The dynamic society which character-
> izes Puerto Rico at present is sharply
> different from what it was not too
> long ago, for this small overpopulated
> Island is experiencing one of the most
> dramatic changes which any society in
> any part of the world might have under-
> gone. Changes which generally take
> scores of years have occurred here in
> two decades.
>   Perhaps the most stark-staring
> assertion on this Atomic Aeon is to be
> found in Sir James Jean's book, This
> Mysterious Universe. He sums up the
> conclusions of "Science" as amounting
> to recognition of "light" as the ul-
> timate constituent of the cosmos, and
> he says that the whole story of creation
> could be told in the opening sentence of
> Genesis: "And God said, 'Let there be
> light.'"
>   Since the birth of humanity light
> has been employed as a symbol of God.
> As light contains very little material-
> ity, it was considered by ancients a
> befitting symbol for them to express
> the incorporeal, pure and holy nature
> of God.
>   The impact of commercial electric-
> ity upon the economy in the agricultural
> zones indirectly or directly affects the
> pattern of economic exploitation of the
> area. Electricity makes possible the

use of electrical equipment on the
farm, as for example, milking machines
and refrigerated tanks. As a result
the agricultural pattern may change
from a seasonal (sugar cane) to a year
round enterprise (dairy). This means
a regular income for the family, a
higher level of living. Electricity
is making possible the mechanization
and/or industrialization of our agriculture which is primordial in a country where land is one of the scantiest
resources.

Rural electrification has made possible the invasion of our rural areas
by industrial buildings. . . .

The effects are numerous:

1. New and diversified jobs are
created.

2. Skilled labor is developed--
sometimes highly skilled.

3. Industry advantageously com-
petes with agriculture in salaries,
creating job shortages in agriculture.

4. When the factory is not erected within the limits of the community
a community emerges around the factory.

5. Industrial jobs are available
for mothers and other women of the
household.

The consequences are many. It is
not proper to appraise them in dichot-
omies such as positive or negative and
good or bad. Nevertheless, the effects
are being experienced in the structure
of the family, the function of its members, and the social institutions of
the community. The power relationship
among rural electrification, industrialization and the people can more easily
be understood if we single out for analysis some of the constituents.

Direct Effects of Rural
Electrification

Economic and social changes in our rural area have been the result of a chain reaction of different projects and governmental programs working together for the betterment of the people.

Notwithstanding, I would not exaggerate if I say that electricity has been the driving force that has put into motion the wheels of progress.

The impact of commercial electricity upon the rural family can be more directly determined by the presence or absence of electrical appliances: kitchen utensils, refrigerators, television sets, radios, and others. The possession of these commodities greatly affects consumption habits as well as the use of leisure time.

Refrigeration has made possible a wider use of perishable goods among the rural families. Meat, fresh milk, and vegetables are being included in the rural family diet.

Radio and television provide for a better use of leisure time. The country store, "the gossip corner," and the batey are losing their importance. Leisure time is now engaged with radio and television that provide education, information, and recreation.

Rural electrification has made possible the organization of night schools for adults, thus providing broader educational facilities.

Side Effects

Up to this point, I have singled out various good and/or controversial concomitants of rural electrification. To my understanding it has also brought about undesirable changes in attitudes.

1. Introduction of the "juke box," or nickel record player, to the farthest rural areas--even ahead of the road--has usurped the tranquility and peace of the rural folk. The love for pleasure, the rural bar, malversation, and drinking, all come together around the "juke box." For bar owners and alcoholic beverage distributors, this might be an asset, but from the moral and economic point of view it is a social cancer.

2. The adolescent group sometimes "hangs around" the bar, playing hookey. This creates an undesirable environment for teenagers, principally girls. In urban areas this situation is in part controlled by established institutions. This social maleficence brings a new phenomenon in the rural area which is as yet untamed by social controls.

You might conclude from the ideas just expressed in the previous section that I am putting human values in rural areas in jeopardy. I merely attempted to point out what may be called the risks of rural electrification and the necessity of making provisions in our social organization for these changes so that we can accept the new without destroying the essential social values needed for a progressive community. We should not forget that the worth of a social system is not to be measured only by the level of living reached in terms of material belongings, but by the opportunity it affords its members to employ the method of scientific knowledge and possession in the management of their lives.

Rural electrification has made it possible for light to reach the farthest corners in Puerto Rico's countryside.

> Let "light" be for us a symbol of eco-
> nomic progress working for the supreme
> values of our social structure.

Previous to 1915, there was practically no rural electricity in Puerto Rico except for a few
short lines which went out from the cities of San
Juan, Ponce, Mayaguez, where there were large private companies. The government entered the field
of electric power in 1915, using water from dams
which were built for irrigation.

Besides the three large electric companies
above mentioned, there were some small municipal
plants, some hydroelectric, and some operated by
internal combustion engines. These, however, only
supplied power for light to the communities in which
they were located and did not reach out into the
rural areas.

In 1925, the first government agency, established in the Department of Public Works, was set
up for the utilization of water resources. In 1933,
and for a few years after that, considerable help
from the PRERA and the PRRA was provided in the establishment of distribution lines, but no further
dams were built until later.

In 1941, the Water Resources Authority was set
up as an independent agency, self-liquidating, so
that it could sell bonds for the development of
water resources in the island, the construction of
power stations and transmission and distribution
lines. Not very much was done for the next five
years due to the scarcity of strategic materials
during the war. In 1946 and 1947, the first appropriation from the Puerto Rican Government was voted
in an amount of $400,000 a year to expand the system.
This appropriation was continued yearly until 1952,
at which time the authority borrowed from the Rural
Electrification Administration of the United States
$6 million at an interest rate of 2 per cent. Since
1952, up to the present date, the authority has borrowed $58 million from the REA.

There are two types of consumers under the
present setup--the large consumers who use a guaranteed minimum and who in some cases pay part of the
construction cost of the distribution lines. There
are also many small consumers who do not use enough
electricity to justify financially the construction
of facilities, and in order to make possible the
supply of light and power to these people, the government pays the authority the difference between
what the facility costs and what the consumers pay.
There is a uniform rate for the whole island, both
rural and urban, and the government subsidy comes
in where the consumption at this rate does not come
up to the costs. The authority operates on a nonprofit basis throughout the island.

In 1963, it supplied electricity and power to
251,123 families averaging 5.2 persons per family in
the rural areas. There are estimated to be 10,000
families who are too remote ever to get service.

The government aids the potential consumer in
paying for the wiring of his house and the purchase
of appliances. Wiring in the average rural house
costs $30 and appliances are sold at a very low
figure. The consumer repays the loan over a considerable period of time and with a minimum interest
charge.

It has been found that actual use goes up rapidly after electricity is available and the people
begin to realize the advantage of having this in
their homes.

In starting rural distribution, the first areas
covered were in fairly high concentrations of population in order to serve the largest number of consumers at a minimum cost and enable the authority to
get some return on its money, which later could be
used for wider distribution. This service was given
to the 58,000 families living in 344 parcela communities and to the 15,000 mutual-aid houses. This is
the type of priority decision which is continually
met by the Planning Board in establishing projects
of various kinds.

The authority has been a pioneer in many aspects of the construction of transmission and distribution lines. They use aluminum instead of copper wire, the aluminum being cheaper and easier to handle, making possible longer spans between poles. The lines are run in a straight line over the mountains and through the valleys and the authority has felt it effective and inexpensive to use helicopters in getting the poles to their final locations.

The authority submits its plans for the year annually to the Planning Board for the PB's final decision on the location and extent of new construction. It also gives quarterly progress reports to the Planning Board and the whole operation is coordinated with the general larger plan of the government for the various communities.

All of this has shown the value of the government taking over a public service of this kind. The private companies never would have branched out into the rural areas as they could not have borrowed money as cheaply as the authority did, nor would they ever find it economical to furnish electricity to widely scattered communities. The authority is self-liquidating on the basis of the low rates which are charged and has not had to ask the government of Puerto Rico for any appropriation for construction since 1952. This program probably represents the greatest change in the standard of living of any of the government operations--the biggest spread between a primitive and a modern way of life.

WATER AND SEWER AUTHORITY

Hydrotopography[23]

Because this study deals with rural communities, the question of water is of special importance. The effect that rivers have had on the development of civilization, ancient or modern, is always fascinating.

Puerto Rico has some 2,000 streams. Although none of them is navigable, most of them small, nevertheless they constitute an important factor for development in supplying potable water, in industrial use, as a source of hydroelectric power, and for irrigation.

The topography of the island explains the difference in water supply between the northern and southern parts of the island. The mountain ranges, running from east to west, are the natural watershed. In two-thirds of the island, from the highest elevation of 4,000 feet, water descends to the north coast, gradually, and rain falls more heavily than on the south coast, where the rivers descend more precipitously and have less volume. The difference is striking when one crosses the mountains from north to south; vegetation changes, the colors become those of a dry region, irrigation becomes important.

In the southwest, a government experiment, "a little TVA," has been under way since 1951. It has already restored 12,000 acres to cultivation (sugar cane land).

Water Supply

Until 1945, the supply of water in Puerto Rico was in the hands of the municipalities, which did not have sufficient funds to keep up with the population increase or provide proper maintenance and replacement of the system. Only six of seventy-five towns had twenty-four-hour water service, others had twelve, eight, six, or even only four hours of service during the twenty-four. There were only fourteen towns which had filtration plants--nineteen towns had deep wells, and forty-two towns had partial-treatment plants. Some 18 per cent of the water supply had no treatment at all. Besides the municipal plants, there were 184 small rural systems, some provided by the municipality, some by the Puerto Rican Government, and some by United States government agencies. They were very ineffectively operated, the rates were too low, there was no

WATER—SUPPLY AND SEWAGE—DISPOSAL SYSTEMS, 1963

Revisado: 31 de diciembre de 1963

actuarial basis for the rates, and there was never
enough money for proper maintenance and replacement.
There were also heavy water losses due to illegal
connections, leaks in the systems, and for various
other reasons. There were no plans, records, or
statistics, and the authorities relied on the memory of the older employees to locate pipes, valves,
etc. There was a frequent turnover of personnel due
to politics and there was also, for the same reason,
a distinct lack of competence. In 1941, it was realized that something had to be done about the water
supply, and the Legislature passed a law consolidat-
ing all of the systems, but legal objections from
the government of the city of San Juan held up carrying out the provisions of the law until 1945.

At that time the insular Supreme Court ruled
that the authority could take over municipal systems
without compensation. At that time, the system was
called the Utilization of Water Resources and was
in the Department of Public Works, but in 1949, the
Legislature created the Authority for Water Resources, which enabled it to sell bonds and to finance necessary construction.

For general administrative purposes, the island
is divided into six districts and sixteen zones
which are generally autonomous, having complete supplies of equipment and personnel.

The first thing the authority did was to establish uniform rates for the whole island, low enough
for the masses of the people, but high enough to
cover costs and amortization. Within three years,
the authority was operating in the black and the deficiencies of the system had been pretty much eliminated. There were two stipulations which were of
great importance. One was a meter for everyone, and
the other was no free water for the government or
its agents. In cases where people were too poor to
have water piped into their homes, there were public
faucets for which the government pays the authority
so much a year. There were 4,000 of these public
faucets in 1962 and more are being installed every
year.

Many other things had to be done to put the system on an efficient operating basis. Meters were purchased and now 92 per cent of the water is metered. The only places where there are no meters are where the consumption does not justify the cost of the meter and on the public faucets. Another immediate need was to clean up the water supply-- provide filtration plants and clean the pipes of sediment and metallic residues. A United States firm specializing in this type of work was hired to check leaks and illegal connections. Another United States firm also was employed to clear the pipes.

The United States Geological Survey was called in to assist in determining underground sources of water, and this help from the United States continues as the need arises. All of the systems were consolidated and interconnected, thus enabling the authority to divert water into the slack areas from flush areas.

Within three years after the consolidation of the water systems, more than 350 kms. of pipe had been installed, and the causes of loss in the various categories had been eliminated.

The start of the construction of filtration plants began in 1950, with various capacities according to the size of the communities. There are now twenty-six of them, and more are being built. The government makes up to the authority the cost of nonliquidating projects, such as the public faucets and some other costs. The hope of the authority is to have all feasible rural areas served by 1967. At the present time, 100 per cent of the urban population has clean, potable water, and more than 50 per cent of the rural population. The following is a chart giving the pertinent figures on the supply of water and the number of sanitary centers which were in operation in 1945, and showing the per cent increase in 1963.

TABLE 12

Water Service Statistics

	Jan. 1945	June 1963	Per Cent Increase
Communities with continuous service of water, 24 hours a day	6	75	1,150
Filtration plants in service	11	41	273
Communities with sanitary sewers	41	72*	76
Mechanical treatment plants for impure water in use	1	39	3,800
Millions of gallons of water supplied daily	49	122	148
Miles of water pipes in service	740	3,580	384
Rural sectors with potable water service	158	1,334	744
Customers for water service	72,000	326,420	353
Number of meters installed	30,000	302,581	909
People supplied with aqueduct water	671,000	1,785,000	166
Public faucets		4,000	
Value of physical plant	$20,000,000	$172,000,000	760

*The sewers for the three remaining towns were under construction in 1963.

HOUSING AND URBAN RENEWAL (CRUV)

Material for this section was taken from reports of CRUV, supplemented by an interview with
Sixto Toro Cintron, Special Assistant to the Executive Director, on February 25, 1964.

Housing is one of the principal activities of
the Planning and Action program in Puerto Rico.
This program, in cooperation with the Planning Board,
is carried out by the Corporation for Urban Renewal
and Housing (known as CRUV). It works with federal
housing programs to "coordinate, carry out and supervise the planning and construction of housing, federal and state, finance lots for building, install services to public housing, special projects, and to
provide technical help for low-cost housing developments by means of mutual aid and encouragement or
through cooperative housing."

The Puerto Rico Urban Renewal and Housing Administration started in 1938 as the Puerto Rico Housing
Authority for all municipalities in the island except San Juan, Ponce, Mayaguez, and Arecibo, which
had their own housing authorities. The authority in
Arecibo disappeared after two years and the other
three were merged with the Puerto Rico Housing Authority in 1957 when it became the Puerto Rico Urban Renewal and Housing Administration. The jurisdiction of the administration is urban only for the
relocation of low-income families. It is financed
by both Commonwealth and federal funds.

With the federal housing programs, it aims to
provide adequate urban housing, creating facilities
and community centers for low-income families. This
housing is mainly occupied by families moved from
slum areas (70 per cent).

This program has completed, or planned for construction soon, housing in all but three of the towns
in the island. It, therefore, touches centers of
population which lie in the rural parts of the island
and is one of the evidences of change which strike

SAMPLE HOUSING-PROJECT PLAN: SALINAS, 1963

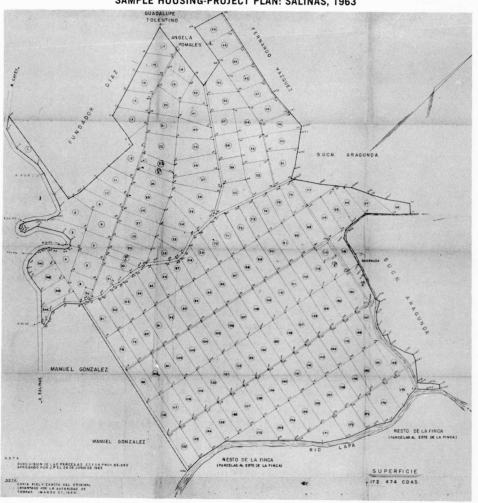

the eye immediately. The pattern of these housing
projects does not appear thoroughly suitable, either
practically or aesthetically, to their surroundings
in the Puerto Rican situation, but they represent a
very great improvement over housing which existed
before, and, because of the genuinely cooperative
relationships with the Federal Government, changes
will be allowed for future buildings which can modi-
fy the present pattern.

The hope of the administration is to eventually
design buildings and individual houses which will
appear like any other urbanization and will not carry the stigma of public housing by their appearance.
At the present time the administration is selling
lots or providing them in usufruct. The lots are
of two kinds according to income rates, the lower-
priced ones having a minimum of utilities and un-
paved streets, and the better lots for those of higher income have full utilities and paved streets. A
shell house is provided at a minimum cost and finish-
ing is done by the cooperative effort of the inhabitants. This, of course, applies to the individual
home but not to the large apartment dwellings.
About 1,000 individual units have already been built
and 3,000 to 4,000 more are needed. The Puerto Rico
Housing Bank originally financed these constructions
from direct loans to prospective owners but now
guarantees the loans which are made by private commercial banks. This service is only available to
those families which do not have sufficient credit
to satisfy commercial banks. The range of income
for these families is between $2,000 and $4,000 a
year.

Another activity which is being studied is rehabilitation on location. It is contemplated that
this operation will be very largely expanded in the
next few years. The purpose of all of this activity
is to "get people out of the slums and the slums out
of the people."

In work on slum problems, every effort is made
to improve the existing sites and the actual houses

where their condition warrants it. There is a recognition of the value of the integrity of a community
and of the disrupting effect of transplanting families from a familiar to an unfamiliar environment.

In both the urban and rural zones, there is
considerable emphasis on centration of housing because of the economy in provided services--sanita-
tion, streets, etc.

Under another plan for individual home building, CRUV provides floor, supports and roof, equipment for the making of concrete blocks, technical
assistance and supervision. The labor is done by
the families themselves. A similar program is carried out in rural areas by the Department of Agriculture under its Social Program. (See section on
Department of Agriculture.)

This means the establishment of 300 rural communities, giving facilities and services which were
lacking before and which could not have been provided for in individual houses isolated from each
other.

Labor is done by the families themselves, a
similar program of "mutual aid" is designed for
those families whose income exceeds the minimum for
public housing but who cannot afford the cost of
private financing. If family members move from a
slum area and sell their house, they use the pro-
ceeds to purchase building materials; CRUV provides
technical advice and supervision in the lots provided for this program.

Another similar program offers an alternative
to persons in the low-cost-housing bracket. This
makes possible improvements and additions to a house
with basic floor area of 500 square feet.

The report on housing under these programs
shows 44,648 units completed, 6,394 under construction, 20,387 planned: total 71,429.

The administration is developing a plan for an
industrial plant to build precast housing compo-
nents which can then be moved to the site and rapidly erected, thus saving labor costs. One of the
principal reasons for the necessity of expanding
these programs is the fact that the price of private
housing is materially increasing and becoming out of
reach for many families.

The administration envisions the progress of
people in government housing as a ladder--first going to government-paid caserios (public housing
apartments in large units) then to individual small
houses and possibly later to the purchase of con-
dominium apartments. It also feels that its jurisdiction will have to be expanded to the rural areas
as well as the urban areas if people are to be per-
suaded to live in the rural areas rather than in the
cities, and it is felt by the government that more
should be done to induce people to stay in the
country.

Plans have been prepared for the continuation
and acceleration of present programs and for new
developments, rural as well as urban, which will incorporate the ideas of the Planning Board (see section on regional development) and all those factors
which take into consideration the cultural patterns
of Puerto Rico and their adaptation and development
in the future.

Administration for the Development
of Cooperatives

The year 1873 saw the first cooperative movement in Puerto Rico with the formation of the Association for Mutual Aid and the Friends of the Public
Good. Some years were very successful, some very
bad. There were many apparently insuperable obsta-
cles which threatened to kill the movement, but the
idea remained alive with the hope of resolving serious social problems.

The first cooperative law was passed in 1920 to
create cooperatives for producers and consumers and

a further law was passed to promote agricultural cooperatives in 1925. In spite of including basic cooperative principles, these laws were inadequate,
but they initiated a period of government action in
favor of the cooperative movement, especially in
agriculture. However, there was no adequate law until 1946.

The arrival of the Reverend J. A. McDonald from
Antingonish, Nova Scotia, sparked a new interest in
the development of active and militant cooperatives.
A commission made up of legislators and executives
was sent to Nova Scotia to study the Angingonish experiment and to see how it could be adapted to Puerto
Rico. Their recommendations resulted in Law 291,
passed in April, 1946, which provided an adequate
legal basis for the development of cooperatives. In
order to further strengthen this development, Law 4
was passed in May, 1957, creating the Administration
of Cooperatives Development. The government fully
recognized its obligation in establishing clear democratic orientation and economic progress through the
free participation of the people in programs of social benefit.

The basic objectives are "to promote a movement
which will serve as an elementary regulation in the
whole economic system of Puerto Rico; which will assure the best possible service to all consumers in
terms of quality as well as price; which will develop between producers the attitudes and necessary
organization for success in creating abundant production, efficient and socially useful; which will contribute to raising to a level of equality the living
conditions of various social groups; and which can
assume in the shortest time possible the responsibility of doing this and providing adequately for the
continued implementation of the objectives above described." (From the Introduction to the Annual Report of the Administration of Cooperatives Development, 1960-61.)

The law further established the cooperative
agency as self-sufficient, with the backing of the

government, but free of government interference.
The Cooperatives Development Administration is the
governing body; it supervises the organization and
operation of the cooperatives, education of prospective organizers, financing through the cooperative bank, and it holds workshops for interested
visiting groups. Further education in the cooperative movement is provided through seminars at the
University of Puerto Rico on the college level and
on the intermediate level in the schools to educate
young people in the cooperative idea.

There are two principal adjuncts of the Cooperative Administration. One is the Cooperative
League, a central organization which coordinates
and orients all other nongovernment organizations
in their functions of developing and strengthening
the cooperatives.

There are several federations of cooperatives
which act to strengthen the integration of the cooperatives in Puerto Rico. They offer services
through centralization which they can provide with
greater efficiency than the cooperatives could realize as independent units, taking into consideration the different types of cooperatives now in
existence, although they work with the Cooperative
League in the execution of educational programs necessary for cooperative development and promotion.

There are three federations functioning:

1.   The Puerto Rico Federation of Consumer
Cooperatives.

2.   The Federation of Credit Cooperatives.

3.   The Federation of Agricultural Cooperatives.

There are 382 cooperatives all told, five times
more than there were in 1945 when intensive development began. Credit co-ops number 222, ten times as
many as in 1945; 91 consumer co-ops--twice as many;
28 agricultural co-ops, twice as many; 25 housing

co-ops and 16 other various types. There are 131,000
members representing over 500,000 people, one-fifth
of the total population of the island.

In 1961, there was a total volume of business
of $75 million, showing a steady progress and growth
but not yet reaching the figure in the total economy
that is hoped for. Farmers are not using them as
much as they could and altogether they are not yet
as significant in their total effect on the economy
as the authorities would like to see them.

Following are the goals to which the people
are reaching:

1. A strong development and expansion program,
serving as an example of good practice in operating
the cooperatives.

2. Creation of a strong cooperative movement
integrated in central coordinated associations and
functioning in close relationship with other cooperative programs.

3. The development of a central system of credit and insurance to provide services to the entire
cooperative movement.

4. Development of an extensive cooperative
housing program which will reduce the cost of living
and also reduce the necessity for government subsidy.

5. Gradual extension of cooperative organization to other fields, where justified by the needs
of the people. Among these are medical and hospital
care, industrial production, cafeterias, schools,
cultural and recreational centers, book stores, drug
stores, etc.

6. The integration of the whole movement in
the Cooperative League.

7. Gradual transfer of development functions
to the movement itself. When this is done the

TABLE 13

Statistical Data on Cooperatives,   1963

Credit Cooperatives - 222
Members - 75,900 in 63 communities
Volume of business - $27,800,000
Capital & Surplus   - $17,800,000
Average loan   - $363

Consumer Cooperatives - 91 in 47 communities--
                         20 urban, 71 rural
4 cooperative supermarkets: members 11,325
                         (6,410 urban, 4,915 rural)
Volume of business - $11,100,000
Sales - 15 times average inventory
Capital & Surplus - $1,500,000±

Agricultural Cooperatives - 28
Members - 41,820
Assets   - $24,700,000
Volume of business - $33,500,000
Capital & Surplus - $9,900,000

Housing Cooperatives - 25
Housing - 16; Lots - 6; Remodeling - 3
Families benefited - 2,700
Spent - $2,200,000
Provided - 534 lots; 386 housing; 111 in construction
Starts in process for 2,300 more families

Other types mentioned before - 16
Assets   - over $1,000,000
Capital & Surplus - $500,000
Volume of business - $1,035,000
Members - 2,024
Types - Gas Stations   4   620 members
        Taxi-Owners Service 2   182
        Graphic Arts   2   129
        Industrial   1   323
        Artisans   1   17
        Drug Consumers   1   500
        Films Arts   1   31
        Life Insurance   1   222
        Health   1   no information

administration need only retain the office of Inspector of Cooperatives to ensure the best interests
of the members.

The function of the Inspector of Cooperatives
is to see to it that rules and regulations are carried out, that cooperatives function normally, to
establish these functions, to establish or dissolve
cooperatives, to examine the books and to receive
statistical information.

Many foreign visitors come to Puerto Rico to
study the cooperative movement and the government
feels a strong obligation to instruct and help them.
They consider it a vital part of the democratic process and are doing everything possible to further
this relationship. To this end the Caribbean Cooperative Confederation was formed in 1957, composed
of representatives of countries bordering the Caribbean Sea, with headquarters in Puerto Rico. Puerto
Rico feels that it must maintain a relationship of
solidarity and cooperation with cooperative movements of other peoples and welcomes this responsibility.

Administration of Parks
and Public Recreation

Thirty years ago there was practically no government interest in, or aid to, recreation. There
was a baseball field in San Juan, operated by a quasi-
government commission made up of interested citizens,
where boxing matches were also held.

In 1941, the Administration of Parks and Public
Recreation was formed to develop all kinds of public
recreation opportunities. The first-year budget was
$3,500 and a goal was set of establishing a park in
every municipality of the island within fifteen
years. It was done in seven years.

There is now a completely diversified program
encompassing communal and cultural recreation, ath-
letics, both amateur and professional, public beaches,

cock-fighting arenas, beautification of public highways, with a budget of $526,000 of which $115,000
comes back in fees, licenses, rents and admissions.

The biggest expense is in the urban areas. The
rural facilities are built with volunteer help plus
a $2,000 grant from the government. There are rec-
reation associations and community centers in the
rural areas.

The low salaries now paid to professional help
in the urban parks and playgrounds prevent the Park
Administration from getting people as competent as
they would like to have.

The administration is planning new recreation
facilities such as swimming pools and community centers in new public-housing developments and also an
enlarged program of public beaches with bathing facilities and cafeterias.

There are now 104 urban and 116 rural baseball
parks, mostly with lights, 84 basketball courts, and
54 other facilities such as volleyball, tennis, and
soccer courts, beaches, woods areas, and lunch rooms,
with a 1962 attendance of 8,247,430.

Effect of Government Programs
on the Ten Communities

The accompanying chart shows the extent to
which government programs affect our ten communities.

The application of government programs is not
the same in all communities. For instance, in the
case of electricity, a higher percentage of families
in more concentrated areas get service than do those
in more sparsely settled areas. This is also true
of water supply and the reasons for this are explained in the sections on water and electricity.
Rural pay telephones are being installed as rapidly
as possible and are now in six of the ten communities studied. The four which do not have them are
rather remote and necessarily the same criteria are
used in providing the service.

Very little low-cost housing--government-owned rental units--have reached these rural areas, but the parcela program is being developed in nearly all of them.

There are excellent paved roads in all the communities, some naturally better than others, but all good enough to permit the use of trucks for market, ambulances, and other necessary transportation. There are more roads connecting municipalities and more feeder roads into or out of isolated areas.

While there are factories in all but three municipalities in Puerto Rico, Hato Tejas, Bayamón, is the only barrio among our ten in which there are one or more factories. However, there are factories in the nearest town to each community and the commuting is relatively simple.

The schools vary considerably, some appearing very much as they were in 1932, others having one or more new classroom buildings. Sanitary facilities are not all they should be, especially as water is readily available. The lunchrooms are well-equipped and serve excellent, balanced meals. There is still a real shortage of classrooms, necessitating a considerable amount of doubling up. The Department of Education is constructing new classrooms as fast as possible and has set a goal of as many more rooms as now exist.

There are regular health centers in four communities and clinical services are provided in the other six. Public welfare reaches all the barrios.

There are agricultural extension agents in most of the communities but in some they cover more than one barrio or Second Unit School. Medianía Alta, Loiza, has none as the land is now destined for housing and recreational development.

The Community Education program only appears in two of the barrios and the Labor Department program is very limited.

CHART 2

Government Services to Ten Rural Areas

	Loiza	Juncos	Cidra	Bayamón	Salinas	Juana Diaz	Adjuntas	Moca	Aguadilla	Arecibo
Water	Partial 50%	Partial 33%	Partial 25%	Almost comp. 90%	Partial 50%	Partial 67%	Partial 20%	Partial 67%	Almost comp. 83%	Partial 40%
Electricity	Partial 63%	Partial 20%	Partial 33%	Complete	Partial 33%	Almost none	Partial 33%	Almost comp.	Partial 83%	Partial 50%
Telephone	Yes	No	No	Yes	Yes	Yes	No	No	Yes	Yes
Low-cost housing	None	Partial 50%	None	None	Partial 7%	None	None	Partial 10%	None	Partial 8%
Social Program Parcelas	Partial	Partial 17%	None	None	Partial 33%	Partial 5%	None	Partial 8%	Partial 67%	Partial 20%
Roads	Good	Good	Good	Good	Good	Good	Good	Good	Good	Good
Recreation	None	None	None	Extensive	Good	Very Good	None	None	Very Good	Good

	In Loiza	In Gurabo & Juncos	In Cidra		In Salinas	In Juana Diaz	In Adjuntas	In Moca	In Aguadilla	In Arecibo
Factories				Yes						
Classrooms	Good	Very Good	Very Good	Very Good	Very Good	Very Good	Very Good	Very Good	Very Good	Very Good
School Lunch	Yes	Yes	Yes	Yes	Yes	Yes	Yes	Yes	Yes	Yes
Health Center	Ltd.	Ltd.	Yes	Yes	Ltd.	Yes	Ltd.	Ltd.	Yes	Ltd.
Public Welfare	Yes	Partial	Yes	Yes	Yes	Partial	Yes	Yes	Yes	Yes
Agri. Ext. Serv.	None	Partial	Yes	Partial	Yes	Partial	Partial	Yes	Partial	Partial
Community Educ.	None	None	Partial	None	None	None	Partial	None	None	None
Dept. Lab.	Partial	Partial	None	Partial	Partial	None	None	None	Partial	Partial
1932 Pop.	2,197	1,020	2,679	3,092	2,628	2,717	1,770	1,800	3,291	4,753
1962 Pop.	4,254	930	3,040	11,427	6,078	2,340	1,712	2,379	3,771	5,665
Pop.	+94%	-9%	+135%	+371%	+131%	-16%	-3%	+32%	+145%	+19%
Households	788	155	486	+371%	1,072	443	331	449	621	1,195

Sources: Reports of the field staff and of the Department of Public Works of the Puerto Rican Government.

Recreation facilities are being expanded as fast as budgetary limitations will allow and now are established in five of the ten areas. It is not unusual to see a baseball field with lights in a rural community.

The chart also shows the 1930 and 1960 populations and the percentage of change in each.

The four tables that follow, Tables 14, 15, 16, and 17, show what the United States Federal Government contributed to various activities in Puerto Rico in 1932 and what it contributed in 1962. They also show the Puerto Rican appropriations for these activities, which in most cases is more than is received from the Federal Government.

No figures are given for the cost of maintaining the various military bases and the Veterans' Administration. The military bases are, of course, much larger than an independent country the size of Puerto Rico would maintain.

TABLE 14

United States Federal Government Contribution
to Public Works and Unemployment
Compensation in 1932 and 1962

	Year and Source		
	1932 Federal	1962 Federal	1962 ELA[a]
Federal Aid to Highways[b]	0	$3,699,129	$9,948,719
Unemployment Compensation (Dept. of Labor)	0	2,819,175	7,743,000

[a]Estado Libre Asociado, or Free Associated State.

[b]Department of Public Works.

TABLE 15

United States Federal Government Contribution
to Health Activities in Puerto Rico
in 1932 and 1962

| | Year and Source | | |
	1932 Federal	1962 Federal	1962 ELA[a]
Hospitals	0	$44,634	$2,700,000
Heart Institute	0	116,932	200,000
TB Control	0	154,350	3,694,700
Mental Health	0	96,177	3,239,451
Public Welfare	0	10,246,519	14,949,628
Venereal Disease Control	0	32,538	28,000
Community Health	0	335,622	76,000
Maternal & Child Health	0	108,716	619,000
Crippled Children	0	108,621	528,000
Cancer Control	0	54,532	143,600

[a]Estado Libre Asociado, or Free Associated State

TABLE 16

United States Federal Government Contribution to
Educational Activities in Puerto Rico
in 1932 and 1962

| | Year and Source | | |
	1932 Federal	1962 Federal	1962 ELA[a]
College of Agriculture & Mech. Arts	$50,000	$186,807	$108,000
Library Assist.		162,226	316,980
School Construction		19,701	5,308,000
Defense Education Activity		536,669	152,000
Vocational	45,000	843,307	5,276,700
Television		200,000	100,000

[a]Estado Libre Asociado, or Free Associated State.

TABLE 17

United States Federal Government Contribution
to Agricultural Promotion in Puerto Rico
in 1932 and 1962

	Year and Source		
	1932 Federal	1962 Federal	1962 ELA[a]
Forestry Cooperation	$2,940	$350	$20,040
Agricultural Experiment Stations	0	877,423	3,632,820
Cooperative Agricultural Extension	0	1,431,962	2,956,480
National Forests	64	2,091	4,850
School Lunches	0	4,669,992	7,932,000
Removal of Surplus Agricultural Commodities	0	6,835,662	0
Commodity Credit Corporation	0	10,029,135	0
Plots (Parcelas)	0	0	60,341[b] 5,147[c]

[a]Estado Libre Asociado, or Free Associated State.

[b]For families.

[c]For public use.

Note: Surplus agricultural commodities and Commodity Credit Corporation contributions are food surpluses distributed to school lunch programs and recipients of public welfare.

Number of Factories Located, Aided and to be Established, and Employment by Municipality in 1963

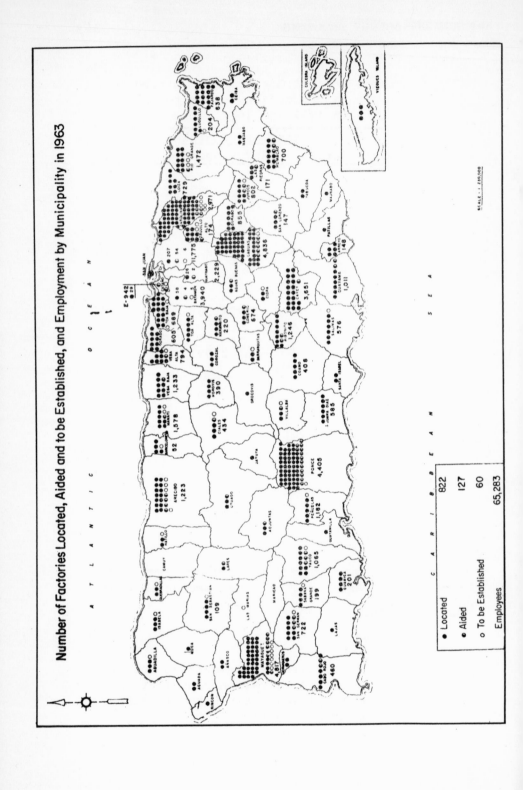

Located 822
Aided 127
To be Established 60
Employees 65,283

Notes to Chapter 4

1. Earl Parker Hanson, _Transformation: The Story of Modern Puerto Rico_ (New York: Simon and Schuster, 1955), p. 59.

2. Jaime Benitez, _Report of the Chancellor to the Superior Educational Council_, July 30, 1964.

3. _Ibid._, pp. 15-17.

4. _The Story of the Division of Community Education_, A Program of Community Development (San Juan, Puerto Rico, 1963).

5. Information from: Lydia J. Roberts, _et al._, "A Nutrition Survey of Three Rural Puerto Rican Communities," _Journal of the American Dietetic Association_, Vol. XLIV, No. 1 (January, 1964); Irwin C. Plough, Nelson A. Fernandez Lopez, Charles R. Angel, and Lydia J. Roberts, _Boletin Asociacion Medica de Puerto Rico_, Vol. LV, No. 12-A (December, 1963).

6. Juan A. Pons, _Puerto Rico: Examen De Su Revolucion y Proyecciones Para El Futuro El Bienestar Social: La Salud_.

7. Tugwell, _op. cit._, p. 70.

8. Elizabeth Wickenden, "Observations on Public Welfare in Puerto Rico," MS, p. 20.

9. San Juan, Department of Health, Social Science Program, _Second Annual Report, 1962-1963_, Introduction.

10. _Ibid._, p. 3.

11. _Ibid._, p. 4.

12. Wickenden, _op. cit._, p. 22.

13. San Juan, Puerto Rico Department of Health, Division of Public Welfare, _Bienestar Publicó Ante_

el Proposito de Puerto Rico. Plan de Diez Anos,
1964.

14. Material taken from Memorandum 63-25, Department of Health, Division of Public Welfare,
May 21, 1963.

15. Wickenden, op. cit., p. 12.

16. The 1960 census showed that among 35 per
cent of the heads of families in the less than $500
income group, none had been to school.

17. Historical material has been taken from
Legislacion Social de P.R. 1936, compiled by Vicente
Geigel Polanco, Director of Division of Economic and
Social Investigation, Department of Labor.

18. Ibid., p. XIII.

19. Ibid., passim.

20. Fernando Sierra Berdecía, The Civil Rights
of Labor and the Public Labor Policy of Puerto Rico
(San Juan, P.R.: Department of Labor, 1960). (Sec.
Sierra died in 1962 and was followed by Sec. Zorilla.)

21. Drawn from Pico, (1962), op. cit.

22. Testimony of Rafael Durand, Administrator
of the Economic Development Administration, before a
special subcommittee of the Select Committee on
Small Business of the U.S. Senate, April 16, 1964.

23. Pico (1962), op. cit.

5

INTRODUCTION TO COMMUNITY REPORTS

An important part of the work done in 1962, as preparation for the present project, was the visits to six of the ten communities by the social workers who had worked in these communities on the 1932 study. Their reports (Aguadilla, Bayamón, Cidra, Juncos, Salinas, Arecibo), reproduced in this chapter, show a real and often subtle understanding of the effects of change in the communities. Because they had actually lived in these places thirty years ago for a period of two years or more; because the experience had been an important part of the lives of these social workers; because their present professional situations give them insight into the planned change at its upper levels, returning to once-familiar localities was a poignant experience. Although what they saw was factually recorded, there lay behind the reports the nostalgia for things past, the impact of personal maturity looking back on youth, and a parallel recognition of actual change and of the reasons for it.

In contrast to these reports stand those of the field staff of 1964. Although all were Puerto Ricans, none of the members of this staff had ever known these communities, only one had any personal experience of rural living in Puerto Rico. What they saw were the ten communities as they are now. Because poverty is still present, there was an element of shock in some situations, there was also an appreciation for the warmth and hospitality of the people interviewed; there was great interest in coming to know something of a different way of

life--what it means to live in rural Puerto Rico
with its difficulties and its rewards. In some
places the natural beauty and luxuriant vegetation
were a new delight, in others the comparative lack
of richness in nature was striking. For all of
them it was a new experience and the comparison
with the past could come only from comparative data
and from the experiences of the past as related to
them in the interviews.

When we ourselves visited the Second Unit
Schools in ten communities, in advance of the field
staff, our view was necessarily superficial but
some of our observations should be noted. For example, some of the schools did not appear to be
very different from thirty years ago and in several
places the principal or some of the teachers had
been identified with the school and the barrio for
many years, yet life in the community had changed.
Teachers often lived in the nearest town and drove
to and from their work; the occupations and interests of parents had changed--the barrio no longer
enclosed their life, even when it remained as the
core of their community. Communication, transportation, available and potable water with few exceptions, often electricity, had transformed or at
least modified the way of life. Where the old
houses remained they were usually painted--some
not completely--expressing to the eye the wish and
the opportunity to bring color into their living.
The appearance of the children was striking--clean-
liness, neatness, healthy color, shoes. The increase in the number of (free) school lunches meant
better nutrition; the program for shoes meant a
change in status as well as protection from some
of the parasitical diseases. In many places there
was a noticeable change or shift in the crops in
the area. Some of these are a result of programs
of the Department of Agriculture, but we noted also
many more small plots of minor crops--particularly
plantains and bananas. We know the marketing of
such minor crops has not been fully worked out but
the increase was obvious. The establishment of
parcelas in many communities has introduced a new
pattern for rural living.

Among our ten communities, Hato Tejas in Bayamón
can no longer be classified as a rural community; it
has become a suburb of a very mixed kind. In outlying parts it retains some rural characteristics in
contrast to the sections nearest to Route #2--one of
the main highways of the island. The municipality
of Bayamón to which Hato Tejas belongs is a part of
the metropolitan area with its own industries, housing developments and congested traffic. Middle-
class growth is apparent everywhere. Hato Tejas
could be studied from the standpoint of a transitional community, suffering the consequences of rapid change with the problems of the city superimposed
in a brief space of time on the rural society. Its
citrus fruit growers have sold their land for high
prices. One or two who remain in this section are
in the business of canning fruit juices; just beyond
lie the acres of pineapples which provide the raw
product.

AGUADILLA--BARRIO SAN ANTONIO

Pop. 1932 - 3,291
Pop. 1962 - 3,771
Households -   621

This is a completely unique community in that
it has been bodily moved twice to make room for
Ramey Air Force Base. It is now part of the barrio
Montana, but keeps its own identity--has its own
post office and considers itself a separate entity.

It is about seven miles from Aguadilla down the
road to Isabela and the community is bordered by
Isabela, Moca, and Aguada.   Due to the moves, practically all the houses are comparatively new and the
community gives the appearance of being well-planned
and is kept very neat. The people do not accept being a part of Montana nor does Montana accept them.

The school is well-equipped and is actually
closer to the people of San Antonio than it was before. There is no information yet as to the number
of children in the school since all the figures we

have available are for the whole of Montana so those
of San Antonio must be estimated on a pro rata basis. Eight new classrooms have been added to the
school since 1942.

The water service is excellent and nearly
everyone has electricity. There is a public telephone but no telegraph office. There is no low-cost
housing but there are 413 parcelas, which means
enough for about two-thirds of the population. The
roads are good and lead to remote areas, but some
of them are not connected yet to the contiguous municipalities. There is a good public-recreation
program and there are also cultural activities connected with the school. There are no factories in
San Antonio but there are three in Aguadilla and the
transportation to Aguadilla is adequate. Health
centers and public welfare services are in full operation, but the Agricultural Extension Service is
only partial. The area concentrates heavily on
raising sugar cane. There is no community education
program and only partial services from the Labor Department.

A Visit to San Antonio

The following is a report of a visit to San
Antonio, Aguadilla, by Mercedes Velez de Perez in
1962. Mrs. Perez as social worker of San Antonio,
Second Unit School, did the work for this community
in 1931-32.

> A place is never the same when you go
> back to it, but if the going back takes
> place following a period of thirty years,
> the changes are very obvious. I recall
> San Antonio very vividly as it was in
> 1930--a closely knit rural "poblado,"
> twelve kilometers away from Aguadilla.
> A good many of its houses were thatched-
> roofed and inside them the furniture was
> quite rustic. The only means of trans-
> portation to and from the place was an
> old bus which made two round trips each

day at specified intervals. Malaria
and tuberculosis were prevalent as well
as gastroenteritis in infants, and
skin and eye infections in children of
school age. Sugar cane cutting provided almost the only source of income
during half of the year, the remaining
months of unemployment being referred
to as the "tiempo muerto" or the dead
season. The one-time important tobacco
and needlework industries for women
were no longer sources of income and
the straw industries were about to die
out. But, in its social cohesiveness,
its leaders were always busy with plans
for the improvement of the community.
The little public square, whose various
flower gardens the ladies in the most
outstanding families took good care of,
the annual celebration of the "fiestas
patronales," and the existence of a post
office station were sources of great
pride among the San Antonians.

Great changes have taken place in
San Antonio as you will see below. Its
inhabitants have been relocated twice
but their strong community feeling has
remained unchanged. They will be nothing else but the dwellers of San Antonio
even when they have twice come to be a
part of two different barrios. One
of its most outstanding leaders rejoiced
over the fact that when the police headquarters substation was established they
succeeded in having it named San Antonio not Montana.

One of the residents of the old San
Antonio (who was in part of the 1932
Cost of Living Study) described the most
visible changes in the following way:
Those were very backward times, the
1930's. Imagine, we used to put
brown sugar in our coffee and I felt
embarrassed over having to say so
in the study [referring to the Cost

of Living Study] . Our houses were
lighted by kerosene burners, since
only the school building and the
richest family in the poblado had
electric light. And as for food,
we only ate meat on Saturdays, and
then, only pork, as beef fillet was
unheard of. The only desserts we
had were homemade ones like coconut candy and "dulce de ajonjoli"
whereas now everybody can have cake
and ice cream and other nice desserts which are easily bought in
the supermarket and kept in the refrigerator. People now drink fresh
milk, not then. Another big change
concerns educational facilities;
you hear nowadays of many poor children going to high school and even
college. This was unheard of in
the 1930's.

Speaking of health facilities this same
person commented that, nowadays, no woman
gave birth to a child at home. Everyone,
she claims, is hospitalized at the time
of delivery. (Later I heard the nursing
supervisor in the Public Health Unit comment that although they have the necessary hospital facilities for every woman
to avail themselves of them at the time
of delivery, there are still a good many
who will not consider giving birth to
their children in a hospital. A great
deal needs to be done along this line by
way of education, she explained.)

As was mentioned before, the San
Antonio poblado has been moved twice
because of the establishment of the Ramey
Base. The first relocation occurred in
1939, when its inhabitants were moved to
Barrio Aguacate where the little "Poblado
de San Antonio" was resettled. There
it remained until 1959, when again the
need to expand the facilities at the Air
Base forced the dwellers of San Antonio

to move to Barrio Montana, the site where
they now are. They tell me that some
people in San Antonio are afraid of the
possibility of having to move again.

An employee of the Administration of
Social Programs in the Department of Agriculture explains that the new San Antonio has had the benefits of modern
planning and zoning methods. Houses are
not scattered irregularly as they used
to be in the old place. They follow a
well-devised relocation plan; each family
has been granted a lot of from 350 to 500
meters.

Streets have been paved by the municipality and all the necessary public services have been provided, such as electricity, individual water facilities for each
house, a post office and a police station,
and schools up to the fourth grade after
which the children move to the school in
Barrio Montana. Other resources in the
community are: a free school feeding
center, a playground, two churches (one
Protestant and the other Pentecostal), a
moving picture house, and a commercial
center which includes several supermarkets, warehouses, laundry, bakery, and
clothing stores. There is also a public
telephone in the neighboring community and
fire extinguishing facilities in every
street corner of the poblado.

There is, furthermore, a very active
citizen's committee whose plans for the
improvement of the community include the
following: building a public square,
establishment of a consumers' cooperative. Plans also include the building
of a Catholic chapel.

Improvement in housing conditions
is readily seen. Thatched-roofed houses
are no longer seen in San Antonio. Home
surroundings are clean and orderly. Many
homes have flower gardens. Modern furniture has replaced the former primitive
benches and tables. Practically every

house has a radio. An estimate of twelve
out of each hundred homes are equipped
with a television set and a refrigerator. There must be around ten houses
with laundry machines in the poblado.

There are around thirty public automobiles and station wagons which provide
relatively good transportation facilities
to and from Aguadilla. There are also
buses to take children to and from school
in the city. The distance to be covered
is now around seven miles. One of San
Antonio's civic leaders considers that
even with the increased facilities adults
still have difficulty in getting transportation in the morning when they need
to get to the Public Health Unit or to
some other place in town.

There is an individual supply of
water for every house in the poblado.
Water is safe. The greatest achievement
in the health area has been the eradication of malaria which used to be a very
serious problem in this community. Tuberculosis, according to the school social worker and the nursing supervisor
in the Health Unit, is still a serious
problem. Of a caseload of twenty-four,
the social worker reported six tuberculosis cases. "The number of deaths on
account of TB may have decreased," claims
the nursing supervisor, "but there is a
good number of new tuberculosis cases
each year." She also commented that other
health problems are now more evident
than previously, or at least, there
seems to be an increased awareness of
the number of cripples, cancer cases
and heart patients besides diabetes and,
lately, hepatitis. She was very much
concerned with the high incidence of
tooth decay, despite improvement in the
measures such as fluorinization of water,
increased dental facilities, etc. She
was referring, however, to the situation

for the island as a whole since she did
not have data on cases from San Antonio.
Sanitary conditions in the community
seem to have improved considerably.
Every house has its latrine in good,
hygienic conditions, and a few have
toilets. The residents of San Antonio
still have to go to Aguadilla for the
treatment of their health problems.
The health unit and the district hospital provide good health services.
School dental facilities have improved
considerably inasmuch as they are no
longer limited to extractions, but make
provisions for tooth repairing.

Everyone agrees that it is in the
area of education where the greatest
achievements have been made. As already indicated, in San Antonio proper,
there are school facilities for children up to the fourth grade. After that
children attend school in the neighboring vicinity of Montana with grades up
to the ninth. From then on, children
avail themselves of the educational facilities in Aguadilla where they get
their high school education. Up to last
year, for further academic training they
had to make plans to attend either the
university in Rio Piedras, or one of the
colleges in San German or Mayaguez, or
the university in Ponce. Since last
year, the Inter-American University of
San German and the Catholic University
in Ponce have established extension
courses in Aguadilla. School buses take
students to Aguadilla in the morning and
back to San Antonio after school is over.
There are also evening classes for those
who need to work during the day. Scholar-
ship facilities, as well as transportation expenses, shoes for needy children
and other educational resources are now
available to help needy children obtain
their education in accordance with their

ability to learn. A good many of the
children of San Antonio have availed
themselves of these opportunities.

Sugar cane still constitutes the
main agricultural product in the region. Though less land is now available for the growing of cane because
so much had to be taken for the military base, there is still sugar cane
growing in the region. No other agricultural products seem to be grown in
this area.

We have already indicated that the
tobacco, needlework and straw industries are no longer sources of income
for women. Work opportunities, in addition to the ones available during
part of the year in the cane industry,
are those provided by the Ramey Base.
This includes domestic service, jani-
torial jobs, gardening, store clerks,
cooks, bartenders, work in gas stations and transportation facilities as
well as in the existing grocery and
clothing stores, laundry and bakery.

Everyone seems to agree that there
is still a serious unemployment problem
in this community in spite of the work
opportunities available in Ramey Base.
Some of the San Antonio civic leaders
have approached the government officials about the possibility of establishing a factory in the community to
alleviate the unemployment situation
but movement in this direction has met
with no success.

The head of the Employment Service
in Aguadilla and the Work Placement Officer could not supply either employment or unemployment figures for San
Antonio as they do not keep such data
on a barrio basis. However, they are
aware of the unemployment problem in
the area and estimate that around 50 per
cent of its wage earners engage in the

sugar cane cutting in the active season and are unemployed when this is over (June to December). It is then when laborers are eligible under the Compensation Plan for Unemployment in the Cane Industry. Under such a plan an unemployed laborer who has worked sixty days in the cane fields is entitled to a total amount of $31.50, payable on the basis of $3.50 per week for nine weeks. Payments are made every two weeks. Legislation now pending aims to increase to $60 the total amount to be given and to twelve the number of weeks for which benefits may be received.

According to the Placement Officer a group of laborers migrates to the United States during the months of April to August in search of season employment. Some of them are residents of San Antonio, both men and women, who move to and from the States in search of work.

No significant migration from San Antonio to the city of Aguadilla is noticeable. Immigration, rather than emigration, accounts for the change in population figures, according to the civic leader already referred to. He agrees with others that there is some movement of laborers to the United States during part of the "tiempo muerto" in search of work. They are sure to return, he claims.

At the moving picture house, pictures are shown every evening and at the athletic park the baseball games and other sports activities take place. School recreational activities, a Boy Scout troop, and the celebration of the "fiestas patronales" once a year around March constitute the additional recreational activities in the area. The moving picture house is famous for the good pictures it shows but it is said that the place is filled largely with

persons coming from neighboring barrios
and even from towns like Isabela and
Aguadilla, rather than with residents
of San Antonio most of whom cannot afford to attend the movies frequently.

There was general agreement with
regard to the unemployment problem and
the existence of poverty among the
people of San Antonio. A visit to the
Aguadilla Public Welfare Office where
we interviewed the local chief revealed
a total of 140 families from San Antonio who were getting public assistance
because of the existence in the family
of: (1) needy aged, (2) needy blind,
(3) permanent and total disability of the
breadwinner, or (4) dependent children.
There are around 671 families in the community so the number of public assistance
recipients seems very high. The trend
is toward an increase in these figures.
Three years ago the number of public assistance cases in San Antonio was only
80 and last January there were 130, the
average monthly increase having been 9.
There were also four cases of children
who had been referred for child welfare
services because of delinquent behavior.

Further inquiry into this last area
revealed that in the year 1961 and up to
the present, a total of 11 youngsters
had been adjudicated delinquent by the
Juvenile Court in Aguadilla. Four of
them had been placed in the corresponding public welfare institutions.

Several of the persons interviewed
spoke of the delinquency problem, a thing
unheard of in the 1930's. Reference
was also made by several of the persons
interviewed to the problems presented by
a few women whose moral conduct was thought
to constitute a problem in the community.
Although these were thought to be isolated
cases, apparently there is some concern

over the problem they present inasmuch
as the community holds in high regard
its reputation for good behavior among
its citizens.

The civic leader of whom we spoke
above referred to the problem of gam-
bling to which some adults in San Antonio were addicted but considered
that, in general, the San Antonio community is composed of good, law-abiding
citizens. There was a great deal of
pride in him when he made such a statement.

LOIZA--BARRIO MEDIANÍA ALTA

Pop. 1932 - 2,197
Pop. 1962 - 4,254
Households   788

Medianía Alta is a barrio of the municipality
of Loiza. It can be regarded in many respects as
atypical, compared to most of the rural communities
in Puerto Rico, though this difference was more
striking thirty years ago than it is at present, due
to roads, communication, and opportunities for employment in industries in Canovanas.

The barrio is situated in the northeast part of
Puerto Rico, running back in a southerly direction
from the coast and bounded by the municipalities of
Carolina on the west, Rio Grande on the east, and
Juncos on the south. It may be reached by crossing
the Loiza River, by primitive ferry, from the west,
or by improved road from the Sixty-fifth Infantry
Highway from the south.

It is characterized by an almost completely
Negro population and in the past had a reputation
for primitive customs, partly based on fact and
partly on myth. Until recently, a large proportion
of the housing was made up of thatched huts although
even in the 1930's there were some well-built
houses of wood along the road. Coconuts and minor

crops were the main commercial agricultural products
and many of the huts were scattered through coconut
groves. There was, and still is, in addition, raising of minor crops largely for home consumption.

This community has a special character and
charm, which at first view appears to be primitive.
There are few families with a standard of living
which could be considered high, and there is a reten-
tion of old values which relates the village to a
traditional past. This is, however, in process of
change, through the appearance of new occupations,
increasing land values, and the introduction of government services.

In this study, some preliminary work was done
before the decision was made to use our sampling
method. School records revealed the frequent rep-
etion of family names and further investigation
showed some social stratification by family, resulting in prestige for certain names. There is no
striking difference, however, in economic level so
that some interpretation and modification of classification of families had to be introduced to allow
for differences not represented solely by income.
The investigators were struck by the lack of adequate living space for the size of the families.
Most houses have outside latrines and tin tubs for
bathing. Some of the new houses have running water
in kitchens but many families still must carry water
from the public faucet. Kerosene is the fuel most
often used; electricity is used for ironing and for
lighting.

Government services include a health unit, a
first aid unit, a post office, police, a public telephone, school buses, school lunchrooms, breakfast for
preschool children, and milk stations for infants up
to three years of age. The Second Unit School retains much of the character of a community center
and families participate in social events held in
the school and make use of governmental services.

One of our field workers wrote that the population of Mediania Alta is "the prototype of a

conservative people, in spite of all changes and im-
provements--they retain their rural characteristics
and seem happier that way."

This community is made up of several sectors,
differing in facilities of water, roads, and electricity. The Programas Sociales of the Department
of Agriculture has established parcelas (see information on this program under Department of Agriculture). No agricultural agent works in the community now because coconuts are no longer a commercial crop there. The reason given for this was that
land is being acquired by both government and private
interests for other than agricultural purposes.

It was reported that some of the residents go
to the continental United States for seasonal agricultural work in the summer.

Our interviewers were impressed by the friendly
atmosphere, both among neighbors and to the field
staff, and were charmed by the children. There was
a willingness to answer questions, but one of the
interviewers found that the fathers often did not
know the ages of their children and the women knew
little of economic questions.

JUANA DIAZ--BARRIO COLLORES

Pop. 1932   - 2,713
Pop. 1962   - 2,340
Households -   443

The municipality of Juana Diaz is in the center
of the south coast but the barrio of Collores is in-
land in a rural section classified in the 1932 study
as growing mixed or minor crops. The municipality
is bounded by Santa Isabel, Coama, Villalba, and
Ponce. To reach Collores one drives some distance
west and north from the town of Juana Diaz. The
Second Unit School is located close to the road
which continues into the mountain area in the direction of Jayuya and the majority of houses of this
community are situated along this same road. Many

of the people of the barrio go to Juana Diaz or Ponce
to work. Some coffee and some sugar are raised.

The field staff found the area conservative in
its outlook, although the residents are strong sup-
porters of the Popular Party and idolize Muñoz Marin.
They are not much interested in the world outside
their immediate community but are anxious to get government services for their neighborhood. They already have water for 300 of the 443 households and
some parts of the barrio already have electricity.

The field staff felt that, although Collores is
a poor community, it has benefited greatly from the
roads, electricity, and schools of the government
program and also has good churches.

Collores is very beautiful and was made famous
by a poem by Luis Llorens Torres. One of the members
of the staff asked the people whom she interviewed
whether they were familiar with the poem; she found
they were not and could not identify the plants and
flowers mentioned in the poem.

There was great curiosity about the study and
during the interviews neighbors came in to find out
why a certain person was being interviewed. The
people were described as religious, hospitable, com-
municative, and receptive.

Note was also made of many marital unions outside legal marriage, but there was condemnation for
a girl who became pregnant before establishing an
arrangement for living with a particular man.

BAYAMÓN--BARRIO HATO TEJAS

Pop. 1932 - 3,092
Pop. 1962 - 11,427
Households- 2,246

Among the ten barrios of the study, the barrio
of Hato Tejas presents the most striking changes. It
lies on the outskirts of the city of Bayamón, a part

of the San Juan metropolitan area. A large part of
the area manifests urban or transitional characteristics, yet there remains one sector which is still
distinctly rural. One leaves Route #2 (San Juan to
Arecibo) to the south. Roads are paved although
not all houses have immediate access to these roads.
Some major crops are raised and there are some
dairies but sugar cane cultivation is almost gone.
Many government services are in operation. There is
a local dispensary for prescriptions and first aid,
in charge of a licensed practical nurse and visited
by a doctor three times a week. These services are
much used. There is also service from the Public
Health Unit in Bayamón to the adjoining barrio of
Rio Plantación which serves Hato Tejas. Full public
welfare services are in operation through the Bayamón office. The program for electricity is not complete, but service centers are provided for installation of light, radios, irons, and stoves at the
rate of $1 per month.

The school picture is complicated. The Second
Unit is a part of a local complex including a new
intermediate school with 655 students and 26 teachers which offers courses in home economics and industrial arts; in another sector, there is a grade
school with 153 children, 3 teachers--grades one to
three, and another, grades one to six with 345 pupils and 7 teachers. The Second Unit itself has
1,249 students and 33 teachers, using the interlocking system to accommodate this number, and some 440
students eat the school lunch. Industrial arts
serves the seventh, eighth, ninth grades and its
program includes graphic arts, drawing, mechanics
in the seventh grade, with metal working, wood working, and electricity in the eighth and ninth grades.
This is an illustration of the new plans of the Department of Education in preparing students for work
in industry. A new vocational school is also being
built.

The Department of Public Works has let a contract for 3,500 linear meters of curbs and 6,050
meters of sidewalk. Housing developments are increasing and land, formerly agricultural, is being

bought up. These developments contrast with existing poor housing. Even under the excellent program
of Programas Sociales, one member of the staff said
the good houses were as good as the best and the bad
houses as bad as the worst.

There has been an influx of population from the
interior of the island, looking for jobs and for improved living conditions. This has brought a variety
of people to the area and has created the usual problems resulting from the need to adapt to a different
way of life. These problems include dope addiction
and juvenile delinquency.

Opportunities for industrial employment exist
in six establishments: a paper company, a container
company, and manufacturers of coffee grinding machinery, frozen fruit concentrates, hard candy, and
agricultural chemicals.

The reports of the field staff from their interviews reflect the rapid changes which have come
to this community--a greater sophistication than is
found in the rural areas, the enjoyment of more con-
veniences of living (or the prospect of acquiring
them soon), high levels of aspirations of parents
for their children. Incomes on the whole are higher
--new occupations include not only employees of industrial plants, but construction workers, chauffeurs (drivers of public cars), workers in supermarkets (in Bayamón), etc.

Family life is affected by the employment situation. Often both parents are working and the
younger children are left with the grandparents,
neighbors, older children--or are neglected. There
was less of an easy and hospitable welcome to the
field staff; more suspicion, more difficulty in
establishing rapport. The staff reported many consensual or casual marital relationships--men with a
number of women, and women with a number of men,
even in cases where the original marriage had been
legal.

Another matter of interest was the strength of

spiritualism, evaluated positively by one member of
the staff who felt that it solves many problems in
person-to-person relationships, although other comments on religion emphasized its superficial-
conventional character.

A Visit to Hato Tejas

The following is a report of a visit to Second
Unit Virgilio Davila Hato Tejas, Bayamón, Puerto
Rico, 1962, by Emma Purcell de Hernandez, social
worker, 1932, and Zenaida B. Shepàrd, home economics
teacher, 1932.

> Hato Tejas, a suburb community of Baya-
> món, Puerto Rico, was chosen among the
> other barrios of the town of Bayamón in
> 1930, as the site in which to establish
> a different type of school, in those
> days called Second Units. This was
> started in Peabody Rural School. In
> this rural school there were only the
> first, second, and third grades. When
> the Second Unit started it was neces-
> sary to add more grades. By and by the
> school reached the eighth grade. In
> 1932 the first graduation took place.
>   In 1930 the school enrollment was
> about 400 students. At present the
> school has two school levels, the ele-
> mentary and the junior high school.
> From the first to the sixth grades,
> there are 1,196 students; from the sev-
> enth to the ninth grades, there are 498
> students; total enrollment, 1,694 stu-
> dents.
>   Today the school has the following
> organization: a principal, an assistant
> principal, 2 home economics teachers,
> 2 industrial arts teachers, 24 elemen-
> tary teachers (from the first to the
> sixth grades), 16 junior high school
> teachers.
>   Although the school has grown in
> enrollment the buildings are more or less

the same with the exception of a new
two-room vocational building. One room
is an all—purpose laboratory where cooking, sewing, child care, housing and
family relationships are taught daily
by two teachers in an interlocking system. The other room is for the industrial arts teachers. They work in coordination as the home economics teachers do.

In 1930 the social worker had a
full program. Now, in 1962, the social
worker works only one day during the
week in the Second Unit of Hato Tejas.
The other four days she works in other
schools of Bayamón.

The Second Unit has a library (a
small one) for the use of the students
It is opened from 8:00 a.m. to 11:00 a.m.
and from 12:00 noon to 3:00 p.m. The
community can not make use of this library because it closes after school
hours and during the weekends.

The lunchroom is the same old one,
slightly enlarged lengthwise. It provides for a total of 460 students attending in shifts according to grades
and hours they are dismissed from class.
The cooking is done with charcoal as in
1930.

Today there are a great variety of
industries established in the community
of Hato Tejas. Some of the industries
are:
1. Miami Windows Factory
2. Iron Work Shop
3. Men's Trousers Factory
4. Patisserie, or Bakery for Pastries
5. Cement Blocks Factory
6. Cannery for Juices with Fruits
    "La Famosa"
7. Furniture Making Shop
8. Duco Paint and Auto Body Repair Shop
9. Gasoline and Auto Parts Garage
10. Repair and Mechanic Auto Shop

The social worker informed us that
unemployment does not exist, due to the
establishment of factories in the community and in the suburbs of Bayamón.
On the other hand, the agricultural aspect of the community has completely
disappeared. The citrus fruits and the
flowers which made Hato Tejas famous in
1930 have gone during the years. We
were informed that a son of an old continental family still living in the community has developed on his own farm a
business of selling flowers and ornamen-
tal plants.

The new military road built during
the last war divides Hato Tejas lengthwise into two parts from north to south.
The traffic of automobiles is mostly on
the new road. The buses coming from
Corozal, Morovis, Toa Baja, Vega Alta
and Ciales, however, always come through
on the old road to give better service
to the community.

The telephone service now is auto-
matic and gives service to the whole
community.

Hato Tejas has a drive-in theater
which the local people enjoy. It is
always filled to capacity. There is
also a cock-fight center. The night
clubs play an important part of recreation in Hato Tejas. There are quite
a few established such as Las Tres Palmas,
El Castillo and El Toronjal, etc.

Hato Tejas has a self-service supermarket and many small grocery stores.
It has a pharmacy and a large hardware
store.

There are about five churches in
the community. One is Roman Catholic
and the rest belong to different Protestant sects.

In contrast to 1930, today everybody has electricity and running water.

Sanitary conditions are greatly improved by the use of running water.
Television provides recreation at home
for the family. Electricity is used
by many families for cooking and house-
cleaning.

In 1930, most people used water
pumps and natural wells for their water
supply. Now water is brought to the
community by an aqueduct.

The community now has the following additional governmental and private
facilities: U.S. sub-post office, police
substation, health dispensary, park and
recreational center, three barber shops,
two restaurants, one flower shop, one
funeral parlor.

The progress and development of
Hato Tejas is considerable; it has been
the attraction for poor country people
living near the town of Bayamón. These
people move to Hato Tejas searching for
work in the factories, but they are
contributing to the development of slum
areas scattered through the community.

A housing-development project of
about 2,500 houses has already been
started on one of the largest farms.
It is called Gascot Urbanization. This
project should give work to hundreds of
people who live in Hato Tejas and in
nearby towns.

The social problems found today in
Hato Tejas by the social worker are
very different from those found in 1930.
The night clubs, the factories and many
other trends resulting from high living
standards have completely changed the
community and the problems among school-
age children.

The services of a full-time social
worker are urgently needed in the community.

CIDRA--BARRIO BAYAMÓN

Pop. 1932 - 2,679
Pop. 1962 - 3,040
Households -   486

Bayamón, a barrio of the municipality of Cidra, is in the lower mountainous section in the east-central part of the island. Cidra is bounded by the municipalities of Aguas Buenas, Caguas, Cayey, Aibonito, and Comerio. The main roads are good and the Second Unit School of Barrio Bayamón is on the main road (primary carretera) to the town. The climate is cool and pleasant.

In the 1930's, the area was classified as a fruit-growing section--pineapple and citrus. Many men left at the time of the _zafra_ to work in sugar cane. Now, the chief crop is tobacco, with some sugar cane also grown. There are some small craft industries, making sandals, rings, etc., from native materials. One factory, making brassieres, is in operation in the town; two others have been closed. In the barrio of Bayamón, houses are widely scattered; a considerable number of the inhabitants work in the towns of Cayey and Caguas. Both these towns are tobacco centers. Much of the tobacco and sugar is raised on the lands of large owners, but small farmers still cultivate one or two acres of tobacco. The large sugar company transports workers by truck to other areas to work. In tobacco growing the small growers do not belong to the cooperatives, but are supplied with materials at a uniform price by the large growers.

Government facilities in fair measure have reached Barrio Bayamón; 123 of 486 families have water and 147 have electricity. Access roads have been built, but there are no low-cost public housing, public telephones, parcelas, or public recreation facilities.

The field staff found the community poor and lacking certain facilities. Sanitary conditions,

even in the school, are poor, transportation difficult, and there is no public telephone. There is a
health unit in the town of Cidra. Overcrowding in
homes was noted.

The Second Unit School (550 students) has some
specific problems. The dropout rate is very high
(over 200 children of school age are not in attendance). An excellent study was made on this subject, giving distance from school, poverty, low educational level of parents as some of the reasons for
dropouts and suggesting remedies. Parents, however,
have aspirations for better education for their children.

The shoe program is limited--only 75 pairs had
been received whereas the study showed a need for
over 250. The lunchroom serves 98 per cent of the
students. The new principal of the Second Unit is
very conscious of the present needs of the school
and has the energy and the imagination to bring
about real development, with the cooperation of the
Department of Education.

Reports of the field staff agree on the warmth
and hospitality of the people of the barrio, also in
their feeling that, in spite of local needs, the general situation is better than it was in the past.

A Visit to Barrio Bayamón

The following is a report of a visit to the rural school of Cidra-Bayamón, May 13, 1962, by Isabel
Laguna de Colorado, social worker, 1932.

> The school district of Cidra used to
> be part of the Cayey school district.
> At present they have a high school. Be-
> fore, the students used to go to Cayey
> or Caguas high school.
>   The Protestant Church has a small
> school in Cidra. The Catholic Church
> is planning to set up one of their own.
> Previously there were no denominational
> schools in Cidra.

The Second Unit used to have eight
grammar school grades, four high school.
Now they have six-three-three.

At present the Second Unit does
not teach industrial arts.

The lunchroom is quite roomy and
very clean and a total of 280 students
and six teachers have lunch there.
The food served seems to be of good
quality.

The registration of the Second
Unit at present is 368 students in the
elementary grades and 127 in the intermediate grades, a total of 495 students.
Only the children of the sixth grade
attend school the whole day; the rest
are under the interlocking plan.

The Second Unit has the problem of
dropouts. Following are some of the
reasons for this problem:

1. Families are moving to Cayey,
Caguas and U.S. in search of better working opportunities.

2. An artificial lake has divided the
land, and many families prefer to send
their children to the schools in town.

3. The lack of jobs, and consequently low income of the families in the
community.

4. A negative attitude on the part
of the families. The social worker
visits only one day in the week to the
Second Unit. She is in charge of three
schools. The result is that she becomes
an emergency worker with very little
time, if any, for social case work.

In Cidra there are three factories,
one of which is near the Second Unit.
One factory makes uniforms, the other
pieces for brassieres, and the third is
a tobacco factory. They employ mainly
women. Before there was only one factory, the tobacco factory.

As a result of the type of industry, there is considerable unemployment

among men. The change from sugar cane
planting to dairy industries has brought
still more unemployment for men.

Most of the land used before for
growing sugar cane is now used for raising dairy cattle. Before, the people
planted pineapple and grapefruit and
there was a packing house. Both types
of cultivations have disappeared. Plantains, bananas, oranges, grapefruit,
and sugar cane are now planted on a very
small scale. Tobacco, however, is being
planted to be processed in the above-
mentioned factory.

Water and electricity are now available in most of the surrounding barrios.
Installation work is going on in some
of those not yet included. At the Second
Unit the water was previously brought
from a small stream behind the school.
Now there is a big cement tank where the
water is collected for cooking and drinking.

The elementary school has electricity now, and the intermediate will have
it soon. The day of our visit people
were working on the installation.

Latrines are still in use in the
Second Unit, but they are lacking in the
elementary school. (Only the intermediate school has them.) The elementary
school children have to cross the road
to use the latrines of the intermediate
school, which creates a dangerous situation for small children.

In general the health of adults
and children is much better. There is
a health center at the entrance to the
town, where all children from the Second
Unit are taken care of. In case they
need hospitalization, they are taken to
the Rio Piedras Hospital. There is also
a dental clinic where teeth are extract-
ed or cleaned.

Social Security benefits are a considerable help to some of the older people of the community. Some poor old people and some children are benefited by the help they receive from the Public Welfare Division of the Department of Health. Although children receive shoes from the Department of Education, I saw three of them barefooted at the Second Unit School.

The roads today are much better and more numerous than in the past. There are also more bus lines. The children who cannot pay have free transportation provided by the Department of Education from their homes to school and back.

There are telegraph and telephone offices in town. In the Second Unit rural school, however, there is no telephone, nor is there any telephone booth nearby.

A big housing development has been built in the town. I did not see much improvement in the houses of the barrio, however, nor in the buildings of the Second Unit.

The town as a whole has not increased in population.

In the town there is a public playground, under Parks and Recreation.

The Second Unit proper has a small playground used by the children. At present they are fixing it so they can play baseball and basketball.

I gathered the impression that the community is not using the government resources to the maximum. This aspect ought to be investigated and studied.

ADJUNTAS--BARRIO YAHNECAS

Pop. 1932 - 1,770
Pop. 1962 - 1,712
Households -   331

Adjuntas lies in the heart of the mountains,
east of the center of the island. It is bounded by
the municipalities of Penuelas, Ponce, Utuado,
Lares, Yauco, and Guayamilla.

The reports on Barrio Yahnecas are filled with
the beauty of the place, with its luxuriant vegetation and mountain views and air. It is reached by
narrow, winding mountain roads and to some of the
staff, seemed at first very remote. But they found
that there are many contacts with the town of Ad-
juntas--people working in the town and others going
to the country to work during the coffee-picking
season. There is a problem which appears in many
places in Puerto Rico--complaints about a lack of
employment combined with a shortage of workers for
such occupations as coffee-picking. This is, of
course, explainable in the light of the seasonal
nature of the coffee industry. Transportation was
described as "bad."

Most of the houses appeared old and not comfortable, but many are well-equipped with electrical
facilities and often television. Furniture was reported as adequate compared to some other communities. Schools seemed to be adequate and education
is given great importance. The Second Unit School
is on the road from Adjuntas. It is a little shab-
by--not one which has been modernized; nevertheless,
the atmosphere is good and there is loyalty to the
community.

One family of artists was described--the walls
of the house were covered with paintings by various
members of the family.

Interest in spiritualism is strong "as a philosophy of life" rather than for its cures.

People were described as "smart, receptive and kind." In spite of complaints about employment, the inhabitants of this region want to live in the country. There seems to be a special atmosphere of happiness, perhaps partly due to the climate and beauty of the place and the interest and contentment of people of different classes.

MOCA--BARRIO VOLADORES

Pop. 1932 - 1,800
Pop. 1962 - 2,379
Households -   449

Voladores is about three miles from the town of Moca on the road to San Sebastian. It is bordered by Isabela, Aguadilla, Aguada, Añasco, and San Sebastian. This is a coffee and sugar area, although a good deal of the sugar land is marginal. At the time the field staff visited Moca, there had been a lot of fires in the sugar cane fields, due to disgruntled workers, people thought, or to a group of fanatical Independentistas who were later caught in a cave with a large store of arms and ammunition. Their trial is still pending.

This is a self-contained community with very little outside activity. The majority of the land is owned by two families and there are many agregados.

There is a good parcela program with some land for home gardens; 178 families live in these houses and 47 families are accommodated in a low-cost housing project.

Many of the women are employed in needlework either at home or in factories.

The school is a real center for community gatherings.

A total of 318 out of 449 families have water available, and most have electricity. In cases

where water does not run to the house there is usually a public faucet within a reasonable distance.
There is no public telephone.

Feeder roads are being constructed from the
main road into the remote areas, but again they are
not fully connected to adjoining towns.

There is no organized public recreation in
Voladores.

Only partial health service is in effect, but
there are full public welfare and Agricultural Extension services.

There are no factories in Voladores, but there
is one in Moca. There are no community education or
Labor Department services.

JUNCOS--BARRIO EL MANGÓ

Pop. 1932 - 817
Pop. 1962 - 482
Households - 155

Juncos is situated in the eastern quarter of the
island about midway between north and south coasts.
The township is bounded by Loiza, Gurabo, San Lorenzo,
and Las Piedras. El Mangó is about five miles out of
Juncos on main highway #31 to Naguabo. It is not a
true barrio. It is a rural community in the barrio
of Gurabo Ariba. It is located in very hilly country producing sugar and minor crops. Probably cattle raising would make better use of the land than
sugar.

There are not many services available, no telegraph, post office or police, but there is a letter
drop and a public telephone. The Agricultural Extension Service is excellent. Transportation to
Juncos is very poor and almost nonexistent after
5:30 P.M. People reported that the ambulance service was good and prompt.

Job opportunities are few in the immediate area, but there are nine factories in Juncos.

There is very little understanding of any class structure in Juncos. The people seem to feel that they are all of the same class. The school is a real community center for meetings, social programs, and other activities. Parents are interested in the school, but do not seem to have much hope for higher education for their children. They said it was for the rich--not for them. El Mangó is primarily a community of laborers, some of whom go to the United States during the summer crop season when there is no cane cutting in Puerto Rico. Some of the field staff felt the people were suspicious that they were government agents and would not talk. Other people in the community were cooperative and answered questions freely. All were very hospitable and friendly on a personal level.

There is a good parcela program and a good scattering of privately built concrete housing. One-half of the people have electricity in the house and one-half have running water. Others use public faucets.

Whereas in 1932 there was only one main road, several feeder roads have been built to the north of the highway, but none to the south. One highway, over the mountains, connects El Mangó to Canovanas.

This is a very self-contained community. People stay here with little outside communication and not much interest in what is going on in the rest of the island.

Seventy-one families live in low-cost public housing. There is a part-time health center and part-time application of public health benefits.

A Visit to Barrio El Mangó

The following is a report of a visit to the Second Unit School (vocational) at El Mangó, Juncos, P.R., by Dolores Gonzales de la Cara, social worker, 1932, and Angelina Sandoz de Frontera, home economics teacher, 1932.

As we went to Caguas we both agreed on the progress of recent years indicated by the spacious road and houses built on both sides of the road. Going out from Caguas the progress seemed to have occurred at a slower pace. The road to Juncos has not changed much and one can still see many of the landmarks of thirty years ago, including a cement bench my father had given to the people of Canta Gallo, which was placed at the side of the road where a sidewalk was built for people from this section to sit and talk. The benches had the name, business and date of the person who donated them. This bench was the only one left, and to me it was very interesting.

We went through the town of Juncos directly to El Mangó, and therefore did not have a chance to see much of the town itself, except as we went through. My personal impression of the town is that it has not changed much in its physical aspects. Perhaps, as in many of our towns, changes and developments have occurred on the periphery and not much in the core of the town.

At El Mangó we went straight to the office of the school principal. She was one of the richest sources of information, since she has been working in El Mangó since 1950.

We visited all the school buildings and the school lunchroom and talked to a great number of the teachers. The visit with a member of the community in his barrio store was also very illuminating. Then we visited the dairy owned by a prominent member of the community, who was thirty years ago, and still is, one of the richest landowners.

In summary the information obtained
and our own observations are as follows:

Great physical developments in these
schools--new buildings, more teachers,
larger enrollment of students.

Enrollment 1950   370 children
           1962   452 elementary school
                      241 girls
                      211 boys
                  312 intermediate school
                      160 girls
                      152 boys
           total 764 children

Teachers, 1950 -- 9
Teachers, 1962 --18; 6 males, 12 fe-
               males; B.A. and Nor-
               mal School.

One of the present teachers was a student from that Second Unit School.

The principal informed us there are
no more teachers because of lack of room
facilities, which is pointed out as a
major problem, although they have two
new concrete buildings and one durotex
structure. Students attend in double
shifts up to the sixth grade. In the
intermediate school they have the departmental system. Vocational training is
limited to home economics for girls and
agriculture for boys.

Social services are provided from
town one day a week. That this service
is limited is also emphasized as a great
drawback.

The children have an art teacher
and a music teacher once a month. Vocational orientation also comes from
the high school in town.

We observed the improvement of the
school lunch. We saw what menu was being prepared, the cleanliness of the
women working in the kitchen, and their
methods of preparation. There are seven
cooks and helpers in charge of food

preparation and food is served in trays
--cafeteria style. Around 350 children
get lunch free. They no longer pay the
1¢ they used to for lunch. The storage
room for foods and groceries for the
lunchroom is kept immaculate and in
perfect order.

Many of the women working in the
lunchroom remembered me very well and
we had a long talk about their families
and about life in general in the barrio.

There still is a Parent Teacher
Association which seems to be active.
They meet once a month.

A mutual-aid housing community
developed in El Mango has greatly increased the number of school children.
The main problem is schoolroom accom-
modation.

Juncos has developed into an industrial town with a great number of
light industries, many of them located
close to town, but on the road going
to El Mangó. Many women, especially
mothers, are working in these industries. A smaller number of men also
work in industries, but the majority
of men still work mainly in agriculture.

All the informants and our own
observations indicate an improvement
of the standards of living: children
look well dressed, healthy. There are
more opportunities for work.

A great portion of the land that
used to be dedicated to sugar cane is
now used for cattle raising. The two
main landowners are still there and
they have established big dairies now.

We did not have much opportunity
to observe or get information in the
area of sanitation and health. One
thing that attracted our attention was
the existence of latrines on one side
of the row of school buildings. On

one side they have built two sets of modern washrooms and flush toilets, one for teachers and a separate one for students.

Houses close to the road are built of concrete or blocks. We could not see any thatched-roofed houses. There is also a cemetery in the community.

Children have free transportation offered by the Department of Education through a contract with a bus line owner known to this part of the island in the field of bus transportation for many years. The whole community has good transportation facilities by means of publicos.

Through the rural electrification program new power lines have been extended farther into the community to where the row of hills starts. Up to this point, houses are wired for electricity. Most families have radios and some have television sets.

The school has a telephone which was pointed out to us as an indication of progress. They also have a loudspeaker system to communicate with all the students.

There has been great improvement in water supply and people do not have to walk far to get water.

A tremendous increase in the number of churches, especially Protestant churches, was pointed out as a major change in this community: Church of God, United Evangelists, Seventh Day Adventists and a few others. The comment was made that it is relatively easy to be a minister in one of these religious sects and for the ministers to use their homes as churches.

In general, if we were to picture graphically changes in this community, our image would be as follows:

To us there are still areas in
which not much change can be noticed
and some in which definite changes
have occurred.

It would be very interesting and
fascinating to measure with as many
scientific methods as possible what
has really happened in the past thirty
years.

I consider that our short visit
was not long enough to make adequate
observations or for the collection of
impressions and certain data, but it
gave us a feeling of the process of
change which is not, however, following an even pattern.

SALINAS--BARRIO LAPA

Pop. 1932 - 2,628
Pop. 1962 - 6,078
Households - 1,072

Barrio Lapa is located on Highway #1 about six
miles northeast of Salinas, which is on the south
coast. It is bordered by Guayanilla, Cayey,
Aibonito, Coamo, and Santa Isabel. It is one of
the communities which has doubled in size since the
1932 study was made, possibly due to the proximity
of a large army training center which, however,
caused the displacement of many people.

Lapa has a good parcela program, again due to
the necessity of moving families.

Work is rather hard to get as it is a strictly
sugar cane cutting and beef pasture area. Cane cutting lasts only from January to June, and the number
of people necessary for grass cutting is limited.
There are no factories in Lapa, although there are
six in Salinas.

This is a very dry area, irrigation being necessary for successful agriculture. The small lot

owners do not have access to irrigation water; therefore, home gardens are limited. Many of the people are unemployed about one-half of the year unless they come to the United States for the summer crop season.

There is an excellent school and the people show great interest in citizen's committees and other activities largely centered in the school.

There is a public telephone, but no telegraph. One-half the families have running water and about one-third have electricity. There are also public faucets.

Highway #1 is the chief road; a few feeder roads have been built but not as many as they need.

The sugar company, Aguirre Central, is the chief landowner and employer, though there is, as stated before, some work in connection with beef cattle.

There is a low-cost housing project of sixty-eight units. There is a part-time health center and full operation of public welfare and Agricultural Extension Service.

A Visit to Barrio Lapa

This is a report of a visit to the Lapa Community of Salinas, 1962, by Pepita Vazquez de Garcia, social worker, 1932, and Lucila C. de Palancos, economics teacher, 1932.

> Progress catches the eye as one starts on the improved road and all along with the new small but modern houses by the road side. A few of the new constructions are concrete and the people seem to have developed a taste for color and flowers. They have planted geraniums and bougainvillea of different colors. We wondered as we looked at the brilliance

and gaiety of the small front yards,
whether this, too, has some kind of
significance in the lives of the people
living in the new improved houses.

The school was our starting point.
The physical plant impressed us at first
sight as the same old one; but as soon
as we entered the principal's office
and the excitement of the moment and
the greetings were over, we realized
that the school has grown up considerably. There are eighteen schoolrooms instead of the seven we had back in 1932.
The school population has increased
from approximately 300 to 750. Instead of an elementary school there is
now a combination of elementary and
intermediate grades. The students can
thus complete up to the ninth grade and
be ready for either vocational training at the Guayama Vocational School or
for high school in town.

It was surprising to learn how
many students take advantage of higher-
education facilities now and how many
of them have attended and completed college training and are currently working
as professionals.

We found all kinds of basic improvements. For example, electricity, running
water, telephone service, sanitary facilities and gas ranges at the lunchroom
instead of the old wood stove.

The agricultural project, according to the information given to us, was
discontinued because of the aridity of
the soil. The land has been converted
into a playground.

Group organizations like the Future
Home Makers, 4-H Clubs, Police Athletic
League and the School Patrol are func-
tioning. There were none in 1932.

The school population is benefiting from different services we lacked

before such as dental services provided
by the municipal government, ophthalmo-
logical services by specialists at Ponce,
"part-time" vocational guidance services,
a health technician, and physical education programs. We were surprised to
know that the social workers' services
have been reduced to a weekly visit.
Another facility that surprised us pleas-
antly is the transportation of students
to school. At the mayor's office we were
informed of the plans to enlarge and improve this service. Most of the students
had to walk a long distance to go to school
in 1932.

In regard to the community in general, the bird's-eye view we were allowed impressed us even at first sight
with the improvement that has taken
place.

The Federal Government expropriated
a large portion of land for a military
training camp, and a considerable number of families has been moved to the
section of the community known as Cocos.
These families occupy parcelas that rank
from a small piece of land known as a
cuadro to extensions up to fourteen acres.
The law applied is known as the Titles
V and VI of the Land Law of Puerto Rico.
The majority of the houses are concrete
and built under the program of "mutual
help." The new concrete homes we visited are very comfortable in comparison
to the shacks we saw in 1932. They are
nicely furnished and have modern facilities for cooking and recreation. We
saw electric ranges, refrigerators, and
television sets. The pleasant surroundings and carefully tended small
gardens are more easily kept because of
the water facilities. We were proudly
taken by our guides to the consumer's
cooperative with its own concrete building, and self-service carts. Two new

modern schools have been built which add
twenty-one more schoolrooms to the whole
community area.   There is a post office station, a public telephone service, an emergency room with a trained
nurse and a health clinic with a part-
time doctor.   There are three churches
of different denominations.   The athletic park is provided with lights for
night games and recreation and there is
a community center.

Although the means of living are
basically the same in the jobs available during the sugar-cane season and
agriculture on a minor scale, the town
now provides a new source of work with
three factories in operation.   Members
of the community work in those factories
but we were unable to find out in what
proportions during such a short time.

The public welfare program provides public assistance for needy
families of the community.   Three
families are receiving child-welfare
services.

We regret that the time available
did not allow us to carry on a more
thorough study of the community for the
purpose of comparison.   It was nevertheless a most fascinating experience
and one of the kind that strengthens
our hope in our people and in our
future.

ARECIBO--BARRIO SABANA HOYOS

Pop. 1932 - 4,753
Pop. 1962 - 5,665
Households - 1,195

The barrio of Sabana Hoyos was classified in
1932 as a sugar and tobacco producing locality.
Sugar is still important, but, in occupation and

character, the barrio is affected by the growing
city of Arecibo, about twelve miles away. In the
1930's, it was a remote rural area. It still is an
entity and gives no impression of being a suburb,
but there is a variety in its life which was not
possible thirty years ago. Excellent roads connect
it with Route #2 (San Juan to Arecibo) and also with
both the cane land lying to the east and a growing
section of pineapple growing to the northwest--a
section which promises a good deal of development.

The municipality of Arecibo is bounded by
Barceloneta, Utuado, and Hatillo. The city of Arecibo on the coast has fourteen factories promoted
by Fomento, four receiving some help from Fomento
and three to be established; to these must be added
the industries resulting from the growth of private
industry. It is clear that this must affect Sabana
Hoyos, not only in actual employment opportunities,
but in general orientation, and in a demand for education which will prepare the young people for work
in industry as well as agriculture.

Many people are engaged in transportation as
drivers of public cars and trucks. Because of the
increased opportunities for employment, both parents
in a family often work, which creates a problem of
child care.

Sabana Hoyos has more of the air of a small
town--scattered but united. It has telephones,
electricity, and water in a large part of the barrio
and recreational facilities. School facilities are
good and school buses bring the children from distant parts of the barrio.

Three health centers have been established and
there are organizations for community improvement,
for family life, and education. New churches have
been built, including a "Temple de Espiritismo"
(spiritualist). The school here has been a force
in the general development of the community.

A Visit to Sabana Hoyos

The following is a report of a visit to Sabana Hoyos, Arecibo, May 19, 1962, by Candida Campos de Cordova, social worker, 1932.

A magnificent asphalt road has taken the place of the red muddy road I had to travel from Route #2 to Sabana Hoyos Second Unit. On both sides of the road there are houses of better appearance than the few I used to know along this same way. On my left side I see a big sign, "Cooperativa," and a second nice road that connects the road to Florida and Barceloneta. I later learned this cooperative was the first consumers' aid credit cooperative, established by efforts of residents of the community in 1940. On my right I see another sign painted on the walls of a 12' by 10' wooden structure: "Clubs 4-H." This means the girls are organized by home demonstration agents of the Agricultural Extension Service and they have a place of their own to hold their meetings.

The Second Unit occupies the same location as it did in 1932, but instead of two buildings, I find six. In front of the school there is a spacious playground. The appearance of the children has improved tremendously. They look healthy and lively. All wear shoes. From an enrollment of 500 students in 1931 it has jumped to 900. There are about four elementary schools in the surroundings and children from Barrio Muertos no longer come to the Second Unit because they have schooling in their own barrio until the ninth grade, as in the Second Unit.

The Second Unit has twenty-five teachers, of whom only two are vocational teachers.

We used to have thirteen teachers among
whom we had six nonelementary teachers;
two teachers of agriculture, a home economics teacher, a shoemaker, a manual
arts teacher and a social worker. At
present the social worker visits the
Second Unit only once a week. Instead
of one employee in the school lunchroom, there are six at present.

The community has provided about
twelve teachers, five of whom are working in the neighborhood; one works at
the university and another has become
an expert in cooperativism who has
visited Latin America to help in the
establishment of cooperatives.

I found electricity and water
facilities besides the good paved roads
that children take from their homes to
school. All of their houses have sanitary facilities and they use electricity
or kerosene stoves instead of the fogones
of 1930. Most houses have radios or
television sets.

Agriculture is still the principal
occupation, but there are no longer
rich landlords. There are many two- or
three-acre farms and a cooperative runs
the Arecibo Sugar Mill. There is a big
pineapple plantation owned by the government's Land Authority where many
women work. Coffee growers from Utuado
come to pick up workers for their coffee plantations. They provide transportation.

The teacher of agriculture reports
that sugar cane is still the principal
crop but minor crops and vegetables
have disappeared because of high costs
of production and unsuitable marketing
facilities. There are no governmental
incentives for minor crops and farmers
earn more in other agricultural or
industrial projects. There are several

hog and poultry projects and a well-equipped dairy.

The diet of the people seems to have improved. They eat more meat and eggs and drink more milk. Pasteurized milk is distributed every day in the community. The diet rarely includes vegetables or minor crops, however.

The income per family is about $24 a week. The cost of living seems to be higher since they now have to pay for light and water and fuel, but they seem to enjoy life more, have more recreation and make better use of government resources.

From poor laborers on $1 a day wages, most of them have become landowners or laborers on $5 a day wages. Women are helping the family income by working on the pineapple plantations, or in nearby factories or picking coffee in Utuado.

There are health dispensaries in the neighboring barrios of Asomante, Arrozal and Candelaria. The cooperative has a public telephone and there is a post office in front of the school.

Children come to school in buses paid for by the municipal government, if they have some distance to travel.

Montana was a very distant barrio with a very poor road leading to it. Now it has a well-paved, broad road and a community center.

Although there are no factories in this area, residents of the community work at factories in Arecibo. An inquiry among students of the Sabana Hoyos Second Unit revealed the following adult members of the family working in factories:

Among seventh-grade students (about thirty), three mothers, three fathers, two brothers, two aunts who live with the family.

8th grade (about 25), 2 fathers, 2
        sisters, one mother.
9th grade - 5 mothers, 3 fathers, 4
        brothers or sisters.
4th grade - 3 mothers, 3 aunts and 3
        sisters.
5th grade - 3 mothers.
6th grade - 3 mothers, 5 aunts (married),
        1 uncle (married), 1 cousin
        (married).
1st grade - 2 fathers, one mother.

Most of the persons working in factories are married; there seems to be a
majority of women (mothers).

Sabana Hoyos appears to be a very
progressive community; the teacher of
agriculture commented that there still
was poverty because of rising cost of
living, but there is no doubt that fathers and mothers have greater work opportunities, a larger income and many
more of life's commodities. Means of
transportation and communication have
been very much improved and individuals
are receiving the benefits of government agencies and their programs. The
health of all members of the family
seems to have improved as well.

The tendency of women to work for
a living may have affected the unity of
family life; as in other places emigration to the United States has caused
several broken homes and a scarcity of
laborers for the sugar cane industry,
but in general Sabana Hoyos is dynam-
ically moving along with progress and
economic conditions are remarkably
better.

CHAPTER **6** THE SECOND UNIT
SCHOOLS OF
PUERTO RICO

INTRODUCTION[1]

Puerto Rico has traditionally upheld education
as one of its most cherished social values. This is
equally true of its urban and rural inhabitants, of
its rich and poor people. Among those of less economic means one will hear very often this remark:
"I do not mind not being able to leave money or other
material possessions to my children but I certainly
want to give them a good education."

The members of the governing classes have likewise shown great faith in education, as evidenced by
the very liberal budgetary allocations they have always made for the educational program.

In 1898, when Puerto Rico became part of the
United States, it had "but the bare rudiments of a
system of public education." It is estimated that
illiteracy rated as high as 85 per cent of the population. But in 1925, when the first educational survey was carried out by a commission of educators
from Columbia University, the island had an organized
establishment for public instruction comprehending
the principal types of institutions from the elementary school to the professional schools of the university. By then the estimated illiteracy rate was
45 per cent.[2]

The distinguished surveyors from Columbia University were greatly impressed with the island's
gigantic efforts to extend the public school system
during the period 1898-1925. In reference to these
efforts this is what they said:

And the people of Puerto Rico have paid
the cost. The per capita wealth of the
island is only one-sixth that of continental United States. It is less than one-
half that of the least prosperous state.
But out of their slender resources the
people of Puerto Rico have built this mon-
umental establishment from the ground up.
They have erected the schools and have
paid for them. They have created agencies
for professional preparation and have
trained hundreds of their best young men
and women as teachers. They have developed an intricate administrative organization and have manned it chiefly with
their own citizens. And all this has
happened within the short space of
twenty-five years. The accomplishment
has been possible only because the people
of Puerto Rico have been willing to spend
an unprecedented proportion of their annual revenues for this purpose. The current educational budget represents 33.6
per cent of all insular and local dis-
bursements. And the public outlay is
only the gross index of the individual
sacrifice that has been the portion of
even the humblest homes.[3]

In comparing the job done in the educational
field in Puerto Rico with achievements in other parts
of the United States, the surveyors concluded that:

The history of education in continental
United States shows no parallel achievement. The American nation sets great
store by popular education. It takes
pride in the public and private sacrifices that from the beginning of the
Colonial period have been made in this
cause. But both in self-denying devotion to the cause of education and in
the speed with which the instrumentalities of training have been created, the
continent has been surpassed by this
youngest American Commonwealth.[4]

PUBLIC EDUCATION IN PUERTO RICO
DURING THE PERIOD 1898-1925

The public school system established in Puerto Rico was patterned after that of the continental United States. The Commissioner of Education himself was until 1948[5] appointed by the President of the U.S. and received directives from Washington. Until 1930, the main objectives of education in the island seemed to be Americanization, extension of the school system, and the teaching of English.[6] In 1925, the educational surveyors referred to above found out that the school curriculum in Puerto Rico was wholly formal, overemphasizing linguistic and arithmetical skills to the exclusion of certain fundamental materials. In the eyes of the professors from Columbia University, the guiding principles of the educational system had been "the reduction of illiteracy and the attainment of a higher standard of citizenship."[7]

It might be safely said of the curriculum offered by both the elementary and the high schools prior to 1928 that it did not answer the island's needs. With the exception of the commercial courses offered in the high schools of the largest cities, the schools only prepared children for further academic training. The whole idea was for students to continue schooling, to push them on and on till they reached the university which would turn out finished products in the form of teachers, lawyers, chemists, engineers, pharmacists, etc. By 1928, everyone realized that the island had too many professionals and that it did not need to prepare many more. What it really needed was intelligent farmers, efficient carpenters, good housekeepers, industrial workers.

Such a school system stimulated the desire on the part of the students to continue studying professional careers regardless of their financial circumstances or lack of vocational aptitude. The tragic part of it was that having obtained an eighth-grade or high school diploma, the student was in no way better prepared to earn his living than before. Even if he were lucky enough to finish a professional course, the chances that he could get a job were

small, as competition among professionals for the
few jobs available was very great.

As was to be expected, the schools' holding
power was very low. This was especially true of the
rural school, most of whose children dropped out after the second or third grades despite the existing
child labor and compulsory school attendance laws.
It was imperative for the country child to help his
father support the family at an early age. Furthermore, even if the child was very intelligent and am-
bitious, his father saw no logical reason why he
should make sacrifices to keep his offspring in
school when so many eighth-grade graduates were com-
pelled to work in the sugar cane plantations for
thirty cents a day. Was it not better that the child
start earlier to earn his living--thought his father--
as it would be more difficult for him to go back to
sugar cane cutting, after having had the advantages
of an eighth-grade education?[8]

The need for a new orientation of the island's
educational activities was very evident. A new philosophy of education more in harmony with the island's
situation, problems, and needs had to be formulated.
The new generation had to be helped to follow a training course parallel to the vocational interests and
aptitudes of its members as well as in harmony with
the needs of the community. The dignity of labor had
to be stressed. The need to prepare children to serve
Puerto Rico in the manner in which it needed them most
had also to be given thoughtful consideration.

This was most important in view of the very serious social and economic problems Puerto Rico was
facing in 1928. In this very densely populated island
a highly literate and academic school (such as the one
available) could not cope with the following conditions and problems: 85 per cent of the people lived
in the country and depended on agriculture for their
support; the number of landowners was rapidly decreasing; the wealth of the island was in the hands of the
few; malaria, hookworm, tuberculosis, malnutrition,
and gastroenteritis were rampant among the inhabitants but very specially among the rural residents.[9]

Life in rural Puerto Rico was very hard and dull. Unemployment was a serious problem, wages were low, health and recreational facilities almost nonexistent. Educational opportunities were insufficient and inadequate. So people started moving to the towns and cities hoping to improve their lot. Life in the city was also very difficult for the rural immigrant, however, because work opportunities, if any, were very few and employment of irregular duration. There were no industries or factories. Overcrowding, poor housing conditions, slums, spread of contagious diseases, delinquency and dependency among children, and other similar problems ensued as a result of the exodus of the rural inhabitants to the city.

As already indicated, the schools' holding power was very low. This was specially true of the rural school where a very small proportion of the children of compulsory school age (eight to fourteen) stayed in school beyond the fourth grade; where thousands of students dropped school with only two or three years of instruction. Two out of every three rural students attended school half a day each day, this being the system in operation for the first three grades in four-fifths of the rural schools. Most of the estimated 90,000-100,000 children of school age who were not in school came from the rural areas. And those who attended school in the country were very likely to have a teacher with much less academic training and experience than her urban colleague.[10]

In view of the conditions surrounding the rural school system prior to 1925, it is surprising to learn from the General Superintendent of Rural Education at the time that wherever consolidated schools[11] had been established, the upper grades were soon filled.

The situation prevalent in Puerto Rico at the time of this first educational survey led the surveyors to conclude that the rural school was one of the largest, if not the largest, educational problem the people of the island had to meet. Some of their

recommendations with regard to the rural school system were:

1. The Department of Education should work on a
new curriculum for the rural schools, to be organized
as a unit. This was to contain the materials most
significant for life in Puerto Rico. The curriculum
should cover four years of instruction on the assumption that it would provide all the schooling available to rural children, most of whom dropped school
after two or three years of schoolwork. The plan
would be, however, to continue increasing the number
of school years up to a six-year elementary course
which was to be the minimum amount of schooling readily accessible to all children in the rural areas.
(At the time of the survey there were 300
consolidated schools, a good many of which offered
instruction up to the eighth grade. Most of the
rural areas had, however, only the one-room school
offering up to the third grade.)

2. The curriculum for this new rural school
should offer health instruction from the earliest
grades and the following other subjects: nutrition,
practical farming, homemaking, native industries,
and courses dealing with economic, political, and
social conditions.

3. The teaching of agriculture which, up to
the time had been largely confined to vegetable growing, was to concentrate on the important farming enterprises in Puerto Rico (sugar cane, tobacco, coffee,
and citrus fruits) and be extended to include work
in poultry and rabbit raising, bean growing, root
crops and pig raising in some places.

In the face of the island's economic and social
problems and because it was a largely rural society
with an agricultural economy, the educators from
Columbia University concluded that some of the obli-
gations of the rural school at the time were:

> to inform the people more fully of the
> opportunities in agriculture, the ad-
> vantages of rural life, and the new

> problems which town life would present;
> to help them to keep possession of
> their land; to make the cultivation of
> that land more profitable; to teach them
> the value of a diversified diet and how
> gardens might contribute to this; to
> emphasize the importance of raising
> their own foodstuffs; to induce the
> larger landholders to assign garden
> plots to their tenants and to train
> the tenants in the use of such plots;
> to show them the opportunities of im-
> proving their present conditions
> through training in agricultural
> skills and the acquisition of prac-
> tical agricultural knowledge.[12]

ESTABLISHMENT OF THE SECOND UNIT
RURAL SCHOOLS

As indicated above, the one-room rural school offering the first three grades of instruction was the rule in the country prior to 1925. In some rural communities, however, there were consolidated schools with grades one through eight. Consolidation of rural schools had started in 1915 under Commissioner of Education Paul G. Miller, who believed that the country school should also serve as a social and cultural center for the community.[13]

The educational surveyors referred to above had advised officially in their report that the best educational statesmanship should be given to the solution of the rural school problem during the decade following that first survey.

> It is true that the island does not have
> the financial resources necessary for
> the immediate solution of these ques-
> tions. The Survey Commission believes,
> however, that these problems can be
> more adequately met than is the case
> at present. The lowered vitality of
> thousands of rural people, due to

disease, improper diet and unsanitary
living conditions, imposes a heavy tax
on Puerto Rico each year. This loss
is undoubtedly much greater than would
be the cost of maintaining schools in
the rural communities now neglected.
With the cooperation of the public
health agencies of the island, adequate
rural schools would, in a few years,
undoubtedly increase very greatly the
productive capacity of the rural people
by increasing their knowledge and bodily vigor. It would also put them in
a position to bear more intelligently
their share of the political problems
of the island. The extension of the
elementary school facilities to all
its people is a goal that Puerto Ricans
should endeavor to attain in the near
future.[14]

The Insular Department of Education gave the
survey recommendations very careful consideration
and in the year 1926 established a Division of Rural
Education charged with responsibility for all matters concerning the rural school system.[15] That
same year Pedro P. Arán was appointed General
Superintendent of Rural Education.   Arán was
very much aware that if the rural school was to
answer the needs and problems of the country people
a good knowledge of such needs and problems was indispensable. With this in mind a study of 300
eighth-grade graduates from rural consolidated
schools was carried out through home visits in which
a questionnaire with pertinent information was duly
filled out. It was learned from the study that very
few students had enrolled in high school. The weaknesses and deficiencies of the prevailing rural
school system were also shown by the study.[16]

There was no doubt whatsoever but that a new
rural school had to be created and, in an effort to
learn from the experience of other countries, inquiries were made concerning the rural schools of
Mexico, Belgium, Uruguay, Argentina, Chile and of

some areas in the United States which seemed to be
trying to cope with problems similar to those of
rural Puerto Rico.[17]

Following these inquiries, the new type of rural
school was established in 1928. Since it was to accept students who had completed the first school
unit, it was called the Second Unit School.
Arán visualized it as a social and community center
where children, youth, and adults could benefit from
both academic and vocational training. The Second
Unit was to project its activities into the community in an effort to better standards of living, improve housing conditions, promote personal and community health measures, and teach people how to make
adequate use of their leisure time. It was to in-
still in the children a love for the land in which
they grew and from which they got their subsistence.
They would be taught how to increase its productiv-
ity and how to make rural life attractive and happy.[18]

In addition to the academic program, the Second
Unit School was to offer children from the fifth
grade up vocational training in agriculture, home
economics, industrial arts, carpentry, native industries, and several other trades with a view to preparing the students to earn their living and improve
conditions in their home and community.

The new school was also meant to give youths
and adults the opportunity to get training in modern
farming techniques, homemaking, and the improvement
of housing conditions. It would also offer them the
opportunity to share school activities aimed at improving the health, recreational, and cultural standards of the community.

To what extent educators in Puerto Rico had
placed their hopes for the solution of some of the
rural problems of the island in the Second Unit
Schools may be gathered from a report submitted in
1930 by Francisco Vizcarrondo, then Deputy Commissioner of Education, at the Columbia Convention
of the National Education Association. In his intro-
ductory statement he said:

> One of the greatest tasks the Department
> of Education has had since its organiza-
> tion has been the solution of the rural
> problem; a solution which will make rural
> life and rural conditions so attractive
> that the present exodus to the cities
> might soon be stopped. With this end in
> view a reorganization was made during the
> year 1928-29 of that part of the rural
> school system where there were consoli-
> dated schools. . . .[19]

In this same report, Vizcarrondo described
the objectives of the Second Unit Schools in the
following terms:

> To be brief, these schools tend to:
> 1.   Elevate the standards of living
> in the rural communities.
> 2.   Increase the productive capacity
> of the island.
> 3.   Put into operation a program of
> social and sanitary betterment, such
> program to take into account the most
> urgent needs of the people living in
> the rural sections.
> 4.   Organize and put into operation
> a program of vocational education.[20]

Great care was taken in the selection of the
communities where the first five Second Unit Schools
were established, as it was desired to have a good
representation of the different topographical regions, agricultural enterprises, and socio-economic
structures. The communities selected were:[21]

1.   San Antón, Carolina, because of its proximity to San Juan, a region representing miscellaneous
activities: grazing, poultry, electricity, agriculture, automechanics, etc.

2.   Sabana Hoyos, Arecibo, a sugar cane region
of the absentee-ownership type.

3.   San Antonio, Aguadilla, a sugar cane region
of small landowners.

4. Lares, Lares, a coffee region.

5. Angeles, Utuado, a coffee region.

The Staff

The Second Units were conceived, planned, and administered by and from the central office of the Insular Department of Education. The vocational and other special teachers were selected and appointed by the central office which also was responsible for their promotions and transfers. Their salaries were paid from insular funds.

The academic staff was supervised by the school principal and other local supervisory personnel, but the vocational and other special staff received technical orientation from the main office.

Great care was exercised in the selection of both the academic and the special vocational teachers. The former were expected to have the same academic training as the urban elementary teachers. This in itself was an improvement over the traditional method of selection of rural teachers. Their salary was likewise equivalent to that of elementary urban teachers.

The vocational staff was also selected with great care. These teachers were expected to have good professional training in their respective specialized fields. Both the academic and the vocational staff were supposed to be firm believers in the philosophy of the new school and to be very much aware that the Second Units had been designed as community centers through which rural life and conditions were to be improved.

The staff of the Second Units was composed of the following personnel: the school principal or teacher-in-charge, teachers of academic subjects, teachers of agriculture, home economics, industrial arts, native handicrafts (industrial work), shoemaking (in some Second Units), barbering (in some Second Units), and a social worker and a janitor.[22]

School Sites, Buildings, and Classrooms

Since the new school was to be both a vocational school and a community center, special provisions had to be made in terms of space, land, vocational shops, and equipment. Each Second Unit had at least five acres of land in which to carry out its agricultural program and other academic and vocational activities.[23] In addition to the regular schoolrooms necessary for academic instruction, space and equipment had to be provided for the home economics laboratories and the manual arts shop as well as the shops for the other trades to be taught.

An assembly room was an indispensable requisite since the program of work of the Second Unit included frequent meetings with parents, young people, and other community members. In the absence of an assembly room, two adjoining schoolrooms separated by a folding door were used whenever large meetings had to be held.

Space had also to be provided for a playground for children and for the offices of the principal and the social worker as well as for the school lunchroom. The latter was an indispensable facility inasmuch as a good many students had to travel long distances and were required to attend school on a full-day basis. So a hot lunch had to be provided for them as well as for other children who, although living near, were eligible for this service because of their difficult financial situation.

The Curriculum

In the traditional rural school teachers had to follow strictly courses of study prepared by the supervisory staff in the central office or by committees of teachers under the supervision of the central office staff. Contrary to that established practice, the staff of the Second Units was authorized to adapt the courses of study to the current needs, conditions, and problems of the school community with which they were expected to be very well acquainted.[24]

The school day consisted of a morning and an afternoon session and the time available, 360 minutes, was equally divided between the academic and the vocational subjects. The former included English, Spanish, health, physical education, arithmetic, and social and elementary science.[25]

The vocational courses offered were at least the following: practical farming, which included animal raising; home economics; manual arts; and native industries. Other trades like auto mechanics, toy making and repairing, shoemaking, and metal work were offered in some schools in accordance with the needs and conditions of the community and the availability of adequately prepared teaching staff.

The work in agriculture and home economics presupposed that the students would carry out home projects. These aimed at having them practice at home what they learned in school and at adapting the training offered to their home needs and personal circumstances. Both the agriculture and home economics teachers were expected to visit and supervise these home projects. This brought them in closer contact with the parents and community in general. They were also expected to organize classes for groups of young boys and girls as well as for adults in the community in accordance with their special interests and needs.

In describing the objectives for the course on industrial arts, this is what Francisco Vizcarrondo said in his report to the NEA in the year 1930:

> The need to develop industries in Puerto
> Rico as a means of supplementing the
> island's income from agriculture has
> been pointed out again and again by econ-
> omists and by students of the island's
> social and economic problems. The Second
> Unit School has tried to direct its edu-
> cational activities following these recom-
> mendations. So it offers the so-called
> industrial course which aims to develop

in children skill and intelligence in
making and marketing industrial products. Teaching projects are organized
according to the community needs.
Utilizing native raw materials, such
articles as rugs, baskets, hats,
brooms, cushions, lace, etc. are made
by the girls attending these classes.
Some of these articles are kept by the
boys and girls and utilized to improve
their home conditions while the rest
are sold in the small local and outside larger markets, the profits being
distributed among the children.[26]

The Social Work Program

Because the Second Unit School was to be a social and educational center for the community's
activities, there had to be a member of the staff
whose main efforts were to be channeled toward bringing the home and the school together. So a special
teacher was assigned to this job. Under the administrative title of social welfare teacher, she was
expected to perform the following duties:

1. To help make the Second Units attractive
and valuable social centers.
2. To help improve the social, moral and sanitary conditions of the neighboring homes.
3. To organize and direct the work of the
Parents' Association.
4. To organize and direct the athletic activities of the girls.
5. To organize and direct the clubs that were
to work for the improvement of the community's
health.[27]

The purpose of the social worker's visits to
the families was mainly educational. In accordance
with Circular Letter No. 35 of the year 1930, issued
by the Insular Department of Education, home visits
by the social worker had the following objectives:

1.   To prevent the raising of hogs in places too near the homes.

2.   To prevent the use of water from rivers or brooks without boiling it.

3.   To foster the cultivation of minor crops.

4.   To stimulate the establishment of home gardens.

5.   To educate families with regard to the nourishing value of vegetables and their place in the diet.

6.   To instruct them as to the practical values in the prevention of diseases.

7.   To instruct families in the means of preventing communicable diseases such as (a) typhoid fever; (b) hookworm; (c) tuberculosis.

The annual report of the Insular Department of Education for the year 1929-30 described the work of the school social worker thus:

> An important feature of the Second Unit
> is the social worker who visits the
> rural homes and gives parents and pupils
> advice on health, social and education
> matters. She[28] is the liaison officer
> between the school and the community.
> She reports to the municipal director
> on the needs of the rural communities,
> to the health officers on medical matters.

Up to the school year 1930-31, the social workers were selected by the Director of Rural Schools in the Department of Education who was also responsible for the technical orientation of the work to be carried out by them. In 1930, a trained social worker from the mainland who was then living in Puerto Rico was appointed Special Supervisor of Social Work in the Department of Education.[29]   Important changes and new developments in the social work program of the Second Units followed this appointment. Special plans were immediately made for the recruitment and training of a group of thirty young women in preparation for the appointment as Second Unit social workers of those who proved to be well qualified for such position.

Great care was taken in the selection of this group of workers and in the plans made for their four-summer-session training plan. The Supervisor of Social Work was determined to develop a training program which would fit the Puerto Rican situation and to offer courses rich in subject matter related to the island's needs, problems and resources. Developing a Puerto Rican technique and not just copying courses given in other countries was the leading idea back of the plan.[30]

The main purposes of the first summer session were:

1. To give the students an idea of the general principles and techniques of social work.
2. To study the most outstanding health problems in Puerto Rico.
3. To study the social and economic problems of the island, especially those affecting the rural zone.[31]

Upon completion of this first summer course, twenty-seven workers were assigned to Second Unit Schools and one to a private plantation where, under the auspices of the School of Tropical Medicine, she was charged with the responsibility for a research and demonstration project related to the eradication of uncinariasis.

The new group of social workers was full of enthusiasm and zest. What they lacked in formal social work education[32] they more than made up with their great desire to do a good job, their enthusiasm and devotion to the cause of rural development, their imagination, resourcefulness, and creativity. The workers were free to create, experiment, learn about rural needs and problems, and start new projects to answer the varying social needs and maladies in their respective communities. Their supervisor was a constant source of inspiration.

Realizing that a good knowledge of the community was the basis for a sound program of work, she instructed them to make a survey of fifty families

selected from the different geographic sections and
income groups from among the families having children in the Second Unit.[33]

A sampling plan showing types of land holding,
agricultural products, housing conditions, etc. was
submitted to the Supervisor of Social Work before
the final selection of the families was made.

The schedule utilized to get the facts consisted
of several cards, each of a different color. The
main card recorded information on family composition
and personal and social data of its members. Another card asked for information related to the
health of the family, the diseases suffered and the
treatment received, as well as home sanitation and
surroundings. A third card dealt with the economic
conditions of the families and past and present occupations of its members, wages earned, family expenses
and other related data. A fourth card called for information on social and recreational activities of
the family, the use of leisure time and the amount
of money spent for recreation.[34]

At the end of the year the facts collected
through the survey, together with the knowledge obtained through other community contacts, were embodied in a community study report which formed the
basis for the program of activities to be carried
out.

Broadly speaking, the study revealed how serious
the health problems were in the rural communities
due to the poor financial circumstances, low wages,
irregular employment, poor housing, lack of health
facilities, as well as because of the ignorance of
the country people. It also pointed to the great
need to provide wholesome recreation facilities for
the "jibaros,"[35] whose life was completely lacking
in opportunities for wholesome relaxation and
healthy use of their leisure time.

Having found what the main problems were and
realizing that there was an almost complete lack of
local resources (rural schools and a few rural

churches were the only ones available), the social
workers started to orient their activities along
lines which would ameliorate, if not eradicate, existing health, economic, recreational, and other
social problems.

Great imagination and resourcefulness was shown
by this group of young women in the performance of
their responsibilities. They were requested to live
in the communities in which they worked, and this
facilitated their task not only in terms of the additional knowledge they got on how people lived but
also because they were able to carry out activities
in the evenings and this made it easier for young
people and adults to participate in them. They were
able, to a surprising degree, to identify themselves
with the communities and with the people.

The result of it all was a very creative piece
of work in every community where a social worker was
assigned. No two programs were identical, as the
activities carried out had their origin in the conditions, needs and problems, and interests of the particular communities as well as in the existing resources and the personalities of the social workers
themselves.

As was to be expected, health and nutrition received primary attention in view of the very serious
problems of uncinariasis, malaria, tuberculosis, and
malnutrition. Health clinics were established with
the cooperation of municipal or public health physicians and nurses. Health campaigns mostly aimed at
the eradication of uncinariasis and malaria were
carried out. Stimulating family and community interest in the building and use of latrines (there were
communities where 76 per cent of the families had no
latrines), talks to parents and other adults by doctors and nurses, educational programs using films
and posters, and similar activities were carried out
with the help of local, municipal and insular resources.[36]

Infant-feeding stations were established not
only to help improve the daily diet of babies and

young children, but also on an experimental demonstration basis. They provided a good opportunity to
educate mothers and to show the relation between
hygienic measures and health. This was very important, since deaths caused by diarrhea and enteritis
were as high as 246.9 per 100,000.

In some communities model houses were established with the help of the home economics teacher.
A typical home was selected for this purpose and,
through the utilization of native materials for the
construction of household furniture and equipment,
and the acquisition of better health and hygienic
habits, a good example of how to improve housing
conditions was set for the rest of the neighbors in
the hope of stimulating in them the desire to improve their own homes.[37]

The organization of the community for cultural
and recreational purposes was another important
phase of the program of the social worker. This included work with the PTAs, the establishment of
ladies' clubs, young people's groups, and athletic
clubs. The ladies' clubs were generally organized
for cultural and welfare purposes. The conduct of
educational conferences, the organization of the
"Ropero Escolar" and the "Zapato Escolar," and the
creation of an emergency fund to help needy cases of
school children and families in the community were
some of the activities of the ladies' clubs.

Young people's clubs and athletic groups were
organized to help provide opportunities for a healthy
use of their leisure time. Social dances, moonlight
singing parties, picnics, May festivals, musical con-
tests, coffee parties, and athletic activities were
all part of the program of such groups.[38]

Besides her work with groups, the social worker
organized and carried out activities aiming to provide for the special needs of individual children
and families. Because of the total lack of social
welfare or relief agencies in Puerto Rico, this phase
of the social workers' job called for great imagination and resourcefulness to make good use of whatever

few facilities were available and to develop resources where none existed. The local Red Cross Committee, the health facilities, and a few private and
religious groups in some of the towns and cities
were about the only resources available at the time.[39]

The social worker also spent a good proportion
of her time in work directly connected with the
school, such as money-raising activities to help improve the school building or grounds, activities
aimed at beautifying school gardens, and participation in athletic and other activities of the school
children. In addition to these school projects, a
few social workers taught one or two classes at the
beginning. This practice was discontinued during
the 1931-32 school year.

The social work program in the Second Units continued developing along the lines described above,
which combined the three methods of social work--
case work, group work, and community organization--
always trying to have activities conform to existing
needs and problems in the rural areas.

The dominant idea behind the work of the Second
Unit School, let us repeat, was the improvement of
living conditions in the rural communities where
they had been established. Determining what the
local conditions, needs, and problems of such communities were constituted a very important aspect of the
social workers' program. Consequently, research and
demonstration were very important tools in the performance of their work.

In the year 1932-33, four research projects
were carried out by different groups of social workers under the supervision of the central office.
These were as follows: (1) a study on standards of
living in rural communities, (2) a study of the
curriculum of the Second Units in relation to the
program of the social worker, (3) a reanalysis of
the health features of the social work program, and
(4) a study of a limited number of maladjusted children in eight schools.[40]

The 1932-33 Study on Standards of Living
in the Rural Zone of Puerto Rico[41]

Purpose

This study was undertaken in the hope of getting pertinent data as to the way in which country people of different socio-economic levels live. This information was needed by both the social workers and the home economics teachers of the Second Unit Schools to gear their work around conditions, problems, needs, and interests of the residents of the rural areas.

The social worker needed to be well informed on what constituted the accepted community norms as well as on the individual variations in standards of living which existed among families living on the same income. "To understand these variations and to incorporate the higher standard into community life"[42] was one of the social worker's goals.

She was also looking for the type of information which might in time help in the solution of the fundamental problems of her clientele. The social worker was hopeful that, through the findings of this study, she could be useful in pointing out the discrepancies between the existing conditions in the rural areas and a standard of living acceptable in modern civilized societies.[43]

Areas Selected for the Study

Ten rural areas were selected for the study after due consideration was given to the following factors:

1. Representative crop regions: sugar, tobacco, coffee, fruit, minor crops.
2. Different geographical regions: mountain, coastal, plain, irrigated sections, etc.
3. Different systems of land ownership: large company, small company, large individual farms, small individual farms.
4. Local industries.

Sugar cane regions were given the largest representation among areas selected because cane was the most important agricultural product. Tobacco was not considered important because at the time of the study there was very little planting of it. The areas selected were the following:

A. Sugar and tobacco sections:
    Aguadilla (San Antonio)
    Arecibo (Sabana Hoyos)
    Juncos (Mangó)
    Salinas (Lapa)

B. Coffee regions:
    Adjuntas (Yahuecas)
    Moca (Voladoras)

C. Fruit Areas:
    Bayamón (Hato Tejas)
    Cidra (Bayamón)

D. Mixed or minor crops:
    Juana Diaz (Collores)
    Loiza (Medianía Alta)

Number and Selection of Families

In each community fifteen families were selected by the social worker, five from each of three socio-economic levels: high, medium, and low. Families were grouped into these levels on the basis of the social worker's own knowledge of accepted standards of living in the locality. "Theoretically it would have been more accurate to set limits for each income group. This could have been done by finding the incomes of a large scattered selection of families and determining from these data three levels in each community."[44] However, it seemed better at the time to rely on the social worker's knowledge of the families and community since what was high in one locality might have been medium in another.

In the selection of the families the social workers were instructed to see that they met the following criteria:

A.   Families were to be selected from among the fifty included in the survey of the year 1930-31 where this was available.

B.   They were to be families with whom the social worker had been in intimate contact, whenever possible, for a period of two or three years.

C.   Only families willing and able to cooperate with the social worker and the home economics teacher by providing reliable information could be selected.

D.   The wage earner of the families should be working and residing in the communities to be studied.[45]

The social workers also selected one family from each income level (three per community) for special studies to be made by the home economics teacher with regard to an inventory of the household furniture and equipment, the kinds of food consumed, and the daily expenses of the families.

Thus a total of 150 families were selected for the study, fifty from each income level. Thirty families from among the 150 were selected for the three special studies to be made by the home economics teachers in the ten areas.

Date of Study and Field
Personnel Utilized

The study covered a period of eight weeks, during the months of March and April, 1933. These were "zafra" months, the time of the greatest earnings in the sugar cane regions, but on the other hand, the period of lowest income in the coffee areas.

The social workers visited their fifteen families in each of the areas selected for the study and filled in special forms with which they were supplied, containing data such as general information (number of members in the family, ages, civil status, etc.); economic conditions (income and expenditures); housing (number of rooms, floor space, sanitary arrange-

ments, building materials, etc.); and health (diseases, treatment, sanitation, and water supply).

The home economics teacher visited her three
families (thirty for the ten areas) for a period of
eight weeks to check on the accounts of the family
as they had been written down by a responsible member. She also entered the items in the corresponding forms provided for expenses of the families for
food (groceries, dairy and garden products, meat,
fish, etc.); rent (payments for use of house or land,
taxes, interest on mortgages, insurance and major repairs); health (medicines, doctor's fees, transportation to clinics and hospitals, etc.); clothing
(dresses, underwear, shoes, suits, etc.); recreation
("fiestas," "velorios," "rosarios," dances, movies,
and transportation for such purposes); operating expenses (lighting, fuel, soap, equipment repairs,
etc.); and miscellaneous (charity, gifts, education,
periodicals, books, tobacco, etc.).

The home economics teachers also made an inventory of the household furniture and equipment and
gathered information on the foods consumed by the
family, including those utilized as flavoring.

Value of the Study

As will be seen in the next chapter, the study
revealed data relative to conditions under which
most of the Puerto Rican rural families lived in the
1930's. The findings can be summarized thus: large
families; very low incomes, if any; deficient diet;
overcrowded living arrangements; hardly any household furniture or equipment; unhealthy water supply;
inadequate or nonexistent sanitary facilities and no
provision whatsoever for wholesome recreation or
cultural development.

By describing the conditions under which rural
residents lived, the study also pointed toward necessary action to help raise their standards of living.
It suggested possible fields of professional endeavor for both the social worker and the home economics teacher. There was, undoubtedly, plenty that

could be done to help the Puerto Rican "jibaro" attain a higher level of aspiration and regain confidence in his ability to help himself even under prevailing conditions.

In fact, many of the activities included in the
work program of both the social worker and the home
economics teacher in the years which followed the
completion of the study were inspired by the findings of the latter.

The study provided convincing new data to support the Second Unit's efforts to help rural inhabitants improve their living conditions. It validated
the philosophy behind the establishment of this
special type of school and proved how right its
staff, both academic and vocational, was in carrying
out activities which would show the country people
how to improve their health, increase their earnings,
have more attractive and livable houses, make good
use of their free time. Vegetable growing, rabbit
raising, the growing of home gardens by students,
the construction and use of adequate latrines, the
need to boil drinking water and to store it in
adequately covered and protected containers, the increasing use of the school lunchroom as an educational laboratory, the making of home furniture and
equipment out of native materials at very little or
no cost, the enrichment of the courses on health,
nutrition and care of the sick, with materials
stemming from local conditions and needs--and many
other measures--were adequately integrated in the
Second Unit curriculum.

As the liaison officer between the school and
the home, the social worker was the transmitter to
the rural people of the new knowledge obtained from
the study as well as from the research related to
tropical diseases and nutritional value of Puerto
Rican foods which was being carried by the Puerto
Rico School of Tropical Medicine, attached to Columbia University. The findings of the study related
to the foods consumed by the Puerto Rican country
people were shared with this medical research institution which, in turn, continued to cooperate in the

training of social workers with whom they shared the latest knowledge then available on disease and nutrition in tropical Puerto Rico.

Extension and Growth of the Second Unit School Movement During the Period 1928-42

Under the dynamic leadership of Pedro P. Arán and Oscar Porrata Doria, the Second Unit Schools continued to grow in numbers and importance during the period 1928-42. With combined insular and federal funds, the program had been established in 95 schools with a total of 15,782 children by the end of that period.[46]

The Second Unit had been successful in retaining the children in school, so that in the year 1937-38, grade nine was added to the school curriculum, and by 1945, there were 130 Second Units functioning as intermediate schools.[47]

The following expressions will give an idea of what the second unit stood for and of its well earned prestige:

In 1931, Dr. José Padin, then Commissioner of Education, while addressing the Caribbean Seminary, expressed his idea of the role of the Second Unit when he said:

Since I took office about a year ago I have devoted most of my time to the promotion of rural education. Our peasants constitute about 80 per cent of the entire population. For hundreds of years they have lived scattered over the mountain-sides, neglected, forgotten, out of touch and out of step with the rest of the island. The "jibaro," as we call the mountaineer, seems to belong to another world, to a lower cultural level. The future of Puerto Rico depends appreciably on our ability to bridge the gap that separates the retarded "jibaro" from his more fortunate brothers.

The conventional one-room rural
school was not doing much to get the
peasants out of the doldrums. Of every
100 pupils who enrolled in the first
grade eighty-four dropped out before
they reached the fourth grade. This
was due to economic pressure which the
academic character of the instruction
given did not relieve.

We are providing a remedy through
the Second Units. . . . But we cannot
cure social evils by preaching. You
have to raise your people to such a
level of intelligence that they can
see by themselves what is wrong with
them and work out their own salvation.[48]

José C. Rosario, for many years professor
of sociology at the University of Puerto Rico, believes that the Second Unit has achieved the following functions:

1. It has served as a nucleus for
the establishment of small country villages in which appear certain characteristics of progress unknown before,
such as the rural medical centers,
churches, and in some instances post
offices.
2. The work carried out by some
teachers of the Second Unit reaches bene-
ficially to many rural families. I am
referring to the social worker, special
teachers of agriculture, home economics,
carpentry and industrial work. When
this work is carried out with whole-
hearted enthusiasm as in the case of the
Padilla Second Unit in Corozal, these
schools can be considered as a civiliz-
ing influence for the community.
3. The Second Units realize the function of being community centers, realizing
in this way a very favorable social
work.[49]

Blanca Arroyo Herrero, who in 1942 was a social worker in a Second Unit School, expressed with enthusiasm:

> The Second Unit at Sabana Seca is the center of all the activities of the community. The Second Unit sees to it that new avenues are opened to the life of the people in the neighborhood, that medical services are obtained for the neediest, that advice is given when needed about all kinds of matters; when this is done, a social worker becomes really useful.
>
> The first and chief problem that we have met in the country is to teach the "jibaro" how to make use of available resources to improve his way of living. Here the "jibaro" has a deep faith in the school. He has been taught to improve his methods of farming; to follow the advice of the social worker in the treatment of his ailments; to plant crops, and raise domestic animals. He tries to prepare well-balanced meals. The girl students learn in the domestic science classes how to improve their homes.[50]

Rafael Hernández, a 1935 graduate of a Second Unit School, said in 1940:

> I am a farmer now. You cannot imagine how long a time I have been hoping for this. I have three milk cows, a yoke of oxen, a pedigreed sow, six little pigs, thirty-five hens, two bullocks, and a horse. We have had good luck since I left school.[51]

Around this same time, a sixty-one-year-old "jibaro" living in the neighborhood of a Second Unit School expressed his experience thus:

> We were in great despair when the Second
> Unit was established. I borrowed 100
> banana seeds from the school. In a
> short time I had over two thousand. I
> returned those I borrowed and planted
> the rest. I believe not less than 700
> acres of banana have been planted here-
> abouts. There were none five years ago.[52]

And Dr. Rexford Guy Tugwell, then Governor of
Puerto Rico, in his message to the 1942 legislative
session, explained:

> There are certain appropriations recom-
> mended on the budget bill to extend edu-
> cational services. These would increase
> the number of teachers of certain types,
> particularly of industrial arts, and
> would provide educational personnel for
> extending the scope of the organization
> of the Second Units, which have been ad-
> mired by educators everywhere. They are
> Puerto Rico's best contribution, so far,
> to the art of education. They deserve
> better support.[53]

In a very comprehensive article in which he
traces the development of the Second Unit School,
Rafael Bonilla Colón, General Supervisor of the
Insular Department of Education, summarizes what he
considers the outstanding contribution of the Second
Unit Schools in the following terms:

> 1. It is the first school in Puerto
> Rico which provides an education adapted
> to the special needs of the rural zone.
> 2. It has served as a center for the
> demonstration of an educational philoso-
> phy which has been extended to the whole
> educational system in Puerto Rico.
> 3. It has succeeded in increasing
> the holding power of the rural schools
> of the island.
> 4. It constitutes the center around
> which villages and communities have been

built with services such as churches,
medical centers, electricity, post
offices, aqueducts, telephone, etc.
    5. It has performed the role of com-
munity centers.
    6. It has succeeded in improving
home conditions in the community.
    7. It has fostered the financial im-
provement of the country people.[54]

The Difficult Years

The year 1942-43 brought an important change in
the educational system of the island--the adoption
of the so-called 6-3-3 plan in lieu of the traditional eight-year elementary and four-year high school
system. As a result of this change, the Second Unit,
which had been functioning as a well-integrated administrative unit, was broken into two: grades 4-6
constituted the elementary level and grades 7-9 the
intermediate school level. Different time schedules
were established for each level. Vocational training started in the seventh grade whereas before it had
been offered beginning with the fifth grade. This
change was possible in view of the increasing holding power of the Second Unit School.[55]

Supervisory services from the central office
were likewise divided into the two levels, there being supervisors in charge of the elementary school
and those exclusively assigned to help the teaching
staff of the intermediate grades. This change affected negatively the work and orientation of the
Second Units, which were hence deprived of the dynamic and imaginative leadership which had contributed so much to their creative development and tremendous growth. This was revealed in a marked decrease
in the emphasis given to that part of the Second
Unit program which concentrated efforts on the work
with the community.[56]

Moreover, the island had been undergoing great
changes since 1940 which marked the beginning of
Puerto Rico's great efforts at industrialization.

As was to be expected, this had its impact on the
rural communities and in their school program. Interest in agriculture began to lag. Many students
complained that at the Second Unit they were forced
to devote a good deal of their school time to agriculture even when their families owned no land and
they themselves were not interested in farming.
This, they claimed, was done at the expense of other
subject matters which would render them better qualified for admission to the urban high schools. Many
of the Second Unit graduates aspired to continue
high school education, academic or vocational. The
new factories seemed to hold a promise of employment if
they gained industrial skills which they did not
think they were getting at the Second Unit Schools.

The transfer of the Second Unit social worker
to the urban schools was also a great loss to the
program of these rural schools. This, too, came as
a result of changing conditions. New social-service
programs had developed in other government departments as well as in federal agencies whose programs
had been extended to Puerto Rico (FERA, PRERA, WPA,
etc.). The Department of Education itself had initiated an urban social work program in the year
1936-37 by transferring several of its rural social
workers to schools in the largest cities. Salaries
and working conditions were more attractive in the
urban setting in the other agencies. So the Second
Unit Schools began to be drained of their social
workers, and in 1954 the department officially transferred the few remaining ones to the urban schools
with headquarters in the office of the school superintendent. This deprived the Second Unit Schools of
their main contact officer with their communities.
The remaining staff, which had its hands full with
academic and vocational duties, had hardly any time
left for home visitation and other meaningful community contacts.

These were the prevailing conditions in the year
1948-49 when a curriculum study was made by the Institute of Field Studies of Teachers College, Columbia
University, following the request made by the Commissioner of Education of Puerto Rico. With respect to

the situation of the Second Unit School population
and the program it was then offering, this is what
the survey report says:

> The decreasing enrollment in the junior
> high school years of the Second Unit
> Schools deserves serious attention. En-
> rollment figures for 1947-48 furnished
> by the Department of Education indicated
> that almost twelve thousand (11,948) rural
> youth were attending urban junior high
> schools. At the same time only 15,735
> were enrolled in the junior high schools.
> Student-teacher ratios in the rural junior
> high schools, as already noted, are low
> in comparison with those in other schools
> of the island, and were lower than they
> should be for good learning situations.
> The problem appears to have at least
> two facets: the required agricultural
> courses in the Second Unit program prob-
> ably prevented some from attending these
> rural schools, and the conception that
> the offering of the Second Unit Schools
> does not "prepare" students as well for
> the senior high school as does the offer-
> ing of the urban junior high schools
> causes many rural youth to attend the
> urban schools.[57]

To remedy the problem of school mortality in
the rural Second Unit, the surveyors recommended
that the vocational courses in agriculture, industrial arts, home economics, and native handicrafts
be brought together "into an articulated offering
for all students in the early junior high school
years." They also advised that in the later junior
high school years, when some students elected agriculture and home economics, other students might be
offered additional vocational courses. General
business or junior business training was recommended
as another possibility, and appropriate elective
courses in art, music, or science were recommended
for students not wishing a definite vocational
offering.

In the opinion of these surveyors, "some excellent work was being done in the Second Unit Schools with respect to preparing students for senior high school." They referred specifically to the training offered in community problems, agriculture, and home economics on which courses they claimed that the students were generally having "good educational experiences." The survey staff considered that if the offering of the Second Unit was broadened "to care better for individual differences in interests and goals, the rural junior high schools could offer excellent opportunities." They saw "no reason why the work in the Second Unit Schools should not be very acceptable for entrance to senior high schools."

It is evident from the above that the Second Unit School was departing more and more from its role as a vocational training and community center and turning into the traditional type of school. It was also apparent that the Second Unit School had been gradually losing its vantage position in rural community development which had made so many educators from the island and from abroad consider it "Puerto Rico's special contribution to the art of education."

The 1948-49 surveyors from Columbia University must have been thinking only in terms of the school curriculum and not of the Second Unit School as a rural development center when they concluded that:

> The small Second Unit Schools are extremely uneconomical, with their investment in school farms and attempt to offer agriculture, industrial arts, home economics and native handicrafts. The fact that they are now said to be uneconomical does not imply any lack of support for their very promising educational program.[58]

It is evident from the report that the financial element was very present in the minds of the educational surveyors when they tried to evaluate the work of the Second Unit Schools. This is understandable as the island was still struggling with

great numbers of children of school age for whom no
school facilities could be offered. This must have
been the reason why the Department of Education
authorities started to be lenient with school promotions. One still hears the phrase "the era of mass
promotions" as officials could not afford to have
students occupy a seat in the same grade for more
than a year. Room had to be made for those who were
waiting outside. The quality of educational services
must have suffered because of the tremendous job to
be done and the great limitations under which educational authorities were trying to discharge their
responsibilities. The public was very outspoken in
its criticism of the public school and the quality
of the education it offered.

Some of the officials in the Department of Education had a strong conviction that another reason
for the state of affairs within the public school
system was the fact that the school was trying to do
more than its share of services to the community,
that it was performing work which belonged to other
agencies, and that the teachers had their hands too
full with numerous tasks which they carried out by
way of cooperation with other public agencies and
with private organizations.

There was a growing feeling that the school
should channel all its efforts and devote all its
time to its real and true function--teaching--and
that it should strip itself of those other tasks
which it had been performing out of a desire to better answer the needs and problems of the same community which was so critical of its work. Thus, around
the middle of the 1950's, official instructions were
given in this direction. Everyone spoke of the discipline of teaching and the need to turn all efforts
toward improving the quality of teaching.[59] Great
care was to be taken to ensure that teachers were
not involved in too many extracurricular activities
of the kind that would divert them from their main
function.

The great stress under which the Department of
Education officers were laboring must have had its

impact on the work and development of the rural Second Unit Schools. There must have been an awareness
of the fact that the Second Unit was losing ground
and that something had to be done to help it regain
its place of prominence as a leader in community development. This led some of these officials[60] to
initiate in 1958 a very interesting project within
the Second Unit School setting, the purpose of which
was twofold: (1) the acquisition, on the part of
students, of knowledge skills, attitudes, and habits
of social value; and (2) the improvement of community conditions through direct social action.

The activities to be carried out were geared
toward:

1. The improvement of health.
2. The acquisition of skill in communication
and problem solving.
3. The cultivation of creative and aesthetic
ways of life.
4. The promotion of economic proficiency.
5. The enrichment and dignification of rural
life.
6. The formulation and acquisition of aesthetic
and spiritual values.[61]

The new program for the Second Unit Schools was
carried out with the help of a council composed of
the school director and representatives of the teaching staff, the students and adult citizens of the
community.

There were also several committees, each composed of representatives of the school staff, children and parents, and each in charge of a different
aspect of the school program.

The council and committees were held responsible
for carrying out a dynamic and very comprehensive
program which embodied both the academic and the vocational work as well as the activities that had to
be carried out to improve community conditions and
enrich rural life.

The committee in charge of the academic program was asked to suggest the necessary changes in the school curriculum to have it answer the student's needs and to adequately meet local problems and conditions.

This committee decided that the academic program of the Second Unit should be fundamentally the same as that of the elementary urban school, with pertinent adaptation to local needs, in order to render the students eligible for admission into urban high schools, inasmuch as the majority of the Second Unit students wanted to enter high school upon completion of the ninth grade.[62]

The committees which dealt with vocational subjects and other aspects of the Second Unit work were likewise responsible for submitting recommendations for the revision of the content of courses and to recommend the development of activities which would answer community needs.

This demonstration project was very successful wherever it was put into operation, as illustrated by the following examples:[63]

(a) In one community where uncinariasis was a serious problem, a large and very successful educational and treatment campaign was carried out.

(b) In another place, an alumni group approached its need for employment in a gainful activity by renting a thirty-eight acre farm which made it possible for them to engage in a very fruitful farming and animal-raising project.

(c) A community recreation center was established in a third area, utilizing one of the school-rooms which was supplied with books, periodicals, and parlor games of various sorts.

It is to be regretted that this very successful project was not extended to all the Second Unit Schools, as it gave ample evidence of the feasibility of training young people and adults to participate,

in a democratic way, in the joint work which the
school and community must carry out to develop the
rural leadership indispensable for rural development.

Instead of continuing along the lines suggested
by this experiment, however, the department once more
turned to the previous plan of dividing the Second
Unit into two levels for supervisory purposes.
Again this resulted in a weakening of the Second
Unit program of social action and community improvement.[64]

Dissatisfaction with the conditions in which
the training for agriculture was offered in the Second Units led to its reorganization in the year
1958-59. In accordance with the revised program,
the teaching of agriculture was limited to the
eighth- and ninth-grade students and the classes were
given in the morning. This new arrangement made it
possible for the teacher of agriculture to have the
afternoon free for (1) the supervision of the student's home projects; and (2) the teaching of classes
in modern farming techniques and animal husbandry to
young adults and farmers of the community.[65]

Following the request of the Legislature of the
Commonwealth of Puerto Rico, a third study of the
educational system of the island was made in 1958-59
under the direction of the Superior Council of Education. José A. Perez, a supervisor in the Department
of Education, carried out a study of the Second Unit
Schools as part of the general study. Thirty Second
Units were carefully selected as the sample for this
study, which revealed that 76 per cent of the 1958
graduates of those schools had registered in high
schools. Three times as many entered academic high
schools as compared with the ones who started vocational high school training. The fact that there
were, and still are, many more academic than vocational high schools may be one of the reasons for
this.[66]

In his study, Perez had sought to answer two
questions: (1) what was the status of the Second
Unit at the time of the study; and (2) how was

this type of school helping to improve community
life?

The data collected by him showed, among other
things, the following:

1.   The number of Second Units had increased
from 5 in 1928 to 131 in 1958.
2.   The Second Unit School had gone through an
evolutionary process during that period: From a
school which took care of students from the fourth
through the eighth grade, offering vocational courses
starting at the fifth grade, it had developed into a
whole school nucleus which offered education from
the first through the ninth grade, with vocational
training starting in the seventh grade.[67]
3.   The Department of Education did not have a
division in charge of Second Unit Schools.
4.   Over 56 per cent of the teachers in the
thirty schools studied were not qualified for their
job.
5.   In the coffee regions, the problem of student absences was very serious at the time of the
harvest.
6.   Except for the teaching of agriculture in
junior high, the rural Second Unit offered a curriculum identical to that of the urban elementary and
junior high schools.
7.   Great emphasis was placed on the teaching
of health habits, safety education, nutrition, and
recreation.
8.   Vocational classes were giving practical
help in the improvement of family living.
9.   Vocational offerings were very limited.
Training in agriculture would be more effective if
an adequate selection of students were made.
10.   The Second Unit Schools were far from being
community-centered schools in spite of the fact that
activities involving members of the community had
been developed in all of the Second Units studied.[68]

Other findings of the study carried out by
Perez revealed serious problems which the Second
Unit School was facing: among others, poor physical
plants, inadequate equipment, great turnover among

the teaching staff, pupil absenteeism, and lack of
interest of the community in the program of the
Second Unit School.

Despite the problems indicated above, the
Second Unit School's holding power was considered
good by the educators who engaged in the 1959 study
of the educational system of Puerto Rico. Because
of the large number of Second Unit students who entered urban high schools, the study report contains
the following recommendations:[69]

1.   That in those Second Units where agricultural training is offered, this be a required subject for the seventh- and eighth-grade pupils and
that it be only offered to those ninth-graders who
wish to get further training in agriculture.
2.   That elective courses in science, art, or
music be offered to ninth-graders who do not wish to
enroll in the agriculture course.
3.   That other elective courses be offered to
the above students in accordance with the available
facilities.

The idea behind these recommendations was to
strengthen the academic aspect of the Second Unit
program and thus to reduce the disadvantages with
which rural students had to cope in getting admission and adjusting to urban high schools.

The report of the 1958-59 educational study
also contains a recommendation to the effect that
the study made by Perez be extended to cover the
graduates of all the Second Units, to determine:
(1) how many of the Second Unit students enter academic high schools for lack of vocational training
schools; (2) what type of vocational courses would
these students prefer to take; (3) the number and
location of the academic high schools and vocational
training schools needed; and (4) whether the organization and practices of rural intermediate schools
are actually answering the real needs of the rural
population.

"It is an undeniable fact," the report concludes,

"that the rural Second Unit Schools have made a significant contribution to education in Puerto Rico,
to the extent that the limitations under which they
work, have made this possible." The members of the
study commission considered that "the provision of
the resources needed for an efficient functioning of
the Second Unit School would serve as a stimulus to
those particular elements of this school which have
been instrumental in bringing about positive changes
in our rural population."[70]

In his article tracing the development of the
Second Unit Schools, Rafael Bonilla Colón refers
to a socio-economic study made by Dr. Cecilia G.
Davila, of the University of Puerto Rico, and quotes
from her study the following findings which are in
accord with Perez's assertion with respect to the
diminishing role of the Second Unit as a community-
centered school:

1. The teachers of the communities studied limited their work to teaching in the schoolroom. Activities reaching toward the community are not carried out.
2. A large number of families do not visit the
school or know the teachers of their children.
3. There is a marked duplication of services
on the part of the different agencies and an evident
lack of coordination and integration among them.
4. The existing resources for the development
in these communities of an integrated plan based on
cooperative action are not being utilized.

New Hopes for the Future of Rural Education
and the Second Unit Schools

The Department of Education of the Commonwealth
of Puerto Rico is now taking a new look at the whole
problem of rural education in the island. Dr. Angel
G. Quintero Alfaro, Deputy Secretary of Education,
considers "the education of children and of other
persons living in the rural zone in Puerto Rico one
of the greatest responsibilities of the island's educational system."[71]

Of the total school population of the island in the year 1961-62 (567,162 students), 45.6 per cent was attending rural schools.[72] Most of these rural students attended the traditional one- or two-room school. In fact, 85 per cent of the rural schools in Puerto Rico in the year referred to belonged to this type of educational establishment. The remaining 15 per cent were either intermediate or Second Unit schools.[73]

Rural students in 1961 were receiving a type of education which compared unfavorably with that which was being offered in the urban communities because: (1) the rural teacher had less training and experience; (2) in the rural school there was a larger student caseload due to the double-enrollment plan; (3) supervision of rural teachers was less intensive; (4) rural school facilities were inadequate; (5) there were fewer educational resources in the rural areas; and (6) working conditions of rural teachers, in most cases, meant less comfort, greater difficulties, long distances, and transportation costs.[74]

All of this has been the subject of serious discussions on the part of Department of Education officials who, in 1961, initiated a special rural education project in Ciales, a typical rural community. As officially stated, the project was to be carried out in the hope of providing the rural inhabitant with the knowledge, skills, attitudes, and abilities which would enable him to work intelligently toward the solution of his own problems as well as those of his country.[75]

This new plan to improve rural education in the island stemmed from the following concepts:

1. The constitutional mandate to offer every person an education focused toward the full development of his personality and the strengthening of human rights.
2. The nature of rural population, which tends to diminish and to intermingle with the urban community.
3. The joint efforts of the urban and rural

zones to adapt education to conditions in our society, which has undergone important changes affecting its socio-economic structure as well as the content and method of learning.[76]

In accordance with these guiding principles, the image of the rural school envisioned for Puerto Rico was described thus:

1.   A school the curriculum of which is geared around the vital problems of the community, laying special emphasis on preparing the student to master the technique of communication.
2.   A school which, in its multiple relations, is an example of a good way of living, respect to individuals, ideas of responsible citizenship, industriousness, collaboration and other attributes of democratic living.
3.   A school with a physical environment offering desirable conditions of security, hygiene, health and comfort, as well as facilities for study and recreation.
4.   A school, the teaching staff of which, besides fulfilling the prescribed academic requisites for the position, possesses ideals of social cooperation, is well acquainted with the community it serves, has the capacity to understand the customs and idiosyncrasy of the country people, understands the nature of children, and ultilizes this knowledge to teach them effectively.
5.   A school that offers opportunity for participation and social exchange on the part of parents, teachers and students as a means of developing the latent leadership of the rural communities and utilizing it for the improvement of living conditions in them.[77]

The rural-education-improvement plan included the revision of the Second Unit School program and curriculum in accordance with the socio-economic changes which the island has undergone, to adapt the educational offerings to prevailing conditions. Three sectional meetings were carried out in October, 1962, at which school directors, superintendents of schools and their assistants, and general supervisors

from the central office of the Department of Education analyzed the conditions that were affecting the
Second Unit School and described them as follows:[78]

1.   The island's economy has changed from a
purely agricultural to a largely industrial one.
2.   There is an ever-growing tendency, on the
part of women in Puerto Rico, to assume other responsibilities besides housekeeping. This is evident in the rural zone, especially in communities in
or near which the new industries have been established.
3.   The increase in transportation facilities
and in the opportunities for employment have brought
a greater population mobility.
4.   The reallocation of previously isolated
rural families in the newly established rural communities calls for a special adjustment to this different type of communal living arrangement.
5.   The rise in the standards of living and the
extension and improvement of educational opportunities has likewise raised the level of aspirations of
the Puerto Rican society.
6.   Life and resources in rural Puerto Rico do
not offer, in the majority of the cases, the opportunity to earn an income large enough to provide for
a full and abundant life.
7.   An ever-decreasing number of persons will
continue to live in the country and engage in the
production of agricultural and dairy products for the
rest of the population. These rural dwellers are
entitled to an adequate education that will enable
them to fulfill their responsibilities efficiently.

In accord with these conditions and with the
changes affecting rural life and the expectations of
the rural dwellers, the Department of Education is
trying to channel educational efforts in a way which
will equip children to live and adjust well in a
changing society. Officials in that government department believe in giving students the knowledge
and skills that will help them to function well in
the farm, home, workshop, factory, or wherever they
decide to make a living and work. It is acknowledged
by educators in the island that the original emphasis

of the Second Unit Schools in preparing students for
farming and country life was justified at the time
of their creation. At this point, however, the
trend is to eliminate the teaching of agriculture in
the Second Unit Schools and to transfer it to the
high school level. It is estimated that only around
thirty Second Unit Schools will continue to teach
agriculture because they are located in highly agricultural areas. At present only 87 out of the 157
Second Unit Schools in operation are teaching agriculture.

The following are the reasons for this change:
(1) the largest number of Second Unit graduates reg-
isters in urban academic high schools;[79] (2) the
number of Second Unit students who are fourteen
years old or over and, therefore, qualified for admission to vocational agricultural classes, keeps
diminishing because of the increase in the educational facilities which have thus permitted early
admission of students; (3) several Second Unit
School communities have lost their agricultural
character; (4) relatively few rural students belong
to landowning families; (5) the increase in the
level of education aspiration among the rural families, and the desire of parents to have their children enter the professional fields or get training
for white-collar jobs.

Itinerant teachers of agriculture will continue
to offer instruction and advice on modern farming
techniques to youths and adults in those communities
where agriculture will no longer be taught in school.
Agricultural laborers will also continue to benefit
from short courses with specified objectives as part
of the accelerated agricultural program.[80]

The Puerto Rican educators engaged in the revision of the Second Unit School plan work are in
agreement that this school should, for organizational
and operational purposes, be considered a single administrative unit, covering from the first to the
ninth grade. Such a plan will be conducive to a
better utilization of plant, personnel, equipment,
materials, and other school resources. Because of

the "peculiar characteristics" of this type of
school, however, the following general purposes have
been formulated for it within the general Program
for Rural Education:

1. To give the student of the Second Unit School
the knowledge, skills, attitudes, ability, and values
that will facilitate his adjustment to a changing society such as the one he lives in.
2. To prepare the student for responsible and
efficient citizenship by arousing his interest in
the social and economic problems of his community
and by instilling in him ideals of cooperation, service, and responsibility toward school, home, and
community.
3. To stimulate the community toward organizing
itself that it may study its problems, and, in a cooperative and democratic way, find a solution for
them.[81]

Officers in the Department of Education of
Puerto Rico believe that the curriculum of a school,
so conceived, should include subjects selected in
accordance with the needs of the community where the
school is located. Prevocational and vocational
courses should admit boys as well as girls to better
answer the needs in a society in which women are
joining industrial plants in increasing numbers. In
Second Unit Schools located in communities which are
no longer agrarian in character, courses in science,
mathematics, music, language, history of Puerto Rico,
and other similar subjects should form part of the
curriculum in lieu of the vocational offerings.[82]

The Department of Education is likewise convinced of the need to make a study of the community
to be served by the Second Unit School prior to the
formulation of the curriculum to be offered. Such a
study will throw light on the selection, adoption,
and coordination of the educational experiences to be
offered to the student body which should be composed
of both children and adults.

Other features of the proposed revision of the
Second Unit School plan are the organization of

juvenile groups of various kinds to enrich the knowledge and experience of children and the extension of
the educational opportunities, both academic and vocational, that they be made available to young people
and adults in the community.

With respect to that aspect of the work which
deals with the community-school relations, the following recommendations were made by the persons who
revised the Second Unit School program:

1. Develop a program of social, recreational,
and cultural activities aimed at promoting a better
understanding of the school and the community.
2. See that the school, the parents and other
agencies and institutions organize themselves for
the development of activities aimed at the improvement of living conditions in the community.
3. Study the problem of school dropouts in a
group of Second Units where the problem is more
acute, in order to develop a pattern for an action
plan that could be offered as a model to other
schools.[83]

Other recommendations made for the strengthening of the Second Unit Schools include the assign-
ment of a person capable of carrying out both social
work and vocational counseling responsibilities.
They also include the provision of adequate equipment and materials for the teaching of science and
the special preparation of teachers in this particular respect.

There is good evidence already of the interest
of the Department of Education in reviving the spirit
and achievements of the original Second Unit Schools.
The adaptation of vocational offerings to local conditions has been put into effect in several schools.
Examples include one school where children are presently engaged in a poultry project, another school
where students are raising cattle to help increase
the meat supply, and a third school which is giving
training in the repair of agricultural equipment.

The way the Departments of Education, Labor, and

Agriculture are joining forces to help train youths
and adults, in answer to the agricultural and industrial demands made by the different communities, is
also a very promising feature of the schoolwork.

Several special services are now being offered
to help fulfill the level of education   aspirations
of our rural students. Among these are   transportation facilities to help children reach the rural intermediate or Second Unit school or the urban high
school; educational scholarships to needy eligible
candidates; and economic help in the form of the
sale of shoes at reduced prices.

To help improve the quality of education in the
rural areas, the most important step taken has been
the appointment of itinerant supervisors through
which adequate professional help to teachers is being offered. The provision of audio-visual aids
such as TV sets, radios, tape recorders, and film
projectors to some rural schools and Second Units is
still another effort to improve the quality of the
educational experiences offered. This is a long-
range program which will eventually provide each
Second Unit School with these basic educational
tools.

In the field of community-school relationships,
the designation of a central office supervisor to
help the teaching staff develop a constructive relationship between the school and the community is a
very promising step. Officials in the Department of
Education are convinced of the need to have the rural
community make the maximum possible use of the
school's facilities. They believe that a special
staff should be assigned to the Second Units for
work with the community after the regular school
hours and on Saturdays and Sundays.

It is too early to know to what extent the
measures taken so far and the plans outlined for the
strengthening of the Second Unit Schools will suc-
ceed in having these schools regain the great leadership role they used to have in the communities they
served. In connection with the program to improve

community-school relations, it is most important to
determine the nature of the goal to be achieved: Is
the relationship between the school and the community to be geared toward the enrichment of the school
program, the bettering of the school plant, the participation of parents in terms of achieving the educational goals, or is it to be channeled toward the
improvement of the community, the solution of its
problems, the raising of its standards of living as
far as the health, recreational, cultural, and moral
aspects of rural community life are concerned?   In
our opinion, the way in which this question is answered is of tremendous importance in terms of the
future development of the Second Unit School whose
greatest contribution has rested in the ways in
which it has been able to reach toward the community
and influence its residents to improve their lot.

For the Second Unit to regain its leadership
role in the community and to be reconverted into a
true community-centered school, three things are indispensable: a community-centered curriculum, but
one which will relate the community to the world beyond its boundaries; an organizational structure conducive to an active and continuous parent and citizen participation; and a staff which believes hear-
tily in the philosophy that a school should not have
intellectual and spiritual walls but must radiate
its influence in the direction of the community it
serves.

Efforts made by the Department of Education to
provide working conditions for the rural teachers
that will attract and hold them in continued service
would be most profitable. Provision should also be
made for adequate living quarters, within the rural
community, for the school director and the special
staff in charge of direct work with the community
and its leaders. This and the full-time appointment of social workers as part of the Second Unit
staff are indispensable measures that must be taken
if the Second Unit School is to make again the kind
of contribution to rural life and development which
prompted famous educators from Puerto Rico and from
abroad to remark in the past that it was Puerto Rico's
special contribution to the field of education.

Notes to Chapter 6

1.   This report was prepared by Mercedes Velez de Perez while working for the Comparative Studies of Cultural Change, Department of Anthropology, Cornell University, under contract AID/csd-296 with the Office of Technical Cooperation and Research of the Agency for International Development.

2.   The International Institute of Teachers College, A Survey of the Public Educational System of Puerto Rico (New York: Columbia University Press, 1926), p. 1.   (Hereafter cited as Survey.)

3.   Ibid., pp. 1-2.

4.   Ibid., p. 2.

5.   U.S. Public Law No. 362 of 1947 enabled the Governor of Puerto Rico to appoint the Commissioner of Education, now Secretary of Education.

6.   Juan José Osuna, A History of Education in Puerto Rico (San Juan: Editorial de la Universidad de Puerto Rico, 1949), p. 282.

7.   Survey, p. 19.

8.   Mercedes Vélez Herrera, "The Development of the Social Work Program in the Public Schools of Puerto Rico" (unpublished Master's dissertation, University of Chicago, 1943).

9.   Survey, p. 39.

10.   Ibid., pp. 199-201.

11.   Ibid., p. 220.

12.   Ibid., p. 39.

13.   Rafael Bonilla Colón,   Reseña Histórica de la Segunda Unidad y su desarrollo desde 1929 hasta el 1962 (Hato Rey: Departamento de Instrucción Pública, Estado Libre Asociado de Puerto Rico).

14. Survey, p. 200.

15. Division de Investigaciones Pedagógicas, Con-
sejo Superior de Enseñanza, Universidad de Puerto
Rico, Estudio del Sistema Educativo de Puerto Rico
(Rio Piedras: Publicación de la Cámara Representante
de Puerto Rico, 1961), II, 1204.

16. Bonilla Colón, op. cit.

17. Ibid.

18. Vélez Herrera, op. cit., p. 31.

19. Francisco Vizcarrondo, The Second Unit
Rural Schools of Puerto Rico, Pre-Vocational Schools
for Pupils of Intermediate Grades (San Juan: Bureau
of Publications, Department of Education, 1930).

20. Ibid., p. 3.

21. Antonio Rodríguez, Jr., "The Second Unit
and the Rural School Problem of Puerto Rico" (unpublished Ph.D. dissertation, University of Indiana,
1943), pp. 59, 61.

22. Ibid., pp. 78-79.

23. Ibid., p. 84.

24. Ibid., pp. 51-52.

25. Ibid., pp. 79-81.

26. Vizcarrondo, op. cit., p. 5.

27. Ibid., p. 7.

28. Only women were selected for this type of
work as educational officers at that time, since it
was thought that women were better fitted for such
work.

29. Dorothy D. Bourne, who had had graduate training at the New York School of Social Work, where she obtained a certificate in social work in 1917.

30. Vélez Herrera, op. cit., p. 52.

31. American Association of Social Workers, Puerto Rico Chapter, "Professional Education for Social Workers," Memorandum to the Commission on the Establishment of a Pan-American University of Puerto Rico (San Juan: American Association of Social Workers, 1939), p. 5.

32. They all had at least a normal school diploma (two-year college education), but a good many were college graduates.

33. Puerto Rico Department of Education, "Handbook for Social Work. Report on Social Work in the Department of Education, 1930-31" (San Juan: Bureau of Publications, Department of Education, 1932), p. A-2 (1).

34. Vélez Herrera, op. cit., pp. 78-79.

35. The term by which peasants are designated in Puerto Rico.

36. Puerto Rico Department of Education, Annual Report 1930-31, Doc. No. 6-M (San Juan: Bureau of Publications, Department of Education, 1931), p. 65.

37. Puerto Rico Department of Education, Handbook, p. A-2 (1).

38. Ibid., p. A-2 (6).

39. Vélez Herrera, op. cit., p. 74.

40. Puerto Rico Department of Education, Annual Report 1931-34 (San Juan: Bureau of Publications, Department of Education, 1934), pp. 75-76.

41. For methodology and forms used in this study, see Appendix B.

42.   Luz M. Ramos and Dorothy D. Bourne, _et al._, _Rural Life in Puerto Rico_ (San Juan: Department of Education Bulletin No. 1, Research Series, c. 1934), p. 5.

43.   _Ibid._

44.   _Ibid._, p. 15.

45.   _Ibid._

46.   Bonilla Colón, _op. cit._, p. 4.

47.   _Ibid._, p. 6.

48.   Rodríguez, _op. cit._, p. 64.

49.   _Ibid._, pp. 65-66.

50.   _Ibid._, pp. 67-68.

51.   _Ibid._, p. 68.

52.   _Ibid._, p. 69.

53.   _Ibid._

54.   Bonilla Colón, _op. cit._, pp. 8-9.

55.   _Ibid._, p. 6.

56.   _Ibid._

57.   Institute of Field Studies, Teachers College, _Public Education and the Future of Puerto Rico, A Curriculum Survey_ (New York: Columbia University Press, 1950), pp. 385-86.

58.   _Ibid._, pp. 377-78.

59.   Information supplied by José Martinez Almodóvar, high officer of the Department of Education, now head of one of the regional offices of education.

60. Dr. Juan Silva, Erasto Rivera Tosado, and Rafael Ramirez.

61. 'Programa de la Segunda Unidad Rural (San Juan: Editorial del Departamento de Instrucción Pública, 1958), p. 5.

62. Ibid., p. 17.

63. Ibid., pp. 24-30.

64. Bonilla Colón, op. cit., p. 7.

65. Memorandum No. 94 of the Secretary of Education, re the Reorganization of the Program of Agricultural Education, December, 1958.

66. Division de Investigaciones Pedagógicas, op. cit., II, 1206.

67. One of the original Second Unit Schools offers a complete secondary school course.

68. José A. Pérez Ortiz, "A Study of the Rural Second Unit School in Puerto Rico" (part of survey of the Puerto Rico school system in 1958-59).

69. Division de Investigaciones Pedagógicas, op. cit., II, 1206.

70. Ibid., p. 1207.

71. Angel G. Quintero Alfaro, "Notas Sobre la Educación Rural" (San Juan: Departamento de Instrucción Pública, Puerto Rico, September, 1962).

72. "Programa de la Sección de Educación Rural" (San Juan: División de Escuela Elemental, Departamento de Instrucción Pública, 1962), p. 4.

73. Ibid., p. 8.

74. Quintero Alfaro, op. cit., p. 2.

75. Departamento de Instrucción, Puerto Rico, "Proyecto de Educación Rural de Ciales, Informe de Progreso al Terminar el Año 1961-62," p. 1.

76. Quintero Alfaro, op. cit., p. 1.

77. "Programa de la Sección de Educación Rural," pp. 2-4.

78. "Recomendaciones en Torno a la Reorientacion de las Segundas Unidades Rurales" (Hato Rey: Departamento de Instrucción Pública, Estado Libre Asociado de Puerto Rico, 1962-63), pp. 1-2.

79. Out of 1,200 Second Unit School graduates in 1963-64, 800 registered in urban academic high schools, as reported to the writers by Fernando Roca, Assistant Director of the Division of Vocational Education, Department of Education of Puerto Rico.

80. "Plan para la Revisión del Programa de Educación Agrícola Vocacional" (Hato Rey: Departamento de Instrucción Pública, Estado Libre Asociado de Puerto Rico, Marzo, 1964).

81. "Recomendaciones en Torno," pp. 1-3.

82. Ibid., pp. 3-4.

83. Ibid., pp. 7-8.

CHAPTER 7 RURAL SOCIETY

Consideration must be given in any discussion of rural Puerto Rico to the stereotype of the "jibaro." Economically exploited by the landlord, poor to the point of destitution, an idealized picture of the jibaro as a man of personal dignity has persisted. This concept has had a permanent effect on both the public image and the self-image of the jibaro, who cannot be identified with the character of the peasant as popularly conceived in many other countries. The fact that certain economic and social patterns are common in all countries where there is an exploited peasantry must be separated from those special characteristics which in Puerto Rico have their psychological effects on adjustment and adaptation to change.

Visitors to rural areas today cannot fail to be impressed and possibly influenced by the courtesy and hospitality of the jibaro. These are symbols of that "dignidad" which carries such a high value in Puerto Rican culture. Even if it is a myth, that myth has a reality which may be a vital factor in reaction to new situations. It is important to form some tentative judgment, based on observed and recorded attitudinal responses, which will indicate whether the jibaro image weighs more heavily on the plus or minus sides of social progress.

We are not attempting to prove that the jibaro was, or is, necessarily a man of consummate virtue. Problems of sex, of marriage and family relations inherent in the way of life in the country thirty years ago occupied much of the attention of social workers in the situations with which they then dealt. These problems have not disappeared.

Our main contention is that it is not necessary
to create a wholly new character for the country
dweller; that character has been established by the
society of which he is a part. It remains to be seen
to what degree it is an asset--a link between past
and present--or a liability because it is a tie to
the past which cannot be kept.

That the jíbaro will find himself more and more
a part of the transitional group is unquestionable.
This will be due to the process of urbanization with
its accompanying mobility--and to changes in the
forms and techniques of agriculture. Both of these
mean different ways of life with their consequent
effects on values. It becomes important to estimate
whether dignidad, typified by the jíbaro, can be preserved as a value--a quality of the individual which
may animate the growth of the life of the spirit in
the new forms required by new conditions. In discussing this, Tumin says:

> However romantic and quixotic this may
> seem to some economists, this concern
> for the life of the spirit is an im-
> portant factor in much of the Puerto
> Rican resistance to new proposals for
> economic development. At the moment,
> the struggle is more to maintain than
> to augment those elements of spiritual
> tradition that still remain . . . it
> offers evidence of an actual conflict
> between material enrichment and the
> felt threat of spiritual impoverish-
> ment.[1]

We would raise the question as to whether or not
this must continue to be seen as conflict. Is it
not rather part of the universal problem of the
present: a new interpretation of old values, liter-
ally a reincarnation in which new symbols are
created from new material forms?

The whole question of class mobility and changing class structure in Puerto Rico is involved in
this question. On this the following quotation is
pertinent:

". . . positive orientation toward the
norms of a non-membership group is precipitated by a passage between membership groups, either in fact or fantasy,
and the functional or dysfunctional
consequences evidently depend upon the
relatively open or closed character of
the social structure in which this occurs. . . ." This formulation helps
considerably in succinctly systematiz-
ing some of the major factors in the
abilities of low-ranked Puerto Ricans
to define the overall system as fair
and responsive to their needs. . . .
This statement is followed, in the Merton and Kitt article, by some observations to the effect that this form of
anticipatory socialization (that is,
referring oneself to standards observed
in groups of which one is not yet a
member) may be functional for the individual in an open system but dysfunctional for the solidarity of his group
or stratum. . . . The anticipatory
socialization into non-lower-class
group life appears to function to in-
vigorate individual morale and energy
in the various strata. . . . But the
curious and unexpected thing in the
Puerto Rican case is that the issue is
not between competing membership groups:
it is between solidarity with a membership subgroup of the society--and hence
some hostility toward other membership
subgroups--and a reciprocally supporting pair of memberships, one within
one's subgroup or stratum and the other
within the membership group defined by
the total society . . . some intransi-
gent version of any class identification and that kind of class identification which can coexist with and reciprocally support identification with
the total society. In the Puerto
Rican case, it seems eminently possible

for a person to maintain on some counts
an identification with a particular
stratum and, at the same time, to have
an equally strong and nonconflicting
identification with the total society.
It is suggested that this is perhaps a
very good index of an open class system. Mobility is desired and approved,
without any necessary implication that
this involves changing one's class
identity, or that this prevents or im-
pedes the same kind and amount of mobility for everyone else in every other
stratum.[2]

The emphasis should perhaps be taken off the
jibaro as the society changes and as he inevitably
becomes a more integrated part of the larger movements by which the whole low-rank stratum rises.
How this group adapts itself in the years immediately ahead will be a matter of great interest. As
the level rises economically, will its members be
able to carry with them the characteristics which
have been given such high value--whether fully justified or not--in the jibaro? The answer will depend
on the society as a whole. Will it find a place for
the preservation of the romanticized jibaro character or will this picture become only a treasured bit
of history? The answer will be decided by the movement of Puerto Rico toward its designated goals and
the degree to which it can amalgamate economic growth
with the idealism expressed in the goals of Operacion
Serenidad, following Operation Bootstrap in the program of development for Puerto Rico.

That the "solidarity with a membership subgroup"
will disappear seems highly probable to us, but the
fact that Puerto Ricans have in the past been able
to maintain an "identification with the total society,"
even when the economic situation, isolation, and resulting ways of life tended to a separation of the
substratum from the whole, gives promise that it will
be possible to preserve the values which have a long
history of survival.

It seems to us that this will not be done by
the preservation of a class identity but will depend
on the vitality of the qualities themselves and their
potential for incorporation in the value system of
the society.

Among the sixty-seven heads of families questioned
in our depth interviews, the following opinions as to
what determines the social class of a family were
given:

TABLE 18

Informant Opinions as to Social
Class Determinants

Number		1st Place Frequency	2nd Place Frequency	3rd Place Frequency	4th Place Frequency
46	Income	31	8	5	2
27	Education	19	7	1	0
23	Occupation	2	10	10	1
25	Family Name	8	1	--	16
4	Morals	3	--	1	--
4	No information				

The number giving income first place is significant compared with thirty years ago in that it represents new opportunity and presumably different values.
The only comment then might have been given through
some correlation with occupation, i.e., the single
mayordomo who appears in the occupational groups
in the 1932 study, as distinguished from the laborer,
who made up the great majority of the occupations

listed, would have had higher status as well as larger income. We can assume that education was rated
high in the past but that the aspiration in terms of
grade to be completed was not very high. Now, 42
out of the sample 67 depth interviews would like
their children to have a university education or
more, and 43 of the heads of families say that they
have been handicapped by insufficient education.

The low percentage rating for occupation indi-
cates that, in itself, occupation does not carry
high prestige, but when combined with education it
shows 34.8 per cent of the sample saying that it is
now easier to rise in the social scale because of
better education, with an identical percentage saying it is easier to rise because of better jobs and
higher income.

That family name still stands first for 8 of
the 67, and third for one, has some significance.
As the élite group is rare in our whole sample (both
the 245 families of the objective interview and the
67 of the depth interview), this may only reflect
the recognition that an élite still exists in the
society as a whole though not as a practical factor
in our sample. A different kind of sample would
place it higher because it remains an important factor in upper-class consciousness even if its importance is probably diluted by new combinations with
the prestige of profession and income.

We have made an attempt to find the number of
agregados   in the 1930's. No accurate figures
could be found, but for 1940, estimates were given
which varied from 25,000 to 100,000 (it should be remembered that these figures mean heads of families
or single persons, not the total population dependent for a living on the wages of agregados).

A quotation from <u>Porto Rico and Its Problems</u>
gives the following information on home ownership
and home tenure in the rural zones in 1930:

No complete survey of home ownership
among the Porto Rican peasantry has

ever been made. In 1924-25, however,
the Insular Department of Agriculture
and Labor made an investigation that
covered by sample 628 rural wards in
ten municipalities representing all sections of the country, in which it secured
data from 3,622 landowners and 9,455 families of resident laborers, or "agregados,"
as they are called locally. Of the latter
group, 82.2 percent lived in dwellings belonging to landowners for which they paid
no rent; 17.6 percent owned their dwellings (but not the sites); and a fraction
of one percent resided in rented houses.
In most cases, therefore, the agricultural laborer has no rent to pay. He
also has no rights of occupancy except
at the will of the landlord, and is
ever faced with the possibility of
forced removal.

The agricultural laborer who owns
his house is in a slightly better condition. It is doubtful, however, whether
ownership of the hut alone really gives
any greater right to occupancy. Although
no land rental is exacted, obligation to
work on the plantation in times of need
ordinarily is stipulated, just as with
the "jibaro" who occupies a shack which
he does not own. If the landlord wishes
to do so, he can eject a resident laborer
who owns his own hut. In that case the
laborer has the alternatives of dis-
mantling the hut and carting the materials away, of selling out to the owner,
or of abandoning his property. The actual practice in cases of forced removal
varies with the conditions under which
the ejection occurs. Charges have been
made that landowners have permitted
their workers to construct their huts in
order that they may acquire them later
on terms favorable to themselves. (Note:
The Homestead Act was enacted later to
remedy this situation.)[3]

The Brookings Institution report describes the home and life of the jibaro.

> Most of the dwellings hug the mountain
> sides and are raised on poles, not only
> to keep them off the ground but also to
> give them balance and an even foundation.
> They can only be reached on foot, over
> narrow paths. There the jibaro, with
> his family, lives apart. He rarely goes
> to town. His social contacts are with
> the landlord, with the local store--fre-
> quently owned by the landowner--and with
> the school. The school is in many ways
> the only, certainly the chief, source of
> social contact with the world about him
> and with his neighbors. This general
> description is less true of the living
> quarters in the sugar cane region, where
> more "labor colonies" are to be found,
> but even there the little isolated hut,
> set on some ridge above the cane, is not
> uncommon.
>
> An attack upon the problems of the
> rural community should include an attack
> upon this mode of residence. And that
> raises many problems of land ownership
> and overpopulation. It is becoming in-
> creasingly difficult for the jibaro to
> find a place to live. He is not wanted
> unless absolutely needed. One large
> landowner remarked, "the little landowner
> has many relatives." The resident labor-
> er, or agregado, may be a burden. And
> where labor is plentiful and to be had
> at will, there is no inducement for the
> landowner to provide him with a place
> for residence. Any real improvement of
> the very grave condition of the rural
> community will ultimately involve group-
> ing the rural population in some sort of
> village communities--each with a school
> in the center, with some means of social
> organization, some prospect of perma-
> nence--something in the nature of a home

in a group of neighbors instead of a hut
at another man's will on an isolated
mountain side. Until that is done,
neither the rural schools nor the governmental medical and sanitary campaigns
will have their full effect or, perhaps,
be able to achieve the ends which they
are meant to serve.[4]

It is interesting to note the developments which
followed in the Second Unit Schools in the 1930's
and in the plans for parcelas in the 1940's, both
continuing and adapting their programs to more recent changes.

That individual life had a lower value thirty
years ago than at present seems to us unquestionable.
One striking example which constantly came to our
attention then was the sight of a man or boy walking
along a road with a baby's coffin on his head--going
alone to bury it in the cemetery. (We find this mentioned in <u>Porto Rico and Its Problems</u>.) Behind this
lay a fatalistic view of life and death, the lack of
medical facilities and of adequate nutrition as part
of the low economic standards which accounted for
the high infant mortality, the failure of the church
to give comfort and support in time of sorrow to
people who could not pay. (This applied also to the
marriage ceremony and accounted, together with isolation, for a large number of the consensual marriages.)

A striking contrast appears now in the rural
areas, where ambulance service is available wherever
roads make it possible. Mention of this is made in
responses to questionnaires with enough frequency
and emphasis to make it appear as a symbol of the
new importance of life and health.

To examine further the characteristics of rural
life, we must look at the communities where in the
1930's the jibaro was thoroughly typical not only of
the country dweller who worked for a large landowner
and lived mainly in the mountain regions, but also
of the man who lived on cane land in the coastal regions and was economically in a similar situation--

perhaps worse. He did not own his own land; it belonged to the company, and if he had a house of his
own, it was a hut to which he had no legal title.
Often he was not allowed even to have a little patch
of yautia or sweet potatoes. And his work was
seasonal--only in the zafra.

The cane worker presents a somewhat different
picture from that of the jibaro. He has a long history which could be followed through the story of the
sugar industry. This has been told many times and
from many points of view. Sugar was well established
before Puerto Rico became part of the United States.
Its importance to the island has been so great, the
investment so large and so profitable, and the laborers needed so numerous that it has for many years
dominated the economy. The story has much in common
with other sugar islands, but it has been complicated
by political involvements--the U.S. tariff, the 500-
acre law, which theoretically limited the amount of
land owned by one corporation or individual, but for
many years was honored in the breach and only became
effective after the establishment of the PRRA.
Unions first came into the industry when Santiago
Iglesias in 1900 appealed for and received aid from
the American Federation of Labor. There is no single
union for sugar workers, however, to this day. Some
of the unions are strong, in some cases due to connections with individual politicians who identify
themselves constructively with a union and with the
labor movement. The cane worker gains dignity as
well as financial advantage from his participation
in the union.

There is special unemployment insurance for
cane workers. This is of great importance because
of the seasonal nature of the work. But, in spite
of special attention given to the problems of the
laborers, the number of cane workers has fallen from
124,000 in 1934 to 49,000 in 1962. The ratio is
greater than the actual figures indicate, because of
population increase. Mechanization within the industry and competition from other industrial developments account for much of this decrease, resulting
in a shortage of cane workers at present--despite

the general unemployment figures. The hard conditions of work in the cane fields is an important factor in the competition with industries which offer
better working conditions. For technical reasons
and because of soil conditions, mechanization will
be slow compared to Florida, Louisiana, or Hawaii.
This will allow time for adjustment, but it cannot
now help the individual worker greatly, and there is
little incentive to younger workers to take up this
occupation. According to Senator Carrasquillo, who
is active in the largest cane-cutters' union, the
average age of cane cutters is fifty-nine years.
When conditions improve, a different type of worker
may respond to the demand.

Education must be the key to the transition
from traditional to modern society and citizenship--
the growing ability of the individual to participate
effectively in a democratic society as well as to
gain the background, the knowledge and the skills
which will free him from his traditional occupational
and social roles. To mention background is to raise
the question of what should be incorporated from the
past; of what will give continuity to life experience and world view; of what will preserve or give
self-respect through an understanding of a present
rooted in the past.

There must be some recognition that this is an
organic experience; it must be growth--not shock.
Difficulties are increased if new experience is simply
superimposed on old or if the new is accepted and then
the attempt is made to reinstitute old values artifi-
cially. To anyone looking back over the last thirty
years, surely the most striking manifestation of a
new attitude is the now prevalent idea of rights.
These rights are increasingly expected, often de-
manded, of the government. Thirty years ago, only
requests might be made--usually to the landlord or
other employer, or to the commissioner of the barrio.

It will be seen that this new attitude appears
in the answers to questions on employer-employee relationships, on politics and on individual and group
initiative within the barrio. Traditional forms often

remain in which petitions for improvements--roads,
water, electricity--are made but in many cases group
or individual action takes place, meetings are held
to plan the requests, work and money may be contributed. Expectations are different because the channels
for effective action exist, where the emphasis is on
what the community must do for itself--as in the Community Education program--or where requests go directly to the mayor, the president of the barrio, or to
the Legislature. As we point out elsewhere, there
are gaps in the application of general programs and
there are communities where the old inertia remains
in varying degrees. The change does not constitute
a neat continuum; it is part of a growing process, a
transformation in ways of thought proceeding irregularly but in a clear direction.

Whether we are looking at the jibaro in the
mountains, raising coffee or tobacco, or the cane
worker on the coastal plain, we see in each the problems of a rural society in transition.

Notes to Chapter 7

1. Tumin, Social Class, p. 19.

2. Robert K. Merton and Alice S. Kitt, Contributions to the Theory of Reference Group Behavior,
quoted in Tumin, Social Class, p. 197.

3. Victor A. Clark and Associates, Porto Rico
and Its Problems (Washington, D.C.: The Brookings
Institution, 1930), pp. 14, 15.

4. Ibid., p. 36.

CHAPTER **8** SOCIO-ECONOMIC
CHANGE[1]

The descriptions of the ten communities (Chapter 5) show that they differ from each other in many respects. Although they do not cover, in physical characteristics, occupations or ways of life, all the varieties which Puerto Rico presents, they do differ sufficiently to show that the effects of general socio-economic changes in the island are not uniform. They illustrate first of all the fact that not all government programs are in operation in all communities; that there is, therefore, a wide range in physical changes among the ten--roads, electricity, water, housing, schools, shopping facilities, churches, recreation. Availability of employment is unequal with resulting differences in the number of unemployed and in incomes. Interrelated with all these factors is the special spirit and attitude of each community growing out of its own local history, its geographical character, its traditions, its occupations, and its patterns of living. All these affect the position of each community on the path from a traditional to a modern society. Those most closely touched by new ways of life carry their own past with them in recognizable forms and none is wholly untouched by what has happened in the last thirty years.

In 1932, four communities were classified as sugar and tobacco sections (Aguadilla, Arecibo, Juncos, and Salinas); two were coffee regions (Adjuntas and Moca); two were fruit (Bayamón and Cidra); two were mixed or minor crops (Juana Diaz and Loiza). None of these has completely changed, but new policies of the Department of Agriculture and the introduction of industry has greatly altered the emphases and often the life of the community.

284

It should be noted that data for the 1932 study were
collected in March and April, during the zafra.
This influenced favorably the income figures in the
sugar regions. The 1963-64 figures, showing income
in October, November, December, 1963, represent a
period of low income intake in the agricultural regions. That the ten communities in 1932 were all
rural and that they were chosen on the basis of crops
raised in each area makes changes in agriculture and
in occupation of great importance, and these will be
reflected in the incomes of the families.

Because the 1932 study was primarily concerned
with the standards of living, income, and expenditure, we shall take this as the first illustration
of change. This will lead to further analysis which
necessarily goes beyond the considerations of the
1932 study.

In 1932, 24.5 per cent of the sample were in the
group of $25 or less, in monthly income; now 8.1 per
cent. In the income group of $25-$99 per month there
was a drop from 44 per cent to 33.3 per cent in 1963.
In the higher income groups there was a rise; in the
$100-$199 incomes, the percentage rose from 20 per
cent to 29.9 per cent and in the $200 or more, there
was a rise from 11.3 per cent to 28.7 per cent. (See
Chart 3.)

These over-all figures show the kind of progress
we may expect toward higher income levels. There are,
however, striking exceptions in our ten communities
to this general picture. We find in Loiza Medianía
Alta a decrease of 2.4 per cent in monthly income and
in Adjuntas-Yahuecas an increase of 329.5 per cent.
But in 1932, Medianía Alta was one of the three communities showing the highest average monthly income
of $102.46; in 1963, 8 out of 16   families
had incomes of over $100 per month. Loiza in 1932
had 8 families in the $100 or less category and 7
with incomes over $100; in 1963, from a total of 29
families reporting on income, 18 had less than $100
per month; 11 over $100. It also had the highest
percentage of low per capita income--37.5 per cent
had less than $10 per month, as against 19.6 per
cent for the total sample in the ten communities.

TABLE 19

Average Monthly Income--1932 vs. 1963--by Community

		Midpoints:	12.50 Less than 25	50.00 25-99	150.00 100-199	250.00 200 +	Total =	N	x Average
Loiza	1932	N	3	5	5	2	$ 1537	15	102.46
		%	20.0	33.3	33.3	13.3			
	1963	N	4	14	6	5	$ 2900	29	100.00
		%	13.8	48.3	20.7	17.2			
Juncos	1932	N	5	7	1	2	$ 1062	15	70.80
		%	33.3	46.7	6.7	13.3			
	1963	N	2	6	5	2	$ 1575	15	105.00
		%	13.3	40.0	33.3	13.3			
Cidra	1932	N	5	5	5	0	$ 1062	15	70.80
		%	33.3	33.3	33.3	--			
	1963	N	0	5	4	8	$ 2850	17	167.65
		%	--	29.4	23.5	47.1			
Bayamón	1932	N	4	6	5	0	$ 1100	15	73.33
		%	26.7	40.0	33.3	--			
	1963	N	1	13	20	28	$10662	62	171.96
		%	1.6	21.0	32.3	45.1			
Juana Diaz	1932	N	2	7	4	2	$ 1475	15	98.33
		%	13.3	46.7	26.7	13.3			
	1963	N	2	4	9	2	$ 2075	17	122.06
		%	11.8	23.5	52.9	11.8			

Adjuntas	1932	N	8	7	0	0	$ 450	15	30.00
		%	53.3	46.7	--	--			
	1963	N	1	7	3	5	$ 2062	16	128.87
		%	6.3	43.8	18.8	31.2			
Moca	1932	N	2	6	3	4	$ 1775	15	118.33
		%	13.3	40.0	20.0	26.7			
	1963	N	1	5	5	5	$ 2262	16	125.67
		%	6.3	31.2	31.2	31.2	(None + 2)		
Aguadilla	1932	N	5	6	3	1	$ 1062	15	70.80
		%	33.3	40.0	20.0	6.7			
	1963	N	2	5	6	2	$ 1675	15	111.67
		%	13.3	33.3	40.0	13.3			
Salinas	1932	N	1	9	2	3	$ 1512	15	100.80
		%	6.7	60.0	13.3	20.0			
	1963	N	6	13	6	7	$ 3375	32	105.47
		%	18.8	40.6	18.8	21.8			
Arecibo	1932	N	2	8	2	3	$ 1475	15	98.33
		%	13.3	53.3	13.3	20.0			
	1963	N	0	6	6	3	$ 1950	15	130.00
		%	--	40.0	40.0	20.0			

TABLE 20

Average Monthly Income --1932 vs. 1963

Community	Number of Families		Average Monthly Income		Highest Per Cent Change
	1932	1963	1932	1963	
Adjuntas	15	16	$ 30.00	$128.87	329.5
Cidra	15	17	70.80	167.65	136.8
Bayamón	15	62	73.33	171.96	134.5
Aguadilla	15	15	70.80	111.67	57.7
Juncos	15	15	70.80	105.00	48.3
Arecibo	15	15	98.33	130.00	32.2
Juana Diaz	15	17	98.33	122.06	24.1
Moca	15	18	118.33	125.67	6.2
Salinas	15	32	100.80	105.47	4.6
Loiza	15	29	102.46	100.00	-2.4
Totals	150	236	$ 83.41	$132.99	59.4

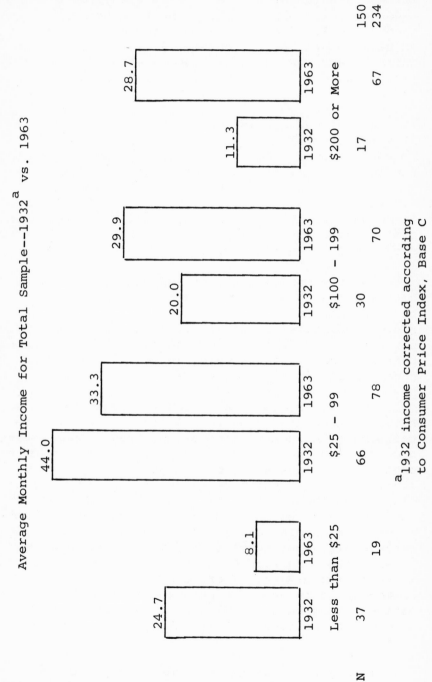

CHART 3

Average Monthly Income for Total Sample--1932[a] vs. 1963

a1932 income corrected according
to Consumer Price Index, Base C

The occupations in the highest income level recorded in Adjuntas in 1932 showed a mayordomo with
wages of $3.50 a week; the highest in Loiza, a mer-
chant with $9.94 weekly income; the medium level in
Adjuntas was a laborer earning $1.75 a week and in
Loiza a farmer with weekly income of $2.24; the low
level showed a laborer getting $1.75 in Adjuntas and
$2.85 in Loiza.

As pointed out in the description of Medianía
Alta (Chapter 5), it was, in 1932, a section of
coconut groves, sugar, and family gardens. It has
retained many of its characteristics but changes are
imminent. Work in new industry[2] is increasingly
available in the towns of Canovanas and Rio Grande.
(Ford Motors will soon open a $15 million precision
ball-bearing factory in Canovanas, Loiza--initial employment 300, eventual--800.)

For the municipality of Loiza as a whole, the
census gives 33 per cent working elsewhere. Nevertheless, Medianía Alta shows 34.3 per cent of unemployed and relief cases in our 1963 sample, and 12.5
per cent in traditional occupations and only 3.1 per
cent--modern artisans--which includes factory and
construction workers.   (See Table 21.)

It seems reasonable to conclude that Medianía
Alta, in greater degree than Loiza as a whole, retains many characteristics of the traditional society,
a conclusion that is reinforced by the proportion of
extended families among our sample--50.8 per cent
(including mixed patterns where grandchildren live
with grandparents or combinations of blood relations
live together) as against 43.7 per cent nuclear families. It is also significant that the highest percentage (12.5 per cent) of the total sample who express dissatisfaction with the present ways of living
is in Medianía Alta. There are many conservative
elements: a tendency to perpetuate old values; farms
divided among children with continued interdependence
between generations; the stability of many old families.

In Adjuntas, where the sample is 17, we find

Loiza Medianía Alta -- Occupation, Education, and Income

Income Group Midpoint	N.	Occupation	Education (Grade)	Monthly Income
0-25	7	Public welfare	0-8 (28 of 30 less than 4th)	7.00-52.50 Midpoint 29.75
	4	Unemployed (Soc. Sec., V. Pension, and from family)	0-12	35.00-63.30 Midpoint 49.15
	2	Traditional rural farm	4-6	50.00-75.00 Midpoint 62.50
25-99	2	Traditional nonfarm (unskilled, fishermen, etc.)	4-6	78.00-106.30 Midpoint 92.15
	3	Modern farm - migrant workers	1-8	50.00-101.00 Midpoint 75.50
	5	Traditional artisans (operators and foremen)	2-12	70.50-158.00 Midpoint 110.13
100-199	1	Modern artisans (operators and foremen)	7	160.
	4	Service workers (laundry, hotel employee, etc.)	6-10	87.50-325.00 Midpoint 206.25
	2	Shopkeepers, own business, own farm	0-8	130.00-200.00 Midpoint 165.00
200+		Prof.	12-16	336.00-500.00 Midpoint 418.00
	30			

TABLE 22

Occupation-Income Classification
(Midpoint used for income)

No.	Occupation	25-49	50-99	100-149	200-249	300-349	350+	Highest
29	Public welfare	29.75						
38	Soc. Sec., Vet., Family aid			137.50				
34	Traditional rural farm lab. and foreman		87.50					
2	Traditional nonfarm		92.15					
12	Modern farm			119.00				
21	Trad. artican incl. foremen				220.75			
59	Modern artisan				229.50			
18	Service workers				201.00			
17	Shopkeepers (own business)					317.00		
8	Professionals						386.00	
7	Elite							1471.25
245	TOTAL							

Bases: Average monthly income $182.02
Midpoint 178.63
Median 169.25

that 29.4 per cent are traditional farm workers--the
main agricultural crop is coffee--with family income
of $40-$120 per month; 17.6 per cent are modern artisans (this includes the workers in industry) with incomes of $115-$200 per month and shopkeepers 11.7
per cent (2 individuals) with incomes of $158-$579
per month.

We believe that Loiza, though closer to the
metropolitan area and undoubtedly in line for a
period of change, represents at present an adherence
to past customs which is reflected in income as well
as in attitude. For twenty-five years or more, 62.4
per cent have lived in this community. Because our
present sample is taken from the areas served by
Second Unit Schools and because in the 1932 study no
landowners who would represent an economic élite
were included, only seven of very high income level
appear in our total sample.

We believe that our highest income level, $200-
$350+, is a realistic representation of the high
average economic status in the ten communities.
There is in Hato Tejas, Bayamón, a wealthy canner
who happens to live in the geographic limits of the
barrio, but whose pattern of living is distinct from
that of the community as a whole. In the same way,
a landowner representing the old type of wealth in
one or two of the other communities, might have been
found. But as the latter group--the landowners--was
not included in the 1932 sample, there would have
been no comparability for the thirty-year period.
We also found that income levels in the ten communities for the high group ($200-$350+) vary in 1963
from a percentage of 11.8 per cent families in Juncos
to 47.2 per cent in Cidra. (See Tables 19 and 20.)
In all our considerations of income figures those
communities most dependent on seasonal agricultural
crops are least reliable because of our decision to
take the three months October, November, December
of 1963 as our period for income data. This was
done in order to get as much reliability as possible
from the memory of respondents. The study now being
made by the Department of Labor will undoubtedly supply more accurate figures, less dependent on local

conditions and seasonal factors. There are, of course,
always factors other than those of memory which affect
the accuracy of income figures--hesitation to disclose
exact amounts for fear that the purpose is related to
tax increase and general reluctance to reveal personal
financial situations.

The most significant material index of socio-
economic change is the source of income. In Table
21 (p. 291) we have included recipients of public
assistance and unemployed, who may be receiving pensions, Social Security payments or help from relatives, as well as those classified by source of wages,
salary or income from their own business. Of our
sample, a total of 72.7 per cent received no financial assistance, and 50 per cent of all heads of
families are farm laborers or foremen, operatives or
housewives (31 women). Income figures are highest
among shopkeepers and professionals--with the exception of the seven elite--a total of 25 persons--then
the modern artisans, traditional artisans and foremen, and service workers, totaling 98 persons.

The differences in the amount, character and
variety of expenditures show changes of the kind
one would expect with increased income. Because
these rural families still fall into the low income
level, the proportion spent on food remains high.
In 1932, the average amount spent on food by the 150
families of the study was $48.43; in 1963, the aver-
age for the 245 families was $85.23. As noted else-
where, the family size in the two samples has, during the thirty-year period, decreased from 7.2 in
the 1932 sample to 5.5 in 1963, operating not only
numerically as an increase of per capita income but
in other aspects--such as living space--to increase
comfort, to raise the standard of living. Of the
1963 sample, 82 per cent report eating better and
this is substantiated by the increased use of meat
and milk in the diet, 42 per cent reporting that
they eat meat three times a week, 18 per cent from
four to six times, and 10 per cent more than six.
Milk shows an equally important increase.

TABLE 23

Consumption of Meat and Milk, 1963

| 1963 | 3 Times | 4-6 Times | More Than 6 | Liters | | | None |
				3	2	1	
Eat meat weekly	42%	18%	10%				
Drink milk daily				13%	31.5%	26%	2.5%

Buying on credit has become an important fac_ tor in budget analysis. Whereas some 57.6 per cent buy furniture and appliances on credit, only 4.1 per cent use credit to buy a house or car. (The low percentage of loans for building may be due to the development of parcelas and mutual aid programs with their special financing arrangements.)

TABLE 24

Use of Credit Facilities

To buy furniture and appliances	57.6%
To buy house or car	4.1%
Other purposes	6.2%
Do not use	30.6%
Monthly payments on debts and loans	59.6%
Nothing monthly	29.0%
Easy to buy on credit but hard to get loans	21.2%

TABLE 25

Expenditures

	# Rep. Expend.	% of Total Sample	# Rep. None	# No Info.	Est. Total Month. Expend.	Est. Aver. Month. Expend./n	% of Total Month. Expend.
1 9 6 3							
Food	242	98.8	2	1	20,625.85	85.23/242	.5112
Trans.	176	71.8	64	5	3,272.36	18.59/176	.0811
Rec.	32	13.1	211	2	616.28	19.25/32	.0150
Med.	111	45.3	127	7	3,634.75	32.75/111	.0901
Cloth.	216	88.2	18	11	3,208.33	14.85/216	.0795
Light	208	84.9	32	5	1,274.50	36.13/208	.0315
Debts	146	59.6	71	28	15,464.50	37.43/146	.1354
Other	66	26.9	82	97	1,247.50	18.90/66	.0309
Rent	36	14.7	21/187*	1	390.00	10.83/36	.0096
Water	154	62.8	89	2	613.00	3.98/154	.0151
1 9 3 2							
Food	150	100.0	--		7,264.98	48.43/150	.6198
Rec.	87	58.0	63		521.06	5.99/87	.0444
Med.	120	80.0	30		640.41	5.34/120	.0546
Cloth.	132	85.3	18		1,331.04	10.08/132	.1135

Oper. exp.	126	84.0	24	778.89	6.18/126	.0664
Other	105	70.0	45	707.47	6.74/105	.0603
Rent	44	29.3	106	476.06	10.82/44	.0406

* 21 people reported no expenditures for rent; 187 people were reported as owning their homes.

1. The 1963 estimated total monthly expenditures were derived in the same manner as the 1932 totals except that the midpoint of the intervals reported in the tables was used as the best estimate of actual expenditures.

2. The 1932 total monthly expenditures were taken directly from expenditure tables by combining the totals of the three groups.

3. The average monthly expenditures were obtained by dividing the actual number of people reporting expenditures in each category. This n is shown with the averages.

4. All figures are corrected for price index by multiplying 1932 figures by 2.23.

No items appear under expenditures in 1932 for light or water. Items such as candles or fuel for light (kerosene lamps) were included in operating expenses. Electricity and water now appear as normal expenditures.

Under transportation, 8 per cent of total income was spent, or an average of $18.59 per month in 1963. In 1932, no item was included for transportation. Life was centered in the local community and there was no opportunity to work outside the neighborhood-- poor roads or no roads--except in those cases where cane workers left home for the period of the zafra.

Amounts spent on recreation were, in 1932, $5 per month--in 1963, $19.20. Present responses on recreation are unsatisfactory. They do not show use of radio and TV as recreation, although we find in 1963 that 43.3 per cent of the families have radio and television; 42 per cent have radio only; 2.5 per cent television only. It is difficult to separate traditional from modern forms of recreation; younger people among respondents have no basis for comparison with the past. Such an item as "going to dances" meant something quite different in the traditional society from the present. Only such occasions as velorios are easily identifiable.

We have no reliable information on clothing items--in terms of actual garments purchased--to explain an increase from $8.86 per month for each family in 1932 to $13.10 per family in 1963.

Among our 245 families, we find that the head of the family is male in 211 cases (or 86.1 per cent of the sample, 13.9 per cent female). Among those reporting, 73 per cent of the heads of families were between 20 and 60 years of age, and 42 per cent were between 40 and 59. The size of the family is 5.5 as compared with 7.2 in 1932 (high income level 8.1, medium 7.7, low 5.9) and with a present island-wide average of 4.8. We have no facts on the composition of the families in 1932. The larger number in each household may be assumed to have represented the extended family which was without doubt the

common pattern in the 1930's.   Among the families
studied in 1962 the nuclear family represents 50 per
cent of the sample; the extended 23 per cent.

TABLE 26

Age and Occupation of Head of Family, 1964

Age of Head

		Number	Per Cent
Largest Age Group	40-49	53	21.6
Next	50-59	49	20.0
	30-39	48	19.6
	60-69	43	17.6
	20-29	29	11.8
	70+	20	8.2
Under	20	1	.4
	X	2	.8

Sex of Head of Family

Men	211	86.1
Women	34	13.9

Occupation

Farm laborers and foremen	48	19.6
Operatives, etc.	45	18.4
Housewives	31	12.5
Artisans, foremen	22	9.0
Salesmen, owners business	18	7.4

In the age group of 40 to 59 years, 25 had completed the fourth grade, 18 the sixth. The educational levels of our sample show that the largest number (54) had third- to fourth-grade education and in age
ranged from 20-69 years; next came those with no education (44). There was no one in this group under
30 years of age; the largest number with no education
lay in the age groups 60 and above (33). Only 25
(10.2 per cent) of the total sample had had any vocational education.

Among the sample families, 38.8 per cent now read periodicals and books, 19.2 per cent read periodicals only, and 3.3 per cent read books only. It is doubtful whether there was any reading at home in 1932, except for schoolwork for children.

Knowledge of English is rated as follows by the interview report: 14.7 per cent "good" down to 4.5 per cent "very poor," and 60.4 per cent have no knowledge.

People appear to have much more knowledge of what is going on around them, both on and off the island. They give as reasons that it is due to radio, TV, relatives in the United States, more social visiting and gossiping, better communications and transportation, more education.

Use of the post office is indicated by 72.7 per cent; telephone or telegraph--new facilities since 1932--are used by this percentage also. In any study of a change from traditional to modern society, communication has more importance than its convenience or, as in the case of radio or television, its recreational aspect.

Because in 1932 there were no large landowners included among those interviewed, the term "farmer" is ambiguous. The situation in 1963 is materially different. Some 66 per cent of the respondents own from a cuadro to fifty or more cuerdas. Nearly half of these own less than four cuerdas. The same great change is observed in home ownership. Formerly, even if an occupant had built his house, it was on the landlord's property and he could be evicted at will. Now, 213 of the 245 families interviewed reported that they owned their homes, 169 of them having built them themselves, either individually or by mutual aid.

The most common rural dwellings in the 1930's were huts, most of them with thatched roofs, but some with galvanized iron roofs. A tin roof in 1930 was somewhat of a status symbol. It was cleaner than a thatched roof, which harbored rats, but it was also

much hotter. There were some wooden houses with tin
roofs, but in general the housing was very poor, inadequate, and unsanitary. In 1963, there were 75
concrete houses, 123 wood and zinc, but of a much
better quality, and usually painted, and a scattering of others made of both concrete and wood.

Most of the huts in 1932 had a living room and
one or two bedrooms and outside kitchens, whereas
now the majority--80 per cent--have from three to
seven rooms. Unmarried male and female members of
the household sleep in separate rooms in 50 per cent
of the families studied. In 60 per cent of the families, the married couple has a room of its own and
23 per cent do not. In 17 per cent of the cases,
there is no married couple.

A total of 66 per cent now have running water in
the house and 18.5 per cent use public faucets. The
remainder have a variety of water sources--deep wells,
relatives, the river, etc. Half of the families have
a latrine, but no shower or toilet. Only 11 have no
sanitary facilities. This is a marked difference
from 1932.

Some 86   per cent have electricity, about
half with hanging ceiling lamp, the other half--no
lamp--and 11 per cent still use kerosene or candles.
As outlined in another chapter, there are still families, and probably always will be, too remote to
get electricity.

A quotation from the 1932 study Rural Life in
Puerto Rico illustrates the difference in regard to
cooking facilities, water supply, latrine and sleep-
ing arrangements.

> All of the houses have some sort of
> kitchen. In the great majority it is
> just an open shack attached to the main
> house. Cooking generally takes place in
> the open air. A built-in sand table
> with three stones for cooking with wood
> or a portable anafre for charcoal are
> the common types of stoves. The brick

or concrete fogon found in the better
houses is built-in, and these, like the
sand table, are not listed as part of
the furniture because they are part of
the house.

The effect of such housing conditions on specific health problems is
obvious and not a mere matter of speculation. Correlations of certain facts
are significant; 63-1/3% of the 150 families obtain water from surface wells,
brooks, rivers, and ditches, and the
death rate from diarrhea and enteritis
in 1932 was 246.9 per 100,000 as against
26 per 100,000 as the highest rate in
continental United States.

In the 150 families an average of
four persons slept in one room. And the
death rate from tuberculosis was 297.3
per 100,000 as against 127.8 as the highest in the States. Infestation from
hookworm is over 90% in many rural sections, and among the 150 families only
54% have latrines of the approved type,
and 28% latrines of the unapproved
types; one has a toilet, 18% have no
latrines, and information was lacking
on the remainder.[3]

In 1962, the largest number of families inter-
viewed--46 per cent--use kerosene for cooking. The
next largest number--37 per cent--use bottled gas.
Wood, charcoal and electricity are the other fuels
used, in about equal numbers of families. As for
ironing, 204, or 83 per cent, use electricity, 13.5
per cent use charcoal in a goose, and the rest, fire-
wood.

A total of 150 (61 per cent) have no oven,
59 (24 per cent) have ovens and use them for meats,
vegetables, cakes, etc. Bread is not made at home.
Twenty-six have ovens but do not use them.

In obtaining information on household equipment,
no questions were asked about the number who owned

refrigerators. This was an oversight, but from observations of the field staff, many of the houses
had them. They were not always used to the full,
however; one refrigerator was observed with no food
in it, but there was one bottle of Coca-Cola. The
old habit of going to the store every day still per-
sists, and many of the people evidently do not yet
realize that food can be preserved as well as cooled
in a refrigerator.

In the 1962 interviews, 57.7 per cent reported
no long-term illnesses in the family. Illnesses reported cover a wide range. As these are based on
the diagnosis of the respondent, we do not place
great reliability on the percentages. Cardio-
vascular, heart, strokes "and others" comprise the
highest percentage--8.8 per cent. A total of 92.7
per cent report no mental disease, and 57.1 per cent
report no one in the family hospitalized during the
year. In the families studied, 69 lost one or two
children before the age of five. Although the 1932
study had no reports on illnesses, it is made abun-
dantly clear by the changes in mortality and morbidity figures over the thirty-year period and by the
emphasis on health problems in the 1932 program of
the social workers and Second Unit School program
that the change in health and sanitary conditions is
most striking. The fact that illnesses reported now
are different is also of great interest and would
warrant further study.

In considering mobility, it is to be noted that
the largest percentage (32.1) of people listed is in
the category of residence for entire life. (See
Table 27.) Taken with the category 25 years or more,
13.6 per cent, it constitutes nearly one-half the
population of the total sample. One would expect
that the nature of the community or the employment
opportunities would affect mobility, but there does
not seem to be any clear pattern. Barrio Hato Tejas,
in Bayamón, shows the lowest percentage (21.9) of
those living there all their lives, which is understandable because it is a fast-growing suburban community and has many newcomers and short-term residents.

On the other hand, San Antonio, Aguadilla, shows the highest percentage (39.9) in the one- to nine-year residence, but San Antonio is not typical because the people of the community have been physically moved twice to make room for Ramey Air Force Base. It is quite possible that some of the people inter- viewed stated how long they had lived in that physi- cal community, whereas they might have lived in the three San Antonios all their lives.

Table 27 shows the distribution of those inter- viewed in the ten barrios in five duration-of- residence periods.

Table 28 shows the nearest location of factor- ies as well as the type of road on which the barrio is located. Bus and public car transportation are available in all ten communities, facilitating ac- cess to jobs and tending to hold people in their com- munities rather than moving into San Juan and other big cities. This transportation is also available for longer distances when there is seasonal work in sugar or other crops.

These factors have also been important in re- ducing emigration to the United States to the point where the net outgo is zero and more and more people are coming back now that the opportunities are bet- ter. This, of course, puts more responsibility on the government to stimulate and attract new industry and business to provide the necessary jobs. The gov- ernment accepts this responsibility and is making excellent progress.

A total of 105 (43 per cent) were born in the barrio in which they now live, and 46 (19 per cent) were born in the same municipality, but in a differ- ent barrio. Fifty-nine (24 per cent) were born in some other municipio. The remainder were born in various places--urban areas or rural--but they could not remember exactly where.

In answer to where they lived before, the great- est number, 72 (29.5 per cent), said they had lived there all their lives. This may mean the same house

as, in the previous question, 105 said they had lived
in the barrio always. Others replied that they had
lived in other barrios, other municipios, and the
United States mainland.

TABLE 27

Length of Residence in Barrio, 1963

Time in Barrio		Less Than 1 Yr.	1-9 Yrs.	10-24 Yrs.	25 Yrs. or More (Not WL)	Whole Life
Loiza	N	1	5	6	9	11
	%	3.1	15.7	18.8	28.1	34.3
Juncos	N	1	2	5	1	8
	%	5.9	11.7	29.4	5.9	47.1
Cidra	N	0	3	5	2	6
	%	0	17.7	29.4	11.7	35.3
Bayamón	N	1	23	18	9	14
	%	1.5	35.2	27.6	13.8	21.9
Salinas	N	1	5	15	3	8
	%	3.1	15.7	46.8	9.4	25.0
Juana Diaz	N	0	3	3	2	9
	%	0	17.7	17.7	11.7	52.9
Adjuntas	N	1	3	4	5	4
	%	5.9	11.7	23.5	29.4	23.5
Moca	N	0	6	5	1	5
	%	0	33.3	27.8	5.6	27.8
Aguadilla	N	1	6	4	0	4
	%	6.7	39.9	26.7	0	26.7
Arecibo	N	2	3	3	3	4
	%	13.3	20.1	20.1	19.9	26.6
Total Nos.		8	59	68	35	73
Per Cent		4.0	21.9	26.8	13.6	32.1

TABLE 28

Geographical Relation of Barrios to Industrial Employment

	Type of Road	Nearest Factory	Distance (Miles)	Employment
Loiza	2	Canovanas 8	10	729
Juncos	1	Juncos 9	5 1/2	802
Cidra	2	Cidra 2	4	?
Bayamón	3	Bayamón 62	3	3,940
Salinas	1	Salinas 6	16	576
Juana Diaz	3	Juana Diaz 6	7	585
Adjuntas	3	Adjuntas 3	15	?
Moca	2	Moca 1	4	?
Aguadilla	3	Aguadilla 3	6	?
Arecibo	3	Arecibo 18	12	1,223

N.B. In some cases, as from Cidra to Cayey, workers go farther than the nearest town to find employ- ment. They also commute to the sugar areas by bus.

Legend: 1. Primary roads
        2. Secondary roads
        3. Municipal roads
                All paved.

Mobility Statistics

31.4 per cent work in the same barrio where they live.
 9.4 per cent work in the town nearest barrio.
13.1 per cent work elsewhere.
26.1 per cent have visited the United States.
 5.3 per cent have visited the United States and
      other countries.
61.2 per cent no member of family has traveled out-
      side United States.
23.3 per cent one trip by one member, or same trip
      by two or more.
17.1 per cent of those traveling went to work.
 6.5 per cent to visit relatives.
 6.5 per cent military service.

Evidently the people are, on the whole, happy
about where they live, 71 per cent reporting that
they would like to continue living there, while 29
per cent said they would like to move. A total of
125 have never moved and the rest have moved for
various reasons--to be nearer their work, to get a
better house, to buy their own home, to be nearer
friends and family.

Of those interviewed, 180 have never lived in
the city; the remainder have had some experience in
urban living; and 230 (94 per cent) of the 245 like
living in the country, the other 15 (6 per cent) prefer the city, but give no reason for the preference.

In response to the question of where they worked,
77 (31.4 per cent) said they worked in the barrio
where they lived. Fifty-five (22.5 per cent) said
they worked either in town or in some other barrio,
and 103 (42 per cent) reported they did not work.
Since the period considered was October, November,
December of 1963, when agricultural work, especially
cane cutting, is slack, this is not surprising.
This is undoubtedly the reason for the higher unemployment rate than the island average throughout our
findings.[4]

Notes to Chapter 8

1.   All figures on income and expenditures are
based on 1932-1963 corrected price index.

2.   Changes are imminent. According to reports,
land is being purchased for several types of development.

3.   Rural Life in Puerto Rico, published by
Department of Education, San Juan, Bulletin #1, pp.
37, 38.

4.   For additional tables on socio-economic
change, see Appendix.

CHAPTER **9** CHANGES IN

ATTITUDES

The expression of satisfaction or dissatisfaction with life at present has great importance as a commitment on the part of respondents. From the data on attitudes it is apparent that replies to specific questions, such as family relations, are not always consistent with this commitment.

Some 67 per cent of the people said they were happier now, giving reasons of better health, education, working conditions, housing, while 16 per cent were undecided, and 15 per cent said they were happier before. Here again, nostalgia may come into the picture. Further, 94 per cent said life was easier now, giving the above reasons for happiness and adding water supply, electricity, roads, hospital facilities, telephone, freedom of speech, better wages, more food, better credit facilities.

TABLE 29

Satisfaction with Life at Present
(Rather Than 30 Years Ago)

Better now	Total 81.6%
(none lower than 70.5%--Cidra)	
Our lives worse now	Total 7.4%
Our lives the same	Total 4.5%
Our lives the same, but some things worse than 30 years ago	Total 4.5%

This opinion prevails even in those communities where incomes remain low and where not all government facilities are offered. In commenting on this

general opinion, we look back to the Second Unit
Schools of thirty years ago where we saw on a smaller scale the results of the interest and expectations engendered by a government program and the
effect on attitudes toward life. Now they feel that
the government cares. This is not without paternal-
istic overtones and a certain amount of transference
from dependence on the landlord to dependence on the
state. Some question certainly arises as to overde-
pendence on government, although, as we have seen,
there is no doubt that planning in Puerto Rico is
organized in a democratic framework and that provision is made for local action, down to the barrio
level, allowing for planning by the municipalities
and cooperation between them and the Planning Board.
But one must look back to the past dependence of the
majority of country citizens on the landlord and the
resulting weakness of individual and local group initiative. An evidence of the intention to encourage
the development of local action appears in the change
from "commisario" to "president" of the barrio, a
change from a party-<u>appointed</u> to a local party-
<u>elected</u> official.

When asked whether change should come quickly
or slowly, 90 per cent said that it should come
little by little through education and training,
government programs, petitions from the people.

An answer to a question in the depth interviews
(Question #11) on future change is interesting. It
gives the responses to the possibility of revolutionary vs. slower changes. A total of 32.8
per cent said "by training and education," and an
additional 10.4 per cent said "by the people, by
petitions, etc." Only 4.5 per cent mentioned rapid
change through the government and its agencies. Although we recognize that the view of the interviewer
may be transferred to the interviewee in many subtle
forms and that the interviewer is not unaffected in
his recording by the general attitude of his respondent, this seems to us to represent a long step from
the replies which would have been made thirty years
ago--an unconscious venture from traditional to modern thinking and a recorded mark on the path to democratic action.

That the people take a more active part in the
affairs of the barrio than they did thirty years ago
is apparent. In regard to specific local action--
the solving of problems of the barrio--47.8 per cent
mention "the traditional way": petitions, complaints
to the mayor, meetings. These traditional forms are,
however, _forms_ and can have new and different meaning
and content stemming from their past significance.
But that, in addition to the percentages quoted, 20.9
per cent participate actively in the solution of
local problems, through election of local committees,
formation of clubs and groups to discuss the needs
of the barrio, is indeed a change of real import.
Meetings are held and petitions and protests are
handled by the president through the proper authori-
ties--69 per cent said this was the modus operandi
now, while 31 per cent said either they left everything to the government or they didn't know how such
matters were handled; 43 of the 67 people questioned
in the depth interview said they took an active part
in barrio affairs.

Landy, in his book _Tropical Childhood_, gives a
strong picture of the power of the Popular Democratic
Party in the community he studied.

> Don Pablo is titular head of PPD and
> runs the municipio with almost unques-
> tioned control. . . . Almost no action
> involving government or law is taken up
> by anyone in Valle Cana without the
> prior consent of the party through Don
> Pablo or his lieutenant.[1]

When he quotes the Vallecaneses saying: "He [Don
Pablo] is like a father to us," we see the party representative taking the place of the good landowner
of the traditional society. The vote cannot be an
expression of new individual freedom in such a case
nor can the community feel the necessity for group
action. The other political parties have little or
no influence. To change this attitude involves more
than the wish to do so, even assuming that the desired methods of the Popular Party are not paternal-
istic. In a small, poor community such as the one

studied by Landy, there is still the lack of initiative, the dependence which long-continued poverty
brings. Perhaps the excellent programs for isolated
communities and community education will in time
reach all such communities; or, perhaps, a new leader, who has had experience or education outside the
limits of the little community or whose own vitality
and ambition give him the courage to rebel, will
alter the leadership pattern. Whether or not the
changes that may come will also alter the political
complexion is not the essential factor. As long as
the Popular Party has a program geared to meeting
continuing needs it may well remain the majority
party. That more attention must be given to the development of democratic methods and to local responsibility is indispensable if the society as a whole is
to move toward a truly representative democracy.

We must, however, recognize again the transitional character which these responses represent--a
developing conception of a democratic society and
the rights and responsibilities in it.

Some communities in the island may retain the
traditional character, even though they may be taking the first steps toward the connection of voting
rights with their needs and desires as citizens.

Daniel Lerner has said in The Passing of Traditional Society:

> Whereas the isolated community of a
> traditional society functioned well on
> the basis of a highly constructive
> personality, the interdependent sec-
> tors of modern society require wide-
> spread participation. This, in turn,
> requires an expansive and adaptive
> self-system, ready to incorporate new
> roles and to identify personal values
> with public issues.[2]

Such communities as the one studied by Landy
are, so far, almost wholly unconscious of the need
for "widespread participation." But our ten

communities in the history of the last thirty years
show, in varying degrees, their awareness of the
world around them and of their potential sharing in
decisions which affect their lives.

To further substantiate our assumption that
there is also greater participation in the processes
of government and more initiative in bringing about
local improvements, we turn to the answers on questions of politics and community action in the questionnaire.

TABLE 30

Attitudes Toward Politics and
Community Action, 1963

Political leaders - good (more concerned)	4.5%
No more fights at elections (before, people were killed; politics are cleaner)	33.9%
The poor get better consideration (before, you had to vote for the rich); more free- dom in voting, more equality in voting; more is done for the general welfare	14.3%
More help is given--foods, schools, housing, etc.	5.8%
Smaller numbers of replies give such reasons as: promises are kept, general improvement under the present government	5.3%

Eighty-four persons (34.28 per cent) gave no
opinion or thought there had been no improvement,
showing indifference or disapproval. The replies
are perhaps more significant in quality than in quantity. Satisfaction seems to be found, among individuals replying, in respect for the voter and his
right to express his opinion, in the orderliness and
fairness of elections. Many people in the past

actually dreaded elections because of the violence
which accompanied them. One woman described her
fear, as a child, of the organized fights that went
on. Votes were bought, voters often voted several
times. The minimum improvement lies in order and
freedom to cast one's ballot; the maximum is implicit in the necessity to make decisions, to find
reasons for such decisions, and to do this free of
economic dependence on "the rich" who made the decisions for "the poor."

The replies to the question of expropriation of
land are pertinent to this new identification with
public issues. When, in the depth interviews, they
were asked how they would feel if the government expropriated their land to make possible a rural resettlement community and thus improve the living conditions of many families, the replies were as follows:

TABLE 31

Attitudes Toward Land Expropriation, 1962-63

	Frequency	Per Cent
Would accept without hesi-tation	3	4.5
Would accept; added comments on civic duty and desire to help others	30	44.8
Would accept--conditioned on payment and another place to live	9	13.4
Would not accept, like, or permit it	14	20.9
Would not accept willingly, but to fight against the government is impossible	11	16.4

Attitudes toward social change are reflected in
replies to questions, in both objective and depth interviews, which deal with personal relations: the
relation to neighbors, of husband and wife, of parents and children.   Replies in these areas of experience give a more ambiguous result than the simpler
responses concerning a comparison of present with
past.   Few would care to go back to the conditions
of thirty years ago, but many, as shown in the attitudinal replies, are very conscious of the problems
which change has brought and with the difficulty
they face in establishing a satisfying value system
in the situation of the present and the goals for
the future.   Some of the same problems are faced in
societies over the world; others are either peculiar
to, or accentuated by, Puerto Rico's own cultural
background--shared in many respects with other Latin
cultures--plus the influence of the United States
over the last sixty-six years.

On the question (#72) concerning neighbors--
"better or worse"--the highest percentage (32.3)
from all communities agree they are "better"; 20 per
cent find them the same; 15 per cent find them
"worse." When they give their reasons for finding
them better, more education, skills, and "civilization" come first (14.3 per cent); other reasons show
scattered percentages. Those who find them "worse"
say that people were more friendly before, helped
each other (11.8 per cent), respected each other.

In asking the respondents about their feelings
concerning hospitality and humanitarianism, we find
an evenly divided opinion, approximately half thinking it was better and the other half disagreeing.
Various reasons were given, such as that thirty
years ago neighbors shared food, visited more often,
helped more in time of sickness--while now they
think more of money and their own concerns. Apparently those who think there is more hospitality today are relying on their feelings, as very few
reasons are given.

The depth interview shows 98.5 per cent who
find people more anxious now to improve their lot,

as a result of better education, less poverty, pride
in occupation (do not want to be laborers)--in other
words, a generally higher level of aspiration. Formerly they were fatalistic, accepting their status
as inevitable, but now they are prouder, more ambi-
tious, eager for learning and hoping for a better
life for their children than they have had themselves.

The reasons given are: improvement in income,
34.2 per cent; educational facilities, 27.8 per cent;
housing, 13.9 per cent. Other replies are distributed among health facilities, communication and transportation, general environment, water and light and
social services of the government. Life is worse
now than thirty years ago, said 13.5 per cent.

Among the persons over forty years old, only
12.3 per cent would like to live as they did thirty
years ago; among those under forty, almost the same
percentage, 12.4 per cent. We had expected to find
a different correlation based on the assumption that
in the older age groups nostalgia for the past would
be an important factor. Of our total sample, 79.2
per cent would not like to live as they lived thirty
years ago; 12 per cent would like to live as they
lived thirty years ago; 5.7 per cent answered "yes
and no"; 2.9 per cent were undetermined. Among the
reasons given were: more facilities, more progress--
roads, schools, etc.--more opportunity to study, more
work, more money, more liberty--"before everyone was
bossed"; does not like to regress--likes to discover
new things, enjoys more things--"before, we walked
barefoot." The highest percentages (47.0 and 31.8,
respectively) in reasons given lie in the categories
of more facilities and more comfort, more work.

That this attitude prevails to this extent is
more striking because unemployment among our sample
is 17.1 per cent--higher by 4 per cent than the
island average of 13 per cent. To understand the
satisfaction with the present, one must compare it
with the past. What was begun in rural areas many
years ago in Second Unit Schools, by the PRERA, the
PRRA, and other agencies, and the great acceleration of all programs in the last twenty years cannot

be measured entirely by the standards of increased
prosperity, marked as this is. In the replies to
all attitudinal questions, optimism is reflected in
concrete hopes for the future and in a consciousness
of rights. This we believe has replaced fatalism in
a large majority of our respondents.

In general most of the people interviewed were
satisfied with their pay and working conditions, but
many said they would change jobs for better pay,
easier work, or more prestige. Others said they
would have liked to change but that now it was too
late.

Some 64 per cent said they had been handicapped because of insufficient education. They could
have been leaders or mayordomos or have earned more,
or have had more prestige. Their aspirations for
their children are a college degree in 63 per cent
of the cases, but all want more than they had. By
the same token, they want better jobs for their chil-
dren--professional positions, teaching, government
employment. Very few want a trade or agriculture.
The white collar job is still the aspiration as it
was in 1932, but to a much greater degree and with
more hope of attainment. Some more realistic and
discerning view of education in modern society is
obviously needed.

In the depth interview, 52 said that employment
possibilities are better now, whereas 10 said there
was no change, 4 that they were worse, and one did
not know. The same proportion in favor gave as reasons the government, labor legislation, education,
modernism, new factories, and the same number saw no
change.

Forty-eight of the 67 respondents in the depth
interview said they would like to have their children
work in agriculture. "It gives satisfaction, it is a
good life, it is profitable" are among the reasons
given. Fifteen did not want that life for their children, and four gave no answer. This is hard to recon-
cile with the answers in the previous paragraph, and
may reflect a love of the land and country which they

would like to pass on to their children. The fact
that agriculture, until recently, has been unprofit-
able, may account for the expression of a desire for
other occupations than agriculture.

When it comes to home life, 28.6 per cent find
parents and children "better"; 23 per cent find both
"worse"; 13 per cent the same as before, and 13.1
per cent better parents, worse children.

A list of reasons given for the situation between parents and children shows the variety, and
hence the conflict, which exists in this period between traditional and modern, between sacred and
secular societies. Among the percentages in these
responses, 10.6 per cent, the highest, speak only of
the lack of discipline. Among those who replied to
the questions, other percentages run from 2.8 to 5.3.
The list of reasons given follows:

Better now: more democracy in the home; before,
the father was the boss and used physical punishment. Parents assume their responsibility
better; care more for their children; have to
support them by law; educate their children better for the future.

Worse now: fulfilled parental responsibility
better in the past. Did not leave children
alone while parents went to work. Parents do
not respect even their own daughters--assault
them. Disciplined their children; now they do
not--or very little. Do not educate them now.

Looking at the children themselves, the parents'
responses show that the highest percentage (27.4)
find more disrespect and disobedience now, delinquency
and unwillingness to help parents. Those who find
children better gave the following reasons: more education; better behavior; children help and cooperate
with their parents; "they deal with each other like
brothers and sisters"; more religious; more helpful
and kind.

In the depth interview, 89.8 per cent believe

delinquency is increasing due to lack of morals,
laws forbidding punishment, general upbringing, opportunities offered by "bad places," too much liber-
ty, and the influence of American culture. In the
relationship of husbands and wives, the highest percentage again is among those who find it worse--
25.8; while 18.2 per cent find it the same;
10.3 per cent find it better; 37.6 per cent "not determined." The reasons are significant. Among those
who find things better now, these reasons are given:
before, they (husbands) were away drinking; now men
and women work and fulfill their responsibilities;
there is more harmony within the family; now they
marry--before, they ran away; they are more religious.

       The reasons of those who find the situation worse
are: before, they used to take their wives out and
have fun together; today they have fun alone; more
divorce (see Table 32) and desertion; they were more
considerate before; did not hit them; too much liber-
ty and temptation now.

       From the depth interviews, further light is
thrown on these responses. The question of the effect on marital relations from women's work outside
the home was asked, and 73.1 per cent found it detri-
mental--"husbands feel uneasy"--for the following
reasons: children are neglected--"woman's place is
in the home"; love of family diminishes--they hardly
see each other; the woman may make undesirable con-
nections--fall in love with someone else; the wife
feels independent--that she has the same rights as
the husband; accepts (unwillingly) the situation as
inevitable.

       Those who approve (20.9 per cent) say: they
like the financial help from the wife; the wife is
happier and they "have an agreement"; they are satisfied.

       Replies to questions in the depth interview on
responsibility for the upbringing of children show
that 28.4 per cent believe that the child belongs to
both parents; they are equally needed and "for discipline there must be marital accord." Others say

TABLE 32

Family Structure

Type	Number	Per Cent
Nuclear	124	50.6
Extended	55	23.0

Size		
4 or less persons	101	41.2
5-8	102	41.6
9-12 or more	42	17.2

Average family, 5.5 persons. This is closer to
average size of family on relief (5.7) than to
average for island (4.8).

Marriages

Year	Number	Divorce Rate
1937	13,964	2.2%
1947	16,779	3.4%
1957	19,044	4.4%
1962	22,769	5.2%

Type of Marriages	Number	Per Cent
In church	110	44.9
Civil	38	15.5
Widower	23	9.5
Consensual--5 yr.	18	7.4
Consensual--not spec.	19	7.8
Sep. (divorce)	9	3.7
Single	8	3.3
Living less than 5 yrs. together	7	2.9
Married ch. or c. unspec.	7	2.9
Divorced	5	2.0

that the mothers are responsible for the girls, the
fathers for the boys. Only 6 per cent say that the
father is the head and authority; 31.4 per cent think
that the mother has more time, is closer to the children, and has more ability to handle them.

"If a girl has a boy friend of whom the parents
disapprove, who should be the one to discuss it with
the girl?"   To this question, 32.9 per cent
answer the father because he is the head, is respected and better informed; 20.9 per cent say the
mother because she is closer to her daughter; 41.7
per cent say both parents, and add "the daughter
should also be heard."

The percentages on all these answers give a
mixed and confusing result from the standpoint of
measurement, but the interest lies in the very differences they show; the clinging to old values and
the recognition of the new; in some cases an idealiz-
ing of the past. Many replies look upon the old
days as better, for example, in matters of sexual re-
lations--which may have been different, but it would
be difficult to prove that they were in any sense
"better."   (This could be shown from actual case
material in the past--the 1930's.)

Table 33 throws further light on attitudes
toward women's independence and gives at least lip
service to old customs.

In the question in the depth interview concerning people's attitude about the rights of others, 41
stated that there is less respect for them, 22 said
there is the same or more, and 4 gave no information.
As a contrast to the custom of word-of-mouth agreements in 1932, all but one of the respondents said
it is safer and better to have signed documents in a
business transaction. Whether the verbal agreement
was violated too often, or whether it is a sign of
changing habits everywhere, is not determined; probably some of both. As in some other categories, it
is difficult to find any correlation in the replies,
especially in the depth interview, with age of the
respondents. Those showing a personal experience

TABLE 33

Depth Interview Question #46--"What About
the Freedom Women Enjoy at Present?"[c]

	Freq.[a]	Per Cent[a]	Per Cent[b]
General answer: Bad: no examples	5	7.0	7.5

General answer:
Bad: women try to manage hus-
  bands; do not mind their
  husbands, etc.
	4	5.6	6.0

Specific answers and reasons:
Bad: woman loses feminine
  qualities, neglects home.
  (Example given--wearing
  slacks, etc.)
	12	16.9	17.9

Bad: they drink and smoke too
  much; keep late hours; night
  spots, etc.
	3	4.2	4.5

Bad: girls go out unchaperoned; come in late at night	7	9.9	10.4

Bad: get corrupted; lose honor
  and respect for self and
  others; undesirable friends,
  etc.
	4	5.6	6.0

Bad: other examples like get-
  ting in trouble with
  police, jail
	4	5.6	6.0

Neutral: examples are pro and con	9	12.7	13.4

Good: women should enjoy these
  liberties; this is a demo-
  cratic country; women have
  same rights as men, etc.
	18	25.4	26.9

Does not know--no information	2	2.8	3.0
Both negative and positive answers	3	4.2	4.5
	71[a]	100.0	b

[a]Multiple count--per cent based on total answers.
[b]Per cent based on 67 cases.
[c]Heads of families interviewed--211 men, 34 women.

with situations in the thirties must be presumed to
be in the older groups. The younger groups either
got their information from parents or other relatives
or they have no information on the subject, even
though they may have opinions.

Of the sample, 92.5 per cent said that the attitude of employers and treatment of employees thirty
years ago was much worse than it is today. Now the
employer has more respect for the employee and his
family (78.8 per cent of 245 replies stated "more respect now"), does not force him to vote his way, pays
reasonably good wages, does not exploit him at the
store, and the hours of work are shorter.

Some 83 per cent like labor unions and believe they have helped tremendously in guaranteeing
a square deal for the workman as well as providing
education, insurance, medical services; 17 per cent
saw no advantages or some positive disadvantages, as
well as real advantages, though the large majority
favored them.

When asked for their opinion on the development
plans of the government (objective questionnaires),
91 per cent said that these programs had improved
the community, 4.9 per cent that they had not, 2.5
per cent that it had brought improvement in some
ways and not others, 1.6 per cent did not know. No
one community shows any striking difference in opinion from others.

From the depth interview there is almost unani-
mous opinion that government programs have helped
the community, made life better, and raised the
standard of living. The reasons given run the gamut
of government services, the chief one being better
schools and more of them, water, electricity, roads,
parcelas. Thirteen items are listed, with no negative opinions. Factories with their accompanying
job opportunities play a major role in these
answers.

Some 82 per cent said they had benefited
from government programs in one way or another. In

all these answers on government help, they do not distinguish between the Federal and Insular Governments. They have no idea which government supplies which part of the benefits, whether it be Social Security, roads, or health centers.

Forty-seven people said the government listens to their requests and gives them fair treatment, and 11 said the government acts independently and their opinions are not considered. A more detailed and precise analysis of these data would be of the greatest interest. To look for correlations between age, education, and socio-economic status in these replies and to examine and compare the ten communities of this study might disclose patterns related to the character of the several communities through a cross-analysis of the variables indicated above. Unfortunately, this is at present outside the scope of this study.

The information on religion has implications that go beyond the data. Further investigation might well relate the factual material to changing attitudes, especially the material from the depth interview, given below.

Of our respondents, 79.2 per cent were Catholic, .8 per cent reported no religion, and .4 per cent gave no information. Between these extremes lie the Protestant denominations--Baptist, Evangelical, Defenders of the Faith, Disciples of Christ, Pentacostal, Jehovah's Witnesses, Methodist, Presbyterian and others--a total of 19.6 per cent.

Spiritualism was considered separately and in some detail. Of the sample, 30.2 per cent were interested and had attended meetings, 16 per cent were not interested, which usually carried with the lack of interest a definite disapproval. No comparison with 1932 is possible except based on experience and, from the memory of this, one could reasonably say that this was an increase.

Interest in spiritualism has increased at all levels since 1932--from gross forms of superstition to intellectual investigation of extrasensory perception. No examples of the latter can be identified in our sample. Statistics referring to the 30.2 per cent who were in varying degrees interested cannot be relied upon because of attitudes of the community toward spiritualism which probably affect replies. Whether those who are interested but did not attend meetings, those who go to meetings, and are interested, who do not say whether they are interested--whether all the degrees of interest express reliable information is very doubtful. The connection with "cures" should be further examined, as well as the connection with religion and the point at which these come together and mutually affect psychological dependence. The interest in this subject and its relationship to spiritual and physical needs make it a subject worthy of further study.

It is our impression that interest in all forms of religion is greater than in the past. The whole subject warrants further study, both qualitative and quantitative. What meets the eye, even in communities distant from urban centers, is the increase in number of churches and chapels and renovation of old churches in the plazas. The depth interview gives the following information: 46.5 per cent believe that people are more religious; 49.2 per cent find that they are less religious--that there is less faith, that people go to church "to socialize"; and 9 per cent link this lack of religion to delinquency and crime. In answer to questions on belief in the power of prayer, masses, novenas, God's power, 38 per cent felt these were greater now; 61.2 per cent less; yet when asked questions on the value of religion, 98.9 per cent expressed a positive opinion. This may be a conventional response but they included a variety of reasons, spiritual, love of God, character formation, social control, and justice.

Notes to Chapter 9

1. David Landy, _Tropical Childhood_ (Chapel Hill: University of North Carolina Press, 1959), p. 54.

2. Lerner, _op. cit._, p. 51.

CHAPTER 10 CONCLUSION

In this study our hypothesis is that planned
change is good: it has brought about a desirable
development. The test lies in a comparison of the
past with the attainments at a given point which is
on the path toward stated goals. We believe that to
make a conscious connection between human needs and
a responsible government is better than to leave the
process of change to undirected forces; that man's
intelligence must itself be the initiating and ac-
tivating factor in the evolutionary process of our
day. We find that where poverty has been the most
important element in a traditional society, material
changes must come first and that decision on priorities in the development of new resources is the
greatest challenge to intelligence. In this process
material satisfactions may be transmuted into new
attitudes. To have one's children live and eat and
grow is the natural desire of parents. To find opportunity and freedom in work brings its own contentment. To have access to knowledge is an incentive
to individual growth and development. Along such
lines our data clearly indicate progress.

When Operation Bootstrap became a strong political and social movement, the decision of the planners
on what programs were both most immediately useful
and also seminal was of crucial importance. The encouragement and growth of industry was considered
essential to any improvement in employment and wages:
the amount of arable land had not for many years been
enough to support the population, much less a rapidly
increasing population; emigration could be a pallia-
tive but not a cure for economic ills; the movement
from country to city was in most cases an indication
of the frustration of life in the country. The conditions necessary for industrial development must

come first, supplemented by relief for immediate
human needs. The degree to which Puerto Rican development is an outcome of planning accentuates the
need to face and to offset its possible adverse effects if the democratic process is accepted--as we
believe it is--as the essential element in the
growth of freedom and individual responsibility.

> Planning, then, is, like any other at-
> tempt to control community life, a kind
> of conflict. . . . We are asked whether
> or not freedom is possible under plan-
> ning. . . . Planning, like all other
> forms of conflict, bears the ever-present
> threat of coercion.[1]

We find few cases which give evidence of clear
definition of conflict, but this cannot be construed
as meaning that no conflict exists. In a study of
an American community, Vidich and Bensman found that

> Instead of facing the issues, they make
> compromises and modify their behavior in
> some cases and reaffirm their traditional
> patterns in other cases. They do this,
> however, without any overt conscious
> recognition of the basic problems.[2]

More sophisticated societies than those represented in our sample show great fear of the effect
of planning on individual freedom, especially, as in
the continental United States, where the history of
local autonomous action and individual freedom of expression is strong. As we have already noted, conflict for Puerto Ricans has, since the beginning of
the American regime, existed because of the difficulty of bringing the two cultures into a satisfactory adjustment.

Superimposed on this difficult acculturation,
planning adds to the complexity of the problem. The
rural communities--less subject to American influences than urban areas--may be fortunate, in an estimate of the degree of conflict, because their
adjustment has not yet felt the full force of the

double problem--it is still, primarily, for the
rural population, adjustment between traditional
and modern values and ways of living. That the influence of the United States has been the most important single factor in the rapid movement from
traditional to modern is not generally recognized in
rural communities, but it is present and adds its
complications to the transition itself.

The Brookings Institution report points out
that aspects of American culture influence local
political units.[3] Historically in the political
life of the community they have been forced to combine two concepts of local government: the English,
continued in the United States, of "wide dispersion
authority," with the centralized administration developed in Europe from the Roman Empire.

How much the dispersed form is essential to
democratic government is a subject for the political
scientists, but we can at least note the difficulties which Puerto Rico still faces in making an
adjustment between two such different concepts and
in finding a practical resolution. At present one
can see that the two views still exist, especially
in rural areas where the psychological effects of
the centralized administration of the past still are
strong. Citizens whose life has been in the small
rural communities tend to transfer the historical
dependence on the landowner or the mayor to whatever
image they have of present governmental authority.

The attitudes we find are clear and cogent illustrations of the gap which exists between Operation
Bootstrap and Operation Serenidad, to enjoy the convenience of running water, to have health and vitality, to see the possibility of better jobs, to have
a road to the nearest town--all these for most
people are easy to accept. To understand that these
very things bring with them problems of modern life,
the discovery that values of the past are often in-
applicable to the present, is a painful difficulty
for adults, a problem for the social psychologist as
well as the sociologist and anthropologist. For the
young people who face the situation of the present

without the perspective which memory of the past
brings may seem a more simple matter, but it is in
fact more complex. The past is theirs too, in history, tradition, and in their relationship to their
parents; they must live in the present and for the
future; because they cannot go back, even in memory,
they must somehow deal with things as they are; they
must assimilate the meaning of the past from which
the present comes.

Democracy by its own nature cannot be coerced.
What can be done is to provide machinery, techniques,
and organization which are both practical and consistent with the principles and purposes which they are
designed to implement. One part of the educational
process must be to interpret their application to
situations and problems which the citizen faces. On
education--and here we use education in its broadest
sense--lies the burden of interpretation, the painful responsibility of bringing to all Puerto Ricans
an understanding of the problems they face and, if
Operation Serenidad is to become a reality, the conscious facing of those problems. Conflict must be
brought into the open and must move toward some new
consensus.

We are very conscious of the possibility that
adaptation to the new forms in a rapidly changing
society could mean impoverishment rather than enrichment of the culture. Something is always lost in
the process of social change--some charming custom,
some spontaneous expression of human warmth may be
gone. On the other hand, some of the self-protecting
hostilities may also disappear. If Operation Bootstrap cannot become Operation Serenidad, the increased freedom of the human spirit will not be guaranteed. But if there can be a synthesis of material
benefits and psychic satisfaction of the effects due
to external causes with a new, or altered, view of
life's meaning, a value system can be created which
will embody the past while directing itself to the
future. New symbols must be found for this synthesis.

Earlier in this study, we mentioned the ambulance as such a symbol. That the ambulance is a

technical improvement over the hamaca (hammock) of
thirty years ago is not merely an argument for technological improvement. The hamaca was the best
means at that time for attaining the necessary end--
help for the sick. The emotional reaction to suffering, the frustration involved in distance from doctor or hospital, were the reactions associated with
the physical symbol. The ambulance today is surrounded by the same emotional aura but with the added
connotation of increased comfort and hope. The con-
notative meaning is thus expanded to include these
emotions.

We believe that new symbols of this kind will
be created through man's ability to adapt himself to
the demands of his environment. Interpretation
through a sense of history, through demonstration of
meaning, can give a broader horizon--a new world view.
Such interpretation must include the aesthetic and
the spiritual--the connection of the artifact of the
past with its mechanical counterpart in the present;
the work of art--whether from the past or modern--
which is "a significant form" for life today. It
cannot be reproduction or imitation. It must embody
meaning which stimulates the creativity which lies
in man's nature and which must not be stultified by
static reference.

This could be the new planning for Puerto Rico.
It must include greater knowledge of the world outside the immediate community, of Puerto Rico's place
in the world--including its political status, of the
relation of means to ends in the development of agriculture and rural life, of industry, of communication, employment, health and recreation, and, most
of all, of education. It must be the new search for
meaning in the contemporary world as it has always
been man's highest search in the past.

We believe that this project has value in bringing to developing countries the help which will enable them to take their places among the more developed democratic societies. We assume that this means,
first, the knowledge and understanding of other cultures and, second, the use of this knowledge and

understanding in adapting modern techniques and economics to the needs of these societies. This is a
creative process involving the transformation of old
values and the identification of meaning in new
forms. Through the growth of new knowledge and experience the vision of freedom and democracy will be
enlarged by the creation of new roles for individuals.

This project has a real, though limited, application to this program. Its findings cannot be applied in toto to other societies; it can only show
what planned change has done and has not done in
Puerto Rico. It can show what has happened during a
thirty-year period in ten rural communities--the
slow beginning and the more recent acceleration
through governmental planning. It must be left to
experts on other societies to discover what information and evidence is applicable to other situations,
many of which may manifest characteristics of our
ten communities thirty years ago.

We are conscious of the fact that Puerto Rico
is in many respects unique, that there has already
been an intercultural adjustment bringing both positive and negative results. But this can be regarded
as a living sample of what happens, in different
forms, when any two cultures are brought into juxta-
position--an illustration of a world-wide condition
which has been, in many cases, precipitated by various forms of foreign aid. Puerto Rico's unique political relationship to the United States--past,
present and future--can be regarded as one example
of the universal effect of political status on economic and cultural patterns which can, in no case,
be ignored. Research and the intellectual curiosity
which stimulates it can look for the adaptations
which will make one experiment, which we find largely successful and important, useful, in concrete
forms, to other situations.

One of the specific questions that has been
brought up during the course of this study is whether
government programs in Puerto Rico can be compared to
or used as an example in other countries because of
the large contributions of the United States Govern-

ment to Puerto Rican programs. The chart shows that, while the United States contribution has been large, the Puerto Rican Government, except for surplus food commodities, has more than matched the United States Government contributions. Military aid to the Latin-American countries probably offsets to a considerable degree United States expenditures for military purposes in Puerto Rico which, of course, are not solely for the protection of Puerto Rico.

The money provided by the United States has certainly been vital to the whole Puerto Rican program. The amount provided in 1932 was negligible compared to today, and it was only after Puerto Rico revised its tax structure and in other ways established itself as a stable financial entity that the Federal Government began to appropriate matching funds to further the reforms and new undertakings of the Puerto Rican Government. Our study shows that a relatively small amount of money per capita--about $33, the present contribution of the Federal Government--can go a long way in improving the economy of a country and the health and happiness of a people when its use is properly planned and properly applied. The Puerto Rican Government budgeted for the 1963-64 fiscal year $449,319,000, or about $180 per capita. This evidences the real facts of Operation Bootstrap and that Puerto Rico is not sitting idly by waiting for handouts.   (We are not in a position in this study to compare these figures with Federal grants to states.)

Essential to this program was the type of leadership in the Puerto Rican Government which could guarantee this stability. This high quality of leadership undoubtedly exists in other countries and, if discovered, could be entrusted to use funds to the best advantage of the country.

Following are some specific government programs which, if interpreted properly and adapted to special conditions in various countries, could be of significant help in furthering the plans of AID and at relatively low over-all cost. They are more fully described in the text of the study.

This interpretation and adaptation might best be done by sending qualified people to Puerto Rico for short periods of observation and study to give them firsthand experience from which to plan and operate their own programs. This could apply both to members of the various AID missions and also to officials of the countries concerned. This would have a somewhat different emphasis from the Point Four Program.

Puerto Rico's use of rum taxes, as described in the section on Puerto Rico Industrial Development Corporation, to establish industrial development, with intelligent planning, demonstrates an objective and realistic point of view toward the correction of the ills of the economy.

When the Puerto Rican Government first "went into business" it was accused of being socialistic and in unfair competition with private industry, but it had to do this in order to demonstrate to private industry that investment in Puerto Rico could be profitable. It stopped as soon as it could--as soon as private industry was convinced--and since then has been stimulating, with tax exemptions, incentive payments, and paying for in-service training, the interest of private firms in establishing branches in Puerto Rico. This development has been going on at a rate commensurate with the ability of the Puerto Rican people to make good use of the new capital, and, with a few exceptions, has been an unqualified success. In a country with more raw materials, basic rather than assembly-type industries could be established, thus giving more work to men. One unfortunate aspect of the Puerto Rican situation is the overbalance of work for women.

The parcela program is one which has been a great step forward in the Puerto Rican scene. It has brought people together in attractive communities, given them good houses to live in, with convenient utilities and services, recreation areas, nearby churches and stores, and has done a great deal to raise their morale and attitude toward life. It has also brought them nearer to their work, to schools

for the children, and to community activities. They
own something themselves and enjoy an economic
freedom unknown to them before. This is a self-
liquidating program at a remarkably low cost to the
government. Whether unique or not, an important factor is the policy of mutual aid in building the
houses. It not only reduces the cost, and the resulting indebtedness, but it brings people together
in a common effort.

The cooperative movement is another self-liquidating government program which has brought great
economic benefits to thousands of people. It is
growing steadily, having proved its worth, and already encompasses a large section of the population.
These programs free the people from the domination
of the big landowners and middlemen, and give them
an economic security they have never had before.

The whole story of the Second Unit Schools has
significance. The idea of the 1930's was new--an
experiment in educational functioning as the chief
factor in change in rural communities. Recent programs show a revival not only of interest but of
creative planning related to new conditions. The
itinerant teachers (principals program) has much to
commend it as an instrument for bringing rural
schools into contact with educational thinking and
its application. Other developments in the "new"
Second Units, described in the chapter "The Second
Unit Schools of Puerto Rico," are focused on the
present situation and offer practical suggestions
for a realistic use of a limited budget to almost
limitless needs.

We still find in the early training of social
workers for work in Second Unit Schools, partially
described in the Introduction, a method and a spirit
which could be adopted or adapted for use in other
places. It engendered a spirit of devotion to a community combined with a sound application of principles of work with groups and individuals which led
to the development, through testing, of a practical
program. Through imagination, meager resources were
expanded, new forces found within the community it-

self and a contribution made to the concept of the
school as a center in isolated communities.

We believe the programs of Community Education
and Isolated Communities are unique and could form a
frame of reference for activities of a similar nature
in other lands. They have fully demonstrated their
value and have highly qualified personnel who could
teach visitors the modus operandi of the programs
and discuss with them their virtues and faults.

Notes to Chapter 10

1. Jessie Bernard, American Community Behavior
(New York: The Dryden Press, 1949), p. 617.

2. Arthur J. Vidich and Joseph Bensman, Small
Town in Mass Society (Princeton: Princeton University
Press, 1958), p. 314.

3. Victor A. Clark and Associates, op. cit.,
p. 114.

APPENDIXES

APPENDIX A

STATISTICAL APPENDIX

TABLE 34

Income by Age

	Less than $25	$25-49	$50-99	$100-149	$150-199	$200-249	$250-299	$300-349	$350 and Up	None	No Info.
Less than 20				1							
20-29		2	6	9	1	2	1			6	2
30-39	1	3	4	8	7	7	1		1	14	2
40-49	1	4	9	10	3	5		1	1	15	3
50-59	4	3	4	4	1	3		1	3	24	2
60-69	2	4	3	5	1					28	
70 or more	1	1		1	1					16	
No info.		1				1					
	9	18	26	38	14	18	2	2	5	103	9

Income is for October, November, December, 1963

TABLE 35

Education by Income

Income*	1-2 Grade	3-4 Grade	5-6 Grade	7-8 Grade	9-11 Grade	4th Yr. H.S.	1-3 Coll.	B.A. or More	None	No Info.	Totals
Less than $25	3	1			1				4		9
25-49	2	7	3						6		18
50-99	7	8	3	2	2	2	1		1		26
100-149	3	7	8	10	7	2			1		38
150-199	3	3	2	1	3				2		14
200-249	1	4	3	4	4	1				1	18
250-299				1	1						2
300-349			1				1				2
350 up			1		1		1	2			5
None	7	23	13	15	3	6	1		30	5	103
Unknown	1	1	2	2	1					2	9
	27	54	36	35	23	11	4	2	44	8	244

*Income average for October, November, December, 1963.
Directors felt that respondents would not give accurate figures for a longer period. This is a period
when there is no sugar cane cutting, no coffee crop,
and in other crops a slack period.

TABLE 36

Age - Education

No.	Age Group	Grade Completed								
		1-2	3-4	5-6	7-8	9-11	4 Yrs. H.S.	1-3 Yr. College	Bachelor or Over	No Education
1	Under 20		1							
29	20-29	2	6	3	7	6	5			
48	30-39	5	12	9	11	6	2		1	1
52	40-49	6	11	13	5	8	2	2	1	2
49	50-59	8	14	5	8	1	2	2		8
43	60-69	2	9	6	4	2				16
20	70 and over	3								17
2	Undet.									
244	Total	27	54	36	35	23	11	4	2	44

TABLE 37

Highest Income Group in Each Community; Highest
Percentage in Given Income Group

Community	Income 200-350+ No.	Percentage	Distribution of Income by Families		
Loiza	5	15.0	8(0-49)	10(50-99)	11(100-350+)
Juncos	2	11.8	5(0-49)	6(50-150)	4(150-350+)
Cidra	8	47.2	5(0-99)	4(100-200)	8(210-350+)
Bayamón	28	42.8	18(0-99)	28(100-250)	20(250-350+)
Salinas	7	22.1	8(0-49)	17(100-200)	7(200-350+)
Juana Diaz	2	12.0	6(0-99)	6(100-150)	5(200-350+)
Adjuntas	5	29.3	8(0-99)	5(100-250)	4(250-350+)
Moca	7	39.1	6(0-99)	8(100-250)	4(250-350+)
Aguadilla	2	13.4	4(0-49)	9(50-150)	2(250-350+)
Arecibo	3	20.2	6(0-99)	6(100-200)	3(200-350+)

TABLE 38

Percentages Out of Labor Force or Unemployed, 1963

Community	Out of Labor Force	Unemployed	Total
Loiza	12.7	25.0	37.7
Juncos	5.9	17.6	23.5
Cidra	6.0	11.7	17.7
Bayamón	15.9	6.1	22.0
Salinas	16.0	12.4	28.4
Juana Diaz	6.2	17.6	23.8
Adjuntas	6.1	17.6	23.7
Moca	11.0	11.1	22.1
Aguadilla	13.3	33.3	46.6
Arecibo	26.7		26.7

TABLE 39

Matriculation in Ten Second Unit Schools, 1963-64*

School District	Number of Second Units	I	II	III	IV	V	VI	VII	VIII	IX	Total
Loiza	Mediania Alta	160	161	224	119	146	168	127	116	114	1,335
Juncos	El Mangó	60	79	69	65	113	85	106	106	84	767
Cidra	Bayamón	63	43	71	74	64	61	47	43	36	502
Salinas	Lapa	73	39	36	36	53	41	210	163	108	759
Juana Diaz	Collores	29	27	54	38	34	60	61	60	44	407
Adjuntas	Yahuecas	45	30	39	31	77	47	58	54	40	421
Moca	Voladoras	40	31	34	58	59	61	67	45	50	445
Aguadilla	San Antonio	134	115	127	147	107	111	130	108	86	1,065
Arecibo	Sabana Hoyos	49	46	69	77	130	123	129	62	71	756
Bayamón	Hato Tejas	182	211	189	254	228	185	251	347	157	2,004

*Commonwealth of Puerto Rico Department of Education

APPENDIX B

INSTRUCTIONS FOR SOCIAL WORKERS

GENERAL INFORMATION ON THE STUDY OF
"STANDARDS OF LIVING IN THE RURAL
ZONE OF PUERTO RICO"
(1933, Dorothy D. Bourne, Supervisor
of Social Work, Department of Education)

The purpose of this study is to give us information as to the way in which the country people, at
different levels, live.

From the standpoint of Social Work this is very
much needed in developing a program suitable to the
needs. For example, if we can correlate a definite
income with certain occupations, housing conditions,
health, etc., we can see better how, within that income, conditions may be improved by education; how
resources of the Government can supplement income
(Department of Agriculture, Department of Health,
etc.); how the better use of time can add to the
health and well-being of the family. As we all
realize, until economic conditions change, we must
look to improving the standard of living under
existing conditions.

This same material is to be used by the committee on Revision of the Rural Home Economics Curriculum. This will insure, as far as Home Economics in
Second Units is concerned, a common background of
knowledge of the living conditions in various typical communities. The curriculum will aim constantly
to see these conditions as they exist and to offer
in the classroom and laboratory practical methods of
attacking the actual problems in our rural communities.

The joint purpose of this study will therefore
insure the harmonious working of the Home Economics
curriculum and the Social Work program. The curriculum will then be based on actual home conditions and
the Social Work program will extend and interpret
the teachings and standards of the school in terms
of community and adult life.

345

The information on foods is a simple qualitative study which will be put at the disposal of the School of Tropical Medicine. The findings of this study will also be used in determining objectives in Home Economics relative to food and diet in rural communities and by Social Workers in the extension of these objectives to the community.

Factors considered in selection of localities:

1 - Representative crop regions: sugar, tobacco, coffee, fruit, minor crops.

2 - Different geographical regions: mountain, coastal plain, irrigated sections, etc.

3 - Different systems of land ownership: large company, small company, large individual, small individual.

4 - Local industries.

Localities selected:

1 - Adjuntas (Yahuecas)
2 - Aguadilla (San Antonio)
3 - Arecibo (Sabana Hoyos)
4 - Bayamón (Hato Tejas)
5 - Cidra (Bayamón)
6 - Juana Diaz (Collores)
7 - Juncos (Mangó)
8 - Loiza (Medianía Alta)
9 - Moca (Voladores)
10 - Salinas (Lapa)

Selection of families:

1 - Number for study: 15 in each selected region.

2 - Distribution: 3 income levels, based on observed standards of living. No more than one family of exceptionally high level and one of exceptionally low level should be included.

After you have selected the 15 families
you will have 5 families from each of the 3
levels, namely:

5 families from level No. I, High
5 families from level No. II, Medium
5 families from level No. III, Low

3 - Method of selection:

    a - From 50 families of Social Workers
        Survey, 1930-31, in localities where
        these surveys are available. (Some
        of these cards were destroyed by the
        hurricane; in a few communities where
        Social Work was begun last year this
        survey was not required.)

    b - Families with whom Social Worker is
        in intimate contact, wherever possible
        covering a period of two or three
        years.

    c - Families who will cooperate with So-
        cial Worker and Home Economics teacher
        in securing reliable information; that
        is, families who will be interested
        and intelligent.

    d - Families in which wage-earner works
        in the community as well as residing
        there.

4 - Out of the 15 families selected, one from
    each income level (high, medium or low)
    should be chosen for the special studies
    to be made by the Home Economics teacher
    for Inventory of Household Equipment Form
    E); Kinds of Foods (Form F); and House-
    hold Accounts (Form G).

DIRECTIONS TO SOCIAL WORKERS

You will see from this that your community is one of those selected for this study. Will you please go over all the material carefully before beginning the work. The value of the study will depend very largely on your selection of the fifteen families.

You will have to use judgment in the use of the survey cards. Wherever possible use them, but it would be advisable after you select your families, to go over the cards for that family and make a list of the information which you will have to get new; that is, you may find that family conditions, or wages or housing, recorded in 1929-30, have changed. If you have the items listed you can correct them when you visit the family.

You will see that the information on foods, on household furnishings and the keeping of household accounts is new. The Home Economics teacher will take charge of this, but will work with only three families, one from each income level. These three families must be among the fifteen chosen for the whole study. The same three families will be used for (1) Inventory of household equipment, Form E; (2) Kinds of food eaten by country people of Puerto Rico, Form F; (3) Household accounts. The three families selected for these three special purposes should be marked with a star wherever they appear on the other forms of the study.

As you will see, after reading over all the material, you and the Home Economics teacher will need to hold frequent consultations and to work closely together on the study as a whole.

INSTRUCTIONS FOR FILLING FORMS S. L.

1 - Most of the information requested in these forms can be acquired from the Survey Cards filled by you for the study of the 50 families in relation to Social Work.

2 - There are few new items inserted for which new information must be acquired. In all cases the information must be brought up-to-date.

3 - Give each family selected for this study a number and keep it throughout all blanks. It should be the same number appearing in the Social Work Survey and Family Face Card.

A - General

1 - Columns 7 and 8 refer to whether the burden of supporting the whole family rests on the man or the woman. Check which.

2 - Column 8: Use the key words on the Family Face Card.

3 - Columns 9, 10 and 11: Just check the source if any relief has been obtained by the family.

4 - Columns 12 and 13: Check which.

5 - Column 14: Give the time in number or fractions of days per week devoted by the head of family to community activities.

6 - Columns 15 and 16: Check if either belongs to any community organization.

7 - Columns 17 and 18: Give the amount of leisure time in terms of days and parts of days per week.

B. Housing Conditions

1 - Columns 1 and 2 should be identical to columns 1 and 2 in Part A.

2 - Column 3: Give size of house in feet thus: 10' x 15'. The width should be the 1st number.

3 - Columns 5, 6, 7, 8 and 9: This information is new. Just give the number of rooms of each denomination.

4 - Columns 10, 11 and 12: Just check which.

5 - Columns 13, 14 and 15: Check the right
column. Columns 14 and 15 call for new information.
Column 13 should include uncovered barrels and other
containers.

C - Economic

The purpose of this information is to find out
what is the total income received by the family and
how they distribute it.

1 - Column 3: Give the weekly amount (money
only) received as wages or salary. In case the head
of family is not a wage earner but a business man or
farmer give his weekly income (average or estimate)
in Column 5 and indicate the fact in Column 19.

2 - Column 4: Give an estimate of the value of
food raised and consumed at home during each week.
The amount in this column represents an income which
is used at home, which, if not raised at home, probably would have been bought somewhere else.

3 - Column 5: Enter here any other income; for
example, value of food raised and sold. Most of the
farmer's income should go in this column.
All income should be reported in terms of
money. The total sum of columns 3 and 5 will give
all moneys available for expenditure.

4 - Columns 6, 7, 8, 9, 10 and 11: Insert in
these columns the proportional part of the weekly income spent for each of the items mentioned.

Food should include all moneys spent for
things which are to be eaten.
Rent should include taxes and any money
paid for the use of property.
Health should include money spent on medicine, doctor's visits, etc.
Clothing should include all expenditures
for personal use such as dresses, shoes, hats, etc.

Miscellaneous includes any other expenses
which cannot be classified among the previous ones.
This should include charity, gifts, etc.

Operating Expenses should include such expenditures as household equipment, light, cleaning
material, etc.

Expenses for transportation should be classified with the item on which the major expense involving transportation falls. Example: Expense for
transportation for the purpose of getting the physi-
cian should be included with Health expenses.

All the information on income and expenses
should be carefully checked and care should be taken
to get as accurate information as possible.

5 - Columns 13, 14, 15, 16 and 17: Fill with
the estimate acquired. If possible consult local
Internal Revenue Office.

6 - Column 18: If the family lives on a farm
for which they pay rent, give the total number of
cuerdas.

D - Health

1 - Columns 3, 4, 5 and 6: Give the number of
persons treated so far for the different diseases.
This information must be brought up-to-date.

2 - Columns 7, 8, 9 and 10: This represents a
new information. Check the source from which they
get water for drinking purposes.

E - Inventory of Household Equipment

This is a new thing. It will be filled by the
Home Economics teacher. One page must be filled for
each family. There shall be 3 such pages, one for
each of the 3 selected families from each level
within the 15. The case number and level should
correspond to that of the rest of the information
for the same family.

1 - Columns 1, 4 and 7: Give the name of the article. Example: Chair, etc.

2 - Columns 2, 5 and 8: Give the kind of article, thus: Wooden, if the article was a chair.

3 - Columns 3, 6 and 9: Give the number of articles of the same class found in the house.

4 - Column 10: Add any other article not mentioned or give any special explanation of information filled.

F - Kinds of Food Eaten by Country People in Puerto Rico

This is new information. It will be filled by the Home Economics teacher. One sheet must be filled for each of the 3 selected families for each day. The information should be gotten for seven days (representing all days of the week; that is, Monday, Tuesday, etc.). The seven days need not necessarily be consecutive.

1 - Column 1: Give the approximate time at which the meal is taken.

2 - Column 2: Give the name of the meal; that is, desayuno, almuerzo, parva, etc.

3 - Column 3: Give the list of dishes served; that is, arroz blanco, habichuelas coloradas, pan y guineo, etc.

4 - Column 4: Name every kind of food used in cooking each dish including small amounts of food used to flavor it, such as calabaza, pimiento, achiote, tomate, etc.

G - Family Account

1 - There are 3 sheets of this kind in the study. One for each of the 3 families chosen from the three different income levels. These three families must be among the 15 chosen for the complete study, and

they must be the same three families as used for the information on Forms E and F.

2 - These sheets will be filled by the Home Economics teachers.

3 - Detailed daily accounts of family income and expenditures will be kept by the Home Economics teacher in order to have complete first hand data to enter weekly on this sheet. This means that she will actually keep the accounts for the three families for a period of 8 weeks or two months, from March 4th to May 5th.

4 - The daily accounts with the weekly totals will be forwarded to the Department attached to the corresponding sheet, not later than May 10, 1933.

5 - Identify each account sheet used with the corresponding Case Number and Level.

6 - Keep a sheet for each one of the expenditures as listed below:

> a - Food: Includes groceries, dairy and garden products, meat, fish, etc. purchased.
>
> b - Rent: Includes payment for use of house, land, etc. Taxes, interest on mortgage, insurance, major repairs.
>
> c - Health: Includes medicines, doctors, transportation to clinics, hospital, etc.
>
> d - Clothing: Includes dresses, underwear, shoes, suits, household linens, etc.
>
> e - Recreation: Includes fiestas, rosarios, velorios, dances, movies, etc.
>
> f - Operating expenses include lighting, fuel, soap, household furniture, equipment, repairs, etc.

g - Miscellaneous: Includes charity, gifts, education, periodicals, books, etc.

Use notebook paper ruled as follows:

Case Number_____   FOOD   Level_____

		Expenditures	
Date	Article	Cash	Credit
April 1	20 lbs. rice at 2 1/2¢	$ .50	
1	9 lbs. beans assorted at 4¢	.36	
1	1 lb. ham at 8¢	.08	
2	1/2 lb. coffee		$ .17
2	2 lbs. lard at 7¢		.14
7	1 lb. brown sugar		.05
	TOTAL	$ .94	$ .36

Enter data daily on corresponding sheet (food, clothing, rent, etc.). Find weekly total of each sheet.

7 - Make a weekly summary of all expenditures:

Case No. _____   EXPENDITURES   Level _____

		Expenditures	
Date	Summary	Cash	Credit
April 1-7	Food	$ .95	$ .25
	Rent	--	--
	Health	.50	--
	Clothing	--	.40
	Recreation	.10	--
	Operating Expenses	--	.25
	Miscellaneous	--	.25
	TOTAL	$ 1.55	$ 1.15

8 - Keep an income sheet. Enter daily all cash
received with date, source and amount. Find the
weekly totals.

Case No. _____   INCOME SHEET   Level _____

Date	Source	Salary Wages	Value of other inc.
April 1	Wage	$ .40	$
2	1 qt. milk sold		.06
3	2 eggs sold		.04
4	10 lbs. batatas sold		.20
5	money borrowed		.25
6	Wage (1/2 day)	.20	
7	Wage	.40	
	TOTAL	$1.00	$ .55

9 - Keep a sheet on the Estimate Value of Food
Raised and Consumed by Family. Enter data daily.
Find weekly totals.

Case No. _____   ESTIMATE VALUE OF FOOD   Level_____
                       RAISED AND CONSUMED
                          BY FAMILY

Date	Kind of Food	Estimated Value
April 1	3 eggs	$ .06
2	2 qts. milk	.12
3	10 lbs. batatas	.20
4	5 lbs. yautia	.10
7	1 mano guineos	.04
	TOTAL	$ .52

10 - After having the weekly totals of the
items of Sheet G, Family Accounts, you are ready to
fill it. No guesses or estimates will be considered.
Only the data from daily accounts and weekly totals
should appear on this sheet.

STANDARD OF LIVING

G – FAMILY ACCOUNTS

Case No. _____   Level _____

Week	Income			Amount of Money Income Spent							
	Sal. or Wage	Value Food Raised	Value Other Inc.	Food	Rent	Health	Cloth- ing	Recre- ation	Op. Exp.	Mis.	Credit
1	2	3	4	5	6	7	8	9	10	11	12
Apr. 1-7	$1.	$.52	$.55	$1.20	--	$.50	$.40	$.10	$.25	$.25	$1.15

Check: It should be noticed that the sum of Column 2, 4 and 12 equals the sum of columns 5, 6, 7, 8, 9, 10 and 11.

Column 3 is a separate item by itself.

STUDY OF THE STANDARD OF LIVING OF COUNTRY PEOPLE
IN PUERTO RICO

Second Unit of _____

A – General

Level (1)	Case No. (2)	Agregado Medianero etc. (3)	Occup. of Head of Fam. (4)	No. in Fam. (5)	Support of Fam. M (6)	Support of Fam. W (7)	Civil Status of Fam. (8)	Relief if Obtained — Municipal (9)	Relief if Obtained — Red Cross (10)	Relief if Obtained — Local (11)	Attend. at Church — Regular (12)	Attend. at Church — Occasional (13)	Time Devoted to Community Activities (14)	Member of Any Community Organization M (15)	Member of Any Community Organization W (16)	Amount of Leisure Time M (17)	Amount of Leisure Time W (18)
High																	
Summary																	
Med.																	
Summary																	
Low																	
Summary																	

STANDARD OF LIVING

B - Housing Conditions

Level 1	Case No. 2	House		Number of Rooms in House						Latrine			Surroundings			Remarks 16
		Size of House 3	Material 4	Bedrooms 5	Salas 6	Bathrooms 7	Dining Room 8	Kitchen 9	App. by Dept. of Health 10	Other Type 11	None 12	Breeding Places for Mosquitos 13	Flower Garden 14	Vegetable Garden 15	
High															
Sum-mary															
Med.															
Sum-mary															
Low															
Sum-mary															

STANDARD OF LIVING

C – Economic

Level [1]	Case No. [2]	Income			Amount of Income Money Spent							Value of Property Owned						Remarks
		Weekly Income Wages [3]	Value of Food Raised for Home Consum. [4]	Value Other Income [5]	Food [6]	Rent [7]	Health [8]	Clothing [9]	Recreation [10]	Op. Exp. [11]	Misc. [12]	Houses [13]	Land [14]	Stock in Store [15]	Livestock [16]	Other [17]	Amt. Land Rented [18]	
High																		
Sum-mary																		
Med.																		
Sum-mary																		
Low																		
Sum-mary																		

STANDARD OF LIVING

D – Health

1 Level	2 Case No.	Number of Persons Treated For:				Sources of Drinking Water				11 Remarks
		3 Hookworm	4 Malaria	5 Tuberculosis	6 Other Diseases	7 Cistern	8 Aqueduct of Artesian Well	9 Other Form Rain Water	10 Brook or River, etc.	
High										
Summary										
Med.										
Summary										
Low										
Summary										

STANDARD OF LIVING

G – Family Accounts

Case Number_____   Level_____

	Income			Amount of Money Income Spent								
Week 1	Salary or Wage 2	Value of Food Raised 3	Value of Other Income 4	Food 5	Rent 6	Health 7	Clothing 8	Recreation 9	Operating Expenses 10	Misc. 11	Credit 12
Mar. 4–10											
Mar. 11–17											
Mar. 18–24											
Monthly Totals											
Apr. 1–7											
Apr. 8–14											
Apr. 22–28											
Apr. 29 to May 5											
Monthly Totals											

_____
(Food, Rent, etc.)

Case No._____   Level_____

Date	Article	Expenditures	
		Cash	Credit
		$	$

Estimate Value of Food

Raised and Consumed by Family

Case No._____   Level_____

Date	Kind of Food	Estimated Value
		$

Income Sheet

Case Number_____   Level_____

Date	Source	Salary Wages	Value of Other Income
		$	$

Expenditures

Case Number_____   Level_____

Date	Weekly Summary	Expenditures	
		Cash	Credit
		$	$

APPENDIX C

AVERAGE CONSUMER PRICE INDEX--ALL ITEMS

Base A (1947-49 average taken as 100) $1.23 in 1957-59
Base B (1957-59 average taken as 100) $ .814 in 1947-49
Base C (1932 average taken as 100) $2.10 in 1957-59

Interpretations:	Year	1947-49 Base A	1957-59 Base B	1932 Base C
	1963	$1.181	$1.062	$2.23
$1 in 1932	1962		$1.054	$2.21
could buy	1961		$1.042	
food for:	1960	$1.26	$1.031	
$2.23 in 1963	1959	$1.246	$1.015	
$2.21 in 1962	1958	$1.235	$1.007	
$2.06 in 1957	1957	$1.202	$ .980	$2.06
$1.76 in 1950	1956	$1.162	$ .947	
$1.00 in 1932	1955	$1.145	$ .930	
$1.28 in 1925	1954	$1.148	$ .936	
$ .74 in 1915	1953	$1.144	$ .932	
	1952	$1.135	$ .925	
	1951	$1.110	$ .905	
	1950	$1.028	$ .838	$1.76
	1949	$1.018	$ .830	
	1948	$1.028	$ .838	
	1947	$ .955	$ .778	
	1946	$ .834	$ .680	
	1945	$ .769	$ .627	
	1944	$ .754	$ .613	
	1943		$ .603	
	1942		$ .568	
	1941		$ .513	
	1940	$ .539	$ .488	
	1939		$ .484	
	1938		$ .491	
	1937		$ .500	
	1936		$ .483	
	1935	$ .537	$ .478	
	1934		$ .466	
	1933		$ .451	
	1932	$ .584	$ .476	$1.00
	1931	$ .650	$ .530	
	1930	$ .714	$ .582	
	1925	$ .750	$ .611	$1.28
	1920	$ .857	$ .698	
	1915	$ .434	$ .354	$ .74

Source: Bureau of Labor Statistics, U.S. Department
         of Labor.

QUESTIONNAIRE FOR 245 HEADS OF FAMILIES

THIRTY YEARS' CHANGE
IN TEN SELECTED
RURAL AREAS OF PUERTO RICO

Family No._____
"Barrio"_____
Municipality_____
Interviewer_____

1. Who is the head of this family?_____

2. How long have you lived in this "barrio"?_____
   _____

3. Where did you live before?_____
                          Sector   "Barrio"

   _____
   Municipality

4. Where did you live five years ago?_____

5. Tell me, do you own this house? Yes____ No_____
   If you own it: If you do not own it:
   a. Did you buy it?   d. Have you rented it?
   b. Did you build it   e. Don't you pay rent?
      yourself?   f. Other_____
   c. Other

6. Kindly observe and indicate the type of construction.
   a. Concrete_____
   b. Wood and zinc_____
   c. Wood and straw_____
   d. Other: _____
             (Specify)

   _____

   _____

7. Let us now talk about the persons who live in
    this house, how many are they?_____

Let us take one by one, starting with the head of
the household:

What is the relationship to the head of the household?	How many years old?	Married or single?	Last grade completed	Vocational training	Where does he or she work?	What religion is he a member of?
Relationship*	Age	Civil Status**	Education	Training on the job	Present occu-	Religion

* For exact relationship with head of family, please
   indicate:

head	brother or brother-in-law
wife	cousin (man or woman)
husband	aunt or uncle
parents or parents-in-law	niece or nephew
son or stepson	no relationship

**For civil status please specify:

single	living together (less
church marriage	than 5 years)
legal marriage	divorced or separated
consensual (more than	married (lives separately)
5 years living together)	widower

8. Where was the head of the family born?

_____   _____
        "Barrio"   Municipality

9. We have already talked about the persons who
    live with you in the house.

    Have you had any other children living apart or
    who are dead? (children of both husband and wife)
    Yes_____   No_____

    If the answer is yes:
        a. How many children have you had alto-
            gether? _____
        b. Are any of them dead?   Yes____ No____

    If the answer is yes:
        a. How many died before they were five years
            old?

    Is there any member of the family who has moved
    but visits you once in a while?   Yes____ No _____

10. Turning now to another subject, I would like to
    know something about the work and living condi-
    tions here.

    a. Do you own any land?   Yes_____ No_____

    If the answer is yes:

    b. Is this land your own or does it belong to
       the Land Authority?   Property_____
       Land Authority _____
    c. How many "cuerdas" do you have?_____
    d. Do you work your land mostly for your own con-
       sumption or for business purposes?
        1. For your own consumption _____
        2. For business purposes mainly _____
        3. For both your own use and business pur-
            poses _____

11. Do you sell any home-manufactured products?
    Yes _____   No _____

    If the answer is yes:
        1. Which? _____

    _____

12. Please tell me, is getting work here in the "barrio"
    a. Difficult? _____
    b. Somewhat difficult? _____
    c. Easy? _____

13. Please tell me, what was more or less the family income including money, agricultural products, help from relatives, and other sources, last month, December? _____
    November? _____
    October? _____

Family Income in 1963

Sources of Income	Dec.	Nov.	Oct.

	husband_____
	wife_____
Salary	others_____
	_____
	_____

Farm (cash)
   or
Business

Interest accrued

Rentals

Horse Races
   or
Lottery

Received from relatives living
in the United States

*Help from relatives, Public
Welfare, and others

Scholarships and other
aids to students

*Please make any other additional comments. Ex: If
 any months were exceptional

14. Now, in terms of the whole year, what was the total family income?

    a. Less than $500.00 _____
    b. From $500.00 to $1,000.00 _____
    c. From $1,000.00 to $2,000.00 _____
    d. More than $2,000.00 _____

15. Would you say that borrowing money or buying on credit are easy or difficult? Easy _____ Difficult _____

16. With respect to the household expenditures ... how much did you spend, more or less, last week on:

    a. Food (for the whole family) _____
    b. Transportation _____
    c. Recreation _____
    d. Clothing (if you cannot give the weekly expenditures, please give us the monthly or yearly figures) _____
    e. Medicines _____

17. How much did you pay last month for

    a. Electricity _____
    b. Water _____
    c. House Rent _____
    d. Clothing _____ monthly _____ yearly _____
    e. Payment of debts or loans _____
    f. Other expenditures _____
    _____

Now let us talk about the health of the family.

18. Does anyone in the household have physical defects? Yes _____ No _____

    If the answer is yes:
        a. What kind of incapacity does he or she have?

19. Has anyone in the family been ill for some time?
    Yes _____ No _____

    If the answer is yes:
        a. Who? _____
                       relationship to head of family
        b. What illness does he have? _____

20. Besides this, was there any case of serious ill-
    ness in the family in 1963? Yes_____ No _____

    If the answer is yes:
        a. What illness did they have?

21. Is there anyone in the family who is mentally
    ill? Yes _____ No _____

22. Was there any person in the family hospitalized
    last year? Yes _____ No _____

    If the answer is yes:
        a. Where was he or she hospitalized?
            1. Municipal Hospital _____
            2. Health Center _____
            3. District Hospital _____
            4. Private Hospital _____

23. Was any child born in this family last year?
    Yes _____ No _____

    If the answer is yes:
        a. Where was he born?
            1. At home _____
            2. In the hospital _____
        b. Who delivered the child?
            1. A doctor _____
            2. A midwife _____
            3. Others _____
                               specify

Let us now turn to another subject:

24. Is the family interested or not in spiritualism?
    Yes _____ No _____

25. Has the family ever attended spiritualist meet-
    ings or centers? Yes _____ No _____

26. What do you think of spiritualism?

    Comments on question 26.

27. Do you or any member of this household receive
    government help? Yes _____ No _____

    If the answer is yes:
       a. What kind of help do you receive?
          1. Money Yes _____ No _____

    If yes: (How much do you receive monthly?)_____
                                             total
          2. Does the family receive federal sur-
             plus commodities? Yes _____ No _____

    If yes: (a) Why does it receive such help?
               (1) Illness or desertion of father
                   or mother _____
               (2) Incapacity _____
               (3) Old age _____
               (4) Blindness _____
               (5) Illness _____
               (6) Other _____

28. Do you or any other family member receive finan-
    cial help from any other source? Yes____ No____

    If the answer is yes:
       a. From what source?
          1. From religious sects Yes ____ No _____
          2. Other _____
                              specify

29. Has any child in the family been placed in an
    institution? Yes _____ No _____

    If the answer is yes:
       a. Why is he in the institution?
          1. Lack of resources _____
          2. Delinquency _____

           3. Behavior problems _____
           4. Physical defects _____
           5. Mental retardation _____

30. Do you get milk from the Public Health Unit?
     Yes _____ No _____

31. Have the children in this family been given
     shoes from the Government's Shoe Program?
     Yes _____ No _____ There are no children _____

Community activities. (Data for the whole family
are to be requested.)

32. What do you do in your leisure time?   Who?
     a. Baseball games_____   _____
     b. Other athletic games: which?

        _____   _____
        _____   _____
        _____   _____
     c. Cock fights _____   _____
     d. Dances _____   _____
     e. Radio _____   _____
     f. Television _____   _____
     g. Wakes _____   _____
     h. Family parties _____   _____
     i. Rosaries _____   _____
     j. Baptisms and weddings _____   _____
     k. Movies _____   _____
     l. Meetings with neighbors _____   _____
     m. Reading newspapers _____   _____
     n. Reading books _____   _____
     o. Dominoes _____   _____
     p. Card games _____   _____
     q. Other recreational activities___
                                            please
                                            specify

        _____   _____
        _____   _____

33. Is the school used for community activities or
     not? Yes _____ No _____ I do not know _____

34. Does the family take part in school activities
    in the "barrio"?   Yes _____   No _____

    If the answer is yes:
        a. What activities have you attended?
           1. Meetings? Yes _____   No _____
           2. Social activities? Yes _____ No _____

35. Can you read and write Spanish? Yes _____ No ___

36. Can you read English? Very well_____
    A little _____   No _____

37. Do you speak English? Very well_____
    A little _____   No _____

    If the answer is yes:
    The interviewer must make the following ques-
    tions in English.
    Let us see if you and I can understand each
    other in English:
        Please, what is the name of this barrio?
        How many children do you have?
        What time to you go to bed at night?

        Understood and answered everything in
           English _____   some _____
        Understood but did not answer in
           English _____
        Did not understand a thing _____

38. Have you ever traveled outside of Puerto Rico?
    Yes _____   No _____

    If the answer is yes:
        a. What countries have you visited:
           United States: Other countries:
                                   please specify

           Date _____   Date _____
           _____   _____
           _____   _____
           _____   _____
           _____   _____

    b. What was the purpose of your trip?
        First time -
        Second time -
        Third time -
        Other times -
    c. When did you return to Puerto Rico?
    d. Tell me, why did you decide to return?

39. Has the family ever lived in town? Yes ___ No ___

40. Would you say you like living in the country, very much _____ a little _____ or that you do not like it _____

41. Would you like to go on living here or would you rather move to some other place?
Stay here _____ Move _____

42. Has the family moved within the "barrio"?
Yes _____ No _____

    If the answer is yes:
      a. Why did it move?
        1. friends _____
        2. work _____
        3. others (specify) _____
      b. Where do you work?
        1. In this "barrio" _____
        2. In town _____
        3. Some other place (please specify)____

43. Speaking of something else, please tell me, how many rooms are there in this house? (Please include living room, dining room, kitchen, bathroom, and bedrooms) _____

44. Do the male and female members of the family sleep in separate rooms? Yes _____ No _____

45. Does the married couple sleep in a room by itself? Yes _____ No _____

46. Does the house have:
    a. toilet?   Yes _____   No _____
    b. latrine? Yes _____   No _____
    c. shower?   Yes _____   No _____

47. What does the family cook with?   48. What does
                                          it iron
                                          with?

    a. wood Yes _____   No _____   _____
    b. charcoal Yes _____ No _____   _____
    c. kerosene Yes _____ No _____   _____
    d. Electricity Yes ___ No ___   _____
    e. gas   Yes _____   No _____   _____

49. Does the house have running water? Yes ___ No __

    If the answer is no:
        a. Do you get your water from the river?
           Yes _____ No _____
        b. Cistern? Yes _____ No _____
        c. Public faucet? Yes _____   No _____
        d. Other _____
                            specify

50. Is there electric light in the house?
    Yes _____ No _____

    If the answer is no:
    What do you use for light? _____

51. Do you have a radio? Yes _____ No _____
    T.V.? Yes _____ No _____ Lamps hanging from
    the ceiling? Yes _____ No _____

52. Is there a public telephone in the "barrio"?
    Yes _____ No _____

53. Is there a telegraph office? Yes _____ No _____

54. Is there a post office? Yes _____ No _____
    Mail box? Yes _____ No _____

55. Do you use the telephone? Yes _____ No _____
    the telegraph? Yes _____ No _____
    the post office? Yes _____ No _____

56. Where does the family make its purchases?
    a. supermarket _____
    b. store _____
    c. street vendor _____
    d. small store _____
    e. others _____

57. Do you roast and grind your coffee at home?
    Yes _____ No _____

58. Do you buy canned foods? Yes _____ No _____

    If the answer is yes:
        a. Which? _____
                        Please specify

59. How many times a week does the family eat
    meat? _____ Fish? _____

60. How many liters of milk, more or less, does the
    family use daily? _____

61. Do you have a stove? Yes _____ No _____

    If the answer is yes:
        a. What do you use it for?

62. Have you bought anything on credit? Yes___ No ___

    If the answer is yes:
        a. Which?
        b. How are you paying them?

63. How many changes of clothes do you have?
    (dresses) What about your husband? (trousers
    and shirts)

    Wife   Husband
    2 or less _____   _____
    3 to 5 _____   _____
    6 to 10 _____   _____
    more than 10 _____   _____

Military Service:

64. Is there any veteran in the house? Yes ___ No __

     If the answer is yes:
        a. How many? _____
     Does any one of you belong or has belonged to
     the National Guard? Yes _____ No _____
        a. How many? _____

65. How many persons in the house voted in the last
     election? _____

66. How many intend to vote in the coming elections?
     _____

67. Have you had any difficulties with the police?
     Yes _____ No _____

     a. Traffic _____
     b. Children _____
     c. Other reasons _____
                      please specify

68. Do you think one lives better or worse now than
     30 years ago? Better _____ Worse _____
     The same _____ Does not know _____

     a. Reasons

69. Do you think there are now more facilities in
     this community than 30 years ago?

	More	Less	The same
a. school	___	___	___
b. for getting a job	___	___	___
c. medical care	___	___	___
d. hospitalization	___	___	___
e. communication			
roads and highways	___	___	___
telephone	___	___	___
telegraph	___	___	___
automobiles and buses	___	___	___
airplanes	___	___	___
f. housing	___	___	___

70.   Would you say that one eats better or worse now
       than 30 years ago?
       Better _____ Worse _____ The same _____

71.   How does politics compare now with 30 years ago?

       a. Why do you think so?

72.   In general, would you say that we are better
       or worse persons than before? For example:
       a. better neighbors
       b. better citizens
       c. better parents
       d. better children
       e. better spouses

       Why do you think so?

73.   Do you think that employers and employees show
       each other more or less respect now? More mutual
       respect _____ Less mutual respect _____

74.   Do you think that because of the government s
       development program life in this community has
       improved on account of services such as roads,
       electricity, agricultural programs, schools,
       health services, employment services, and
       others? Yes_____ No_____ Does not know _____
       Why do you think so?

75.   If the person interviewed is less than 40 years
       old:
       a. Thirty years ago life was different from
           what it is today; from what you have heard
           about that time, would you like to have
           lived then? Yes _____ No _____
           Why do you feel that way?

       If the person interviewed is over 40 years old:
       b. Thirty years ago life was different from
           what it is today. Would you like to be able
           to live as you did then? Yes _____ No _____
           Why do you feel that way?

DEPTH INTERVIEW QUESTIONNAIRE

Thirty Years of Change in
Ten Selected Areas
of Rural Puerto Rico

Family No. _____
Barrio _____
Municipality _____
Interviewer _____
Person Interviewed _____

1. As I was telling you, we are interested in knowing whether there have been changes in the ways
of life and habits of the people nowadays when
compared to the situation which existed 30 years
ago. . . . When you think of how the landlord
treated his squatters and laborers, would you say
that there have been changes in the relationship
or that now landlords treat their squatters and
laborers more or less the same way they did 30
years ago?

Why do you say so?

Do you like it better the way this relationship
is now, or do you think it was better as it used
to be?

2. And, as far as being up-to-date on the life and
happenings in the barrio, do you think there have
been changes?

Do you think that people are more aware now than
they used to be of the needs and problems of
their barrio, or don't you think so?

How do you account for that?

3. Participation

In connection with community problems, how are
these solved? For example, if a road is to be

made or a school built, what steps are taken?

Who, as a rule, assumes responsibility for such action?

4. Participation

Do you think that something could be done to improve living conditions in this community?

What things, for example?

Who, in your opinion, should be held responsible for this?

Do you think that people in the community could do something to improve conditions here?

What about you?

5. Participation

Have people in this barrio in some way participated in meeting the problems of their barrio?

Please tell me, what have they done? (Get specific details of action undertaken.)

For what type of projects?

What about you? Have you somehow taken action to help solve community problems? What have you done?

6. Knowledge of the Outside World

Would you say that people nowadays are better informed of what is happening outside their barrio? Say, for example, of what happens in the nearest town? In San Juan? In the United States? Or in other countries? (Ask them to give examples and reasons.)

7. <u>Participation</u>

   Are people in this barrio given the opportunity
   to be heard on matters which affect them? For
   example, when the government is to undertake a
   project, such as a road or some other thing that
   affects the people of the barrio?

8. I have been told that in former years people
   used to do business without the need to sign
   any documents because people kept their word.
   What do you think of such a way of doing business?

9. Some people say that formerly life was happier
   than today but others do not share this opinion.

   What is your opinion on this? Do you think that
   people are more or less happy now than they were
   30 years ago?

10. We have been talking about people of former
    times. Do you believe that life was less diffi-
    cult than it is now or do you think it is easier
    nowadays? In which ways is it more difficult?

11. In your opinion, should changes in the ways of
    life come suddenly or gradually? For example:
    (To get jobs; to give people land.) How could
    changes be more rapid?

12. Are people nowadays more or less anxious to im-
    prove their lot than people 30 years ago? Are
    they just the same in this respect?

    With regard to: Education of their children
                     Employment opportunities for
                          their children
                     Home equipment and facilities

13. <u>Goals</u>

    Would you change your job if you could?

14. For what type of work would you change your present job?

15. With regard to salaries, are you satisfied with what one gets now or would you say that salaries are unfair?

16. Do you think that you have been handicapped because of insufficient schooling?
    a. Yes _____
    b. No _____
    c. Does not apply _____

17. Up to what grade would you like your children to get in school?

18. What kind of occupation would you like your children to have?

19. <u>On the value of human beings</u>

    In terms of the consideration and respect among people:

    Would you say that people show more or less respect for others now than formerly? For example:

    A. for neighbors
    B. for parents
    C. for teachers
    D. for police officers.
    Explain.

20. One way of showing respect for people is by considering and respecting their rights.

    Do you think that nowadays people show more or less respect for the rights of others? Example:
    Standing in line and waiting for turn
    Refraining from making noises

21. Would you say that people are more or less hospitable with their neighbors than before?

22. <u>Government</u>

Do you believe that government programs have
helped to improve living conditions in Puerto
Rico?   Yes _____   No _____

If the answer is yes:

How?

If the answer is no:

Why?

23. Should the government expropriate your house and
land to make possible a rural resettlement community and thus improve the living conditions of
many families, how would you feel?

24. If you were not allowed to build a house in the
place you would like to build it because this
would interfere with the government plans, how
would you feel?

25. Have you in some way benefited from government
programs?   Yes _____   No _____

If the answer is yes: How?

If the answer is no: Explain

26. Would you say that you have contributed in a way
to the government's programs for your community?
How?

27. <u>Social Status</u>

You know that in every place people fall in different social classes. How many social classes
are there in this barrio?

28. If we were to classify the families in this barrio into four classes - high, middle high, low

middle and low, to which would you say you belong?
High __   High middle __   Low middle __   Low __

29. And the majority of your friends to which class
would you say they belong?
High __   High middle __   Low middle __   Low __

30. As a rule, do you attend dances, social meetings
and parties of the high class __ high middle __
low middle __ or low __ ?

31. What about your children, do they attend social
activities and parties of families belonging to
the high class __ high middle __ low middle __
or low __ ?

32. What determines, in your opinion, the classification of a family in one social class rather than
in some other?
Income _____   Education _____   Occupation _____
Heredity (family) _____

33. Would you say that it is now easier or more difficult to rise to a higher class than it used to
be?
Easier __ More Difficult __ Why? _____

34. Do you think it possible to rise socially?
Yes _____   No _____.   How?

35. Is it right to have these class differences?
What is your opinion on this?

36. <u>Work</u>

Do you think there have been any changes with regard to the employment situation in your barrio
in the last years? Yes __ No __. If the answer
is yes: a. What are the changes?
         b. What in your opinion is the reason
            for such changes?

37. Would you like your children to work in the field
    of agriculture? Yes __ No __. Why?

38. Do you believe it is right for the woman to work
    outside the home? Yes __ No __ A. Why?

    Same question asked with regard to the following:

    In cases of married women
    In cases of married women with children
    In cases of married women without children.

39. What do you think of labor unions?

    a. What are the advantages for the workers?
    b. What are the disadvantages?

40. <u>Family and relationship among its members</u>

    Do you believe that:

    a. Women should always respect (obey) their hus-
       bands? Yes __ No __

    b. Women should ask their husband's permission
       when they wish to go
       1. outside their home? Yes __ No __
       2. visit their neighbors? Yes __ No __
       3. to town? Yes __ No __

    c. That the husband should not inform the wife of
       his earnings? Yes __ No __

41. Do you think that the fact that the wife works
    outside the home affects somehow the marital re-
    lationship? Yes __ No __ How?

    How, in your opinion, does a husband whose wife
    works outside the home feel? Satisfied ___
    Dissatisfied ___. Explain.

42. Who do you believe should have major responsibil-
    ity for the upbringing of the children?
    Father ___ Mother ___ Both ___. Why do you
    feel that way?

For example: If a girl has a boy friend of whom
the parents do not approve, who
should be the one to discuss it
with her.

43. Do you think that nowadays people feel more or
less responsible for:

grandparents   more ___   less ___
aunts and uncles   ___   ___
parents   ___   ___
children   ___   ___

With regards to the size of the family, do you
think that people in this barrio would like to
have many or few children?

44. What is your opinion with regard to the way children behave nowadays?

45. What do you think of the freedom which youngsters
now enjoy?

46. What about the freedom women enjoy at present?

47. Do you think women should smoke?

48. Do you believe in having women drink alcoholic
beverages at home or at social parties in the
barrio?

49. In your opinion, is juvenile delinquency increasing? Yes ___ No ___   What could the reason be
for it?

50. <u>Religion</u>

Speaking now of religion, would you say that
people are now more or less religious than they
were 30 years ago? More ___ Less ___. What
makes you think so? What is the evidence for
this?

51. Would you say that people nowadays attend church
more or less frequently than before?

52. Do people in your barrio expect you to attend church or does it make no difference to them? whether you attend or not?

53. Would you say that nowadays people believe more or less in the value of prayers (novenas, masses, God's power, etc.) than they did 30 years ago?

54. What in your opinion is the value of religion? How can religion help people? In what cases would you say that religion cannot help people?

55. Do you believe that religion gives people more security and self-confidence or don't you think so? Explain.

56. I am going to give you two different ideas and ask you to tell me with which one you are more in agreement:

    Things which are going to happen to one in this life are already predetermined and one cannot do a thing to change them.

    One can, through self-effort, make one's destiny and make decisions to improve and alter one's life stream and future.

57. Does religion prevent you from doing certain things you would like to do or would you say that it does not interfere with your life in a way that affects you negatively?

58. Do you believe that religion makes people more humane towards their neighbors or would you say that it does not affect them in that way?

59. Do you think people are more or less hospitable now than they were before? For example: do they help their neighbors more?

    (Try to find out whether, due to a better financial and employment situation, people are less hospitable or feel less responsible towards their neighbors in terms of helping them.)

APPENDIX F

SELECTED ANSWERS TO QUESTIONS
FROM DEPTH INTERVIEWS

1a. Question: Do you believe that the manner of the
owner with his laborers is different
or is the same as it was 30 years ago?

Answer: It has changed. The laborers were obliged
to do what the owner of the farm said (30 years ago).
They were obliged to vote for the party of the owner
of the farm. They had no choice but to do what the
owners said. . . . When they gave an opinion it became the law. That is over. Today the laborer has
the protection of the government and they have the
right to accept what they want--or move to some other
place of employment. They like it better this way.
Now the laborers have the permission to go on strike
. . . the power to participate in different discussions . . . and also decide if they want to keep
working or not for certain farm owners.

2nd Question: By living in the village and knowing
what goes on every day, do you think
there have been changes? Are people
more aware than they used to be of
the needs and problems of their barrio? How do you account for this?

Answers: In the municipal government they count on
persons who went back and forth for information on
village doings. Now we have more communication between persons and we know everything right away.
They discuss each sector of the village and their
problems and necessities.

Today the village has leaders, social programs,
and smart hillbillies who keep the village informed.

Because of the increase in population we have
more communication of news . . . nobody wants to
miss anything.

When they have public meetings, the village
citizen can express his opinions and try to find so-
lutions to their problems . . . more ease of expression and communication.

The people find out about improvements in different places and they have a constant concern for
improvement. There is a lot of communication among
the people of the village and they are acquainted
with what has been done and what is going on . . .
not only the village but the whole island (is aware).
Today the people participate in everything. They
can give their own ideas and plan on them if they
want. We get information from television and radio.

Now they know less. Before when something happened the people acted quickly. Now when something
happens the people won't even go as a witness.

Because of the increase horizontal and also ver-
tical, people are more related with each other. We
have more communication because of village planning
which consists of streets and highways.

Now the people comment more. Before you were
afraid to talk and concealed things because if the
Patron found out you would be punished. Today we
have the freedom of speech. . . . Today we have
more freedom. . . . We have roads and highways
which facilitate the passing of news.

We know what happens rapidly. Now we know more
because the kids are smart and know about everything
and tell everything. Now they talk more because before you didn't give any importance to it. Today we
are more intelligent and can understand better what
the consequences might be.

. . . don't pay any attention to what is going
on. Before you didn't know as much because you were
isolated and it took longer to get the news. Now we
have more people to spread the news. Now we have
more relation with the people and know about everything. Because you know the people better, they

bring the news to you. Because of the facilities of
the roads the people travel further and see more.

When good things happen you never know of it
but when something goes wrong you find out. Don't
know anything about before--was too young.

We know about what is going on in the village
now, like we did before.

Today you know right away when somebody gets
sick because the people are always gossiping. I'm
always busy with my housework and I don't have time
to find out. . . . I don't know about before.

Now everybody in the village knows about everything before it has happened. . . . There are so
many lazy people sitting around they find out everything. Because of the civilization we have through
the medium of radio, telephone and television.

Today we find out in about five or ten minutes
all that has happened. Before it took years to find
out (awareness) to the civilization by the policeman.
The people get the information before the patient ar-
rives at the hospital.

If (up-to-date) they build a community center,
a park, and a school. Now there is so much vanity
that the children ask for too much. We have money
for all this. This obliges the changes and movements of people so that they know what is happening
in the village.

3rd Question: How do you resolve the problems of
               the village? Who assumes responsi-
               bility for such action?

Answers: The neighbors get together and sign a peti-
tion and go to see the Mayor. Generally, the person
most interested is in charge of this.

4th Question: Do you think that something can be
               done to improve the life in this

community? What things? Who should
be responsible? Can the people do
something. How about you?

Answers: A factory. We have a group of persons who
are in charge of soliciting what is needed. They
get together in a school and when the Mayor comes in
they tell him what they need for the village. Yes
(the people should do something) . . . . Yes (I
should).

Here we need water or public faucets. We need
electric lights; also if we are going to better our
life we should fix the streets and public telephones. . . . I believe that the Municipal Government should be in charge. Nothing (for people to
do). If I could, I would like to have an interview
with someone (to improve conditions).

5th Question: Have people in this barrio partici-
                pated in meeting the problems of
                their barrio? What have they done?
                What types of projects?

Answers: Neighbors get together and dig the ditches
and drains, etc. Also in the project of mutual help.
They work 203 days and if they cannot keep going
they pay 2 or 3 people to finish the work for them.
(I) participated in the project houses and by sign-
ing.

8th Question: In previous days people made negotia-
                tions without signing documents.
                What do you think about this? Can
                one rely in business matters on the
                spoken word or would you say that it
                is advisable now to have the docu-
                ments signed? Why?

Answers: It was a mistake. They made traps. There
were cases where great capital in a family where the
head passed away (the family) did not even know how
much he had. Now with the income tax you have to
keep a record of all expenditures. Documents should

be signed. This is done in front of a lawyer . . .
and even with that they fail. We have seen a lot of
court cases and think that they are not valid. When
the lawyers look at the papers they try to make out
that there are five legs on a cat.

In those days it was all right. They were mus-
tached men and men of their word. Now it has to be
signed. Now the word has no value. If someone
comes with more knowledge, the word is no longer
valid. This means that the other one has to be prepared. . . .

9th Question: Some people say that formerly life
                was happier than today but others do
                not share this opinion. What is your
                opinion on this? Do you think that
                people are more or less happy now
                than they were 30 years ago?

Answers: Before it was easier, they had more consideration for the poor people. Today the people
are too selfish. Before you made less money but you
could do more with it. Everybody had their meals because they cultivated. Now everything is sugar cane.

10th Question: Do you believe that life was less dif-
                ficult than it is now or do you think
                it is easier nowadays? In which ways
                is it more difficult?

Answers: Before you had more difficulties. Now we
have ambulances, roads, and lights, transportation
and medical facilities.

36th Question: Work: Do you think there have been
                any changes with regard to the employ-
                ment situation in your barrio in the
                last years? What are the changes, if
                so: Your opinion for the reason for
                change.

Answers: Now we have to pay double to the people
for the same kind of work that they used to do before for less salary. With the change in atmosphere

and life everything is high and what you make isn't
enough.

Before they had less work. Now they can cut
sugar cane everywhere and they have the facilities
to go to town to look for work. The Government
gives help in sowing and in that way they cultivate
more places and . . . make more work. The Government gives money and fertilizer to sow the sugar
cane and tobacco.

Before you would not find the women working but
now because of so many factories we have women working and more men working.

Before the only place you could find a job was
on a farm, now you can find a job any place even in
construction. Because of the administration of the
Government--it is good.

We have more movement or work. There is construction everywhere and building projects. We owe
all that to the government.

The factories are close. Before all the work
was with sugar cane. Today we have more variety.
Factories are established by Americans.

Today we work less and make more money. Before
you had more work to do but you made less money.
The government and the legislature are the ones that
move all these things.

Now they can go a lot farther to look for work.
There are more facilities for transportation.

Now there is always work. You can leave here
and always find a job in another place. We owe this
to the new government.

We are progressing in work. If you don't work
in one thing you can in another. To the party, Popular Government (reason for change).

We now have factories which didn't exist before.
We have favorable changes in agriculture in modernizing and mechanizing. The community has grown up and
we need better and more opportunities for work so
that the people can win their bread.

There is more opportunity for employment and
more salary. Now everybody wants to own their home
and there are a lot of them under construction.
They have highways, cement and louver factories--
all these you need for construction.

Before most of the work was done by hand, today
we have more machines and more preparation and a
greater variety of work. To the government (reason
for change).

Believe it is equal.

It's easier to find a job. As soon as the people progress they find a better job. Now we have
more factories, more construction and that's why it
is easier. Because of progress. As the years go by
we have advanced culturally and the people want to
know more; the town aspires to more progress.

37th Question: Would you like your children to work
                in the field of agriculture? Why?

Answers: No--once they had a farm and the work came
to a stop.

The environment of agriculture is dismal and
the work is too hard.

We have a farm at El Rosario which we have
leased for many years as no one in the family is interested in living in the country far away from civilization and progress.

They are working in more professions. When I
retire I'll dedicate all my time to agriculture.

You don't have to kill yourself working in agriculture. You still make money.

To do both things. Go to school and find a different job. Agriculture is a good idea for a business.

No, he's not going to like it because he wants to be a mechanic. If he can't afford to go to school he will have to take what he can get. But if he finishes his education he can get a better job.

Yes.

Everything on the outside is so high that if we plant our own crops it will be easier to have something to eat.

That's my pleasure. Work in agriculture.

You have to make provision for bad times.

Because agriculture is a necessity in this country, I would be proud of a son who would help the country through agriculture.

After the lands belong to you, it is good and you can make profit.

Yes, because I am delighted with agriculture.

If he wants it, yes. Cultivation of the farm is good business. Now we don't work on agriculture too much. If you know how to work them you can have success.

38th Question: Do you believe it is right for the woman to work outside the home? Why? Married women? Married women with children? Without children?

Answers: If they don't have any children, they can work out.

The mother has enough work with her children and she should take care of her home. A married woman ought to help her husband.

No. The women to start have the intention of working to help the husband but then after a while they take off and gad about with other men.

The man that gets married should have his wife at home and provide her with what she needs.

People don't have as much respect for women who work outside as they do for those who stay home.

With the understanding that she is to help her husband.

It is necessary in case her husband gets sick.

The baby should not be left alone. When the children are grown up, the problem is the women's. The first obligation of a married woman is her children.

No.

Always if the salary of the woman is necessary to the economy of the home.

The house is not taken care of the same and the wife is not waiting for her husband. (She should not leave the house because the only time she should work out is if she is working with her husband.) He is opposed under all circumstances.

She abandons the house and the children.

Yes, in case of necessity.

It all depends if it doesn't interfere with the education of the children. Any mother should not abandon her children nor leave them with the maid.

It is an advantage for both of them to work before they have any children. After they have children it is better for the woman to take care of the children to insure the tranquility of the home.

39th Question: What do you think of labor unions?
                  Advantages _for_ the workers? Disad-
                  vantages.

Answers: Social security, contribution, etc. We
try to help the Patron with the laborer, as soon as
the Union starts the patron doesn't worry and lets
the Union solve the problems of the laborers and
their families. The Patron stays away from the
Union. If a laborer needs a loan, the Union con-
cedes it and tries to help all they can. Many
Unions stir up hate.

      Sometimes it is good but most of the time it
interferes with the progress of the business--fo-
menting strikes and lack of understanding. They
have insurance, they make claims to the Patron,
raise of salary. The Patron doesn't worry about the
problems of the laborer--without the Unions the Patron and the laborer would work better together with
regulations.

      Don't know. The husband doesn't belong to the
Union (works on the train).

      They're good. Before the poor had no defense,
no one to back them up--today they are protected.
They have Unions that abuse--they steal from the laborers and they go away with the money. The ones of
the Government are good.

      They are necessary because previously the la-
borers were abused.

      They have a limit to the hours worked and a
fair minimum salary. Sometimes the laborers claims
are unjust to business. Example--you never miss the
water till the well runs dry.

      Some benefits for the Patron and for the labor-
ers. They discuss problems without friction between
Patron and laborer. Sometimes the laborers ask so
much from the Patron that it hurts the Patron and
then they close the factories because they can't
agree.

If it weren't for the Unions, the Patron would have no respect for the laborers. If a Union member passes away, they help the widow with money.

Help with money, for accidents, etc. Before there was nothing like this.

The Union has advantages because it makes settlements. They give employment and help unemployment.

They are good. Struggle for the well-being of the laborer. Before, nobody backed them up. Not any (disadvantages).

They are good. In case of necessity the Unions have a meeting and agree to use the funds in case of the sickness of a member. It doesn't have any disadvantages.

It is a defense organization. In union there is strength. Hospitalization, if you get sick, you get sick benefits. Not any (disadvantages).

It is good. By having a Union you can get more power through unity.

It's good. It gives benefits for sickness, unemployment and medicines for the children.

They are good and favor the worker. Favors the worker very much (advantages). There is no disadvantage.

BIBLIOGRAPHY

BIBLIOGRAPHY*

Annotated Bibliography

Brameld, Thomas. <u>The Remaking of a Culture: Life and Education in Puerto Rico</u>. New York: Harper and Brothers, 1959. 478 pp.

   This book is an analysis and appraisal of Puerto Rican culture today. It is addressed to Puerto Ricans and to people in other countries concerned with how a frontier culture seeks to remake itself, especially with how it wishes to enlist education in that remaking.

<u>Community Change: An Action Program in Puerto Rico</u>. September 15, 1953, issue of <u>Journal of Social Issues</u>, Vol. IX, No. 2. Articles by Stuart Chase, "Redesigning an Economy"; Fred G. Wale, "The Division of Community Education"; Carmen Isales and Fred G. Wale, "The Field Program"; Raul Munoz, Belen M. Serra, Angelina de Poca, "Research and Evaluation in a Program of Community Education"; F. Cannell and Stephen B. Withey, "Concluding Comments."

   Discusses this unusual education program in rural Puerto Rico, which is concerned not with personal development of individuals, but with people living together in communities and tries to stimulate them to use their own aptitudes for solution of community problems. Includes results of survey on present socio-economic conditions in rural communities, as well as social and community activity.

---

*Note: This bibliography has not been compiled as a complete list of Puerto Rican studies but has been selected for purposes of this project.

Edel, Matthew. "Land Reform in Puerto Rico, 1940-
      1959," Caribbean Studies (October, 1962 and
      January, 1963).
            Article gives in narrative style the story
      of land reform.

Fernandez Mendes, Eugenio (ed.). "Portrait of a So-
      ciety." Mimeographed book of readings of Puerto
      Rican Sociology. Río Piedras, P.R., 1956.
      (Puerto Rican Collection, University of Puerto
      Rico.)
            Includes following articles: Kathleen L.
      Wolf, "Growing Up and Its Price in Three Puerto
      Rican Subcultures," in Psychiatry, November,
      1952. Article presents contrasting ways in
      which children grow up in three different class
      groups: small rural coffee and tobacco farmers,
      sugar workers, and middle class of small rural
      town. Patterns of adult behavior and training
      of children. S. L. Descartes, "Historical Ac-
      count of Recent Land Reform in Puerto Rico,"
      in Caribbean Land Tenure Symposium, Caribbean
      Commission, Washington, D.C., 1947. John P.
      Angelli, "San Lorenzo: A Case Study of Recent
      Migrations in Interior Puerto Rico," in The
      American Journal of Economics and Sociology,
      January, 1952. Analysis of instability as re-
      flected in population shift of one small seg-
      ment of interior Puerto Rico as people abandon
      rural areas on account of decline of coffee and
      tobacco crops.

Hansen, Millard, and Wells, Henry (eds.). Puerto
      Rico: A Study in Democratic Development. Jan-
      uary, 1953, issue of The Annals of the American
      Academy of Political and Social Sciences. Vol.
      CCLXXXV. 166 pp.
            Includes articles: Luis Muñoz Marín et
      al., "Political Development"; Harvey S. Perloff,
      "Transforming the Economy"; J. Mayone Stycos
      and Reuben Hill, "The Prospects of Birth Con-
      trol in Puerto Rico"; J. J. Galbraith and Caro-
      lyn Shaw Solo, "Puerto Rican Lessons in Economic
      Development"; Teodore Moscoso, "Industrial De-
      velopment in Puerto Rico"; Rafael Pico, "The

Role of Planning in Puerto Rico"; Simon Rotten-
burg, "Labor's Role in Industrialization";
Julian H. Steward, "Culture Patterns of Puerto
Rico"; Francisco Ayala, "The Transformation of
the Spanish Heritage"; Kingsley Davis, "Puerto
Rico: A Crowded Island"; R. G. Tugwell, "What
Next for Puerto Rico?" Also text of constitution of the Commonwealth of Puerto Rico. The
purpose of this collection is to describe in
some detail what happened in Puerto Rico between 1941 and 1953 and explain its significance.

Hanson, Earl Parker. Transformation--The Story of
Modern Puerto Rico. New York: Simon & Shuster,
1955. 416 pp.
The story of Puerto Rican development with
emphasis on the role played by its leaders, particularly Muñoz Marín, and from Introduction by
Chester Bowles, "We are neither radical nor conservative," says Muñoz Marín, "we are merely
realistic. . . ."

Hill, Reuben, Stycos, J. Mayone, and Back, Kurt W.
The Family and Population Control: A Puerto
Rican Experiment in Social Change. Chapel
Hill: University of North Carolina Press, 1959.
481 pp. A cooperative study of the Social Science Research Center, University of Puerto Rico,
and the Institute for Research in Social Science,
University of North Carolina.
Population is still increasing in Puerto
Rico, one of the world's most densely populated
areas. This study concentrates on 633 families
of the lowest income group in an effort to determine why families act as they do re fertility and how they might be induced to change.

Koenig, Nathan. A Comprehensive Agricultural Pro-
gram for Puerto Rico. Washington, D.C.: U.S.
Government Printing Office, 1953. 299 pp.,
tables, graphs, illus.
This two-year cooperative study by U.S.
Department of Agriculture and Commonwealth of

Puerto Rico deals with problems of agriculture
in Puerto Rico against the background of the
people and their land. Gives descriptions and
statistics of progress in rural life and makes
recommendations.

Landy, David. Tropical Childhood: Cultural Trans-
    mission and Learning in a Rural Puerto Rican
    Village. Chapel Hill: University of North
    Carolina Press, 1959. 291 pp. illus.
        Studies 18 families as representative of
    the lower-class population dependent upon sugar
    cane and discusses composition of the family,
    living conditions, health and disease, religion,
    income, family economics, formal education (in-
    cluding rural Second Units), traditional atti-
    tudes toward sex, courtship, and childbearing.

Lewis, Gordon. K. "Puerto Rico: A Case Study of
    Change in an Underdeveloped Area," Journal
    of Politics, XVII (1955), 614-50.
        The thesis is that American occupation and
    control have left a real colonial psychology in
    the Puerto Rican people. Though material trans-
    formation since 1898 has been remarkable and
    planned progress in health, education, agricul-
    tural reform, public works, industrialization,
    etc., has been great, Puerto Rico is still a
    society subordinate in law and fact to the
    American sovereign.

Mills, C. Wright, Senior, Clarence, and Goldsen,
    Rose Kohn. The Puerto Rican Journey: New
    York's Newest Migrants. New York: Harper and
    Brothers, 1950. 238 pp.
        A report on Puerto Rican migration to New
    York City, based on interviews with a member of
    1,113 families, covering some 5,000 persons.
    Compares migrants' new environment in New York
    with former Puerto Rican environment.

Mintz, Sidney W. Worker in the Cane: A Puerto
    Rican Life History. New Haven: Yale Univer-
    sity Press, 1960. 288 pp. illus.

Based on taperecorded interviews with a
cane cutter of a small village of Santa Isabel,
the book tells his life story, partly in his
own words, with background material by author.

Morales Otero, P. et al. "Health and Socio-Economic
Studies in the Tobacco, Coffee, and Fruit
Regions," The Puerto Rico Journal of Public
Health and Tropical Medicine. New York: Colum-
bia University Press (March, 1939).
Study conducted with 2,567 rural families
in tobacco regions, 2,488 families in coffee
regions, and 688 families in fruit regions.
Data on living conditions, health, social con-
ditions, economic conditions.

Perloff, Harvey S. Puerto Rico's Economic Future:
A Study in Planned Development. Chicago:
University of Chicago Press, 1950. 434 pp.
illus. Also London, England: Cambridge University Press, and Toronto, Canada: W. J.
Gage & Co., Limited.
Based largely on a study sponsored by the
Social Science Research Center of the University of Puerto Rico, the book gives historical
background, political and economic developments
since 1898, and appraises the island's industrialization program in terms of modern social
science. The program has developed considerably in the sixteen years since the book was
published.

Petrullo, Vincenzo. Puerto Rican Paradox. Phila-
delphia: University of Pennsylvania Press,
1947. 173 pp.
This book is more or less a popular approach intended to give an over-all picture of
Puerto Rico and its people. It is chiefly concerned with what happens to a people when de-
nied self-government, and examines the future.

Roberts, Lydia J., and Stefani, Rosa Luisa. Pat-
terns of Living in Puerto Rican Families. Rio
Piedras: University of Puerto Rico, 1949.
Presents a picture of living conditions in

Puerto Rican families, based on an island-wide
study of a representative sample of about 1,044
families (601 in rural areas) in 25 municipalities. Findings in 230 tables are for latter
part of 1946, and include sections on housing,
home conditions, health, diets, educational and
cultural advantages, and implications of the
findings.

Rodríguez, A., Jr. The Second Unit and the Rural
    School Problem of Puerto Rico. San Juan, P.R.:
    Imprenta Venezuela, 1945. 238 pp.
        This study was accepted as part of require-
    ments for Doctor of Education degree, School of
    Education, Indiana University. It traces devel-
    opment of the Second Unit Rural Schools from
    their establishment in 1928 as community schools
    and consolidated rural schools of a vocational
    character. Their objectives included improving
    living conditions in rural communities through
    vocational guidance, raising productive capaci-
    ty of the people, and providing a program of
    social and health instruction based on needs of
    country people.

Rosario, José C., and Carrión, Justina. "Rebusca
    Sociológica," Summer School Review. Rio Pie-
    dras: University of Puerto Rico, (July 6, 1937,
    August 2, 1937).
        The first article gives data from a study
    of social and economic conditions of 105 fami-
    lies in a small typical rural community of the
    coffee region. The second deals with the same
    type of data for 105 families in the sugar cane
    region. Both articles include excerpts from
    statements made by the people in colloquial
    Spanish, showing attitudes re family, marriage,
    women, religion, etc.

School of Public Health and Administrative Medicine,
    Columbia University, and Department of Health
    of Puerto Rico. Medical and Hospital Care in
    Puerto Rico. 1962. 425 pp., graphs, tables.
        This report, submitted to the Governor and
    the Legislature of Puerto Rico, is the result

of a three-year cooperative study of patterns
of hospital and medical care of 2,951 families
throughout the island and an island-wide survey
of facilities. It discusses old unsolved problems and new problems just emerging and concludes that, though much progress has been made,
there is still a serious problem of substandard
conditions and care. Recommends a comprehensive long-range plan.

Steward, Julian, et al.   The People of Puerto Rico:
     A Study in Social Anthropology. Urbana: Uni-
     versity of Illinois Press, 1956. 540 pp.
          A cultural historical study of behavior
     patterns of certain of the Puerto Rican people
     with emphasis on modification of cultural form,
     function, and pattern of modern Puerto Rico.
     Concerned especially with features which dis-
     tinguish people engaged in major forms of agri-
     cultural production. It presents its analysis
     in the form of hypotheses applicable to other
     world areas. Intensive analysis of selected
     communities and subcultures: Tabara, a tobac-
     co and mixed crops municipality; San José, a
     traditional coffee municipality; Nocora, gov-
     ernment-owned sugar plantation; Canamelar, a
     rural sugar plantation.

Stycos, J. Mayone.   Family and Fertility in Puerto
     Rico: A Study of the Lower Income Group. New
     York: Columbia University Press, 1955. 332 pp.
          This book discusses the influence of pre-
     vailing sexual norms, family structure, ideol-
     ogies, and other aspects of social structure.
     It represents the first stage of a three-stage
     project on human fertility in Puerto Rico. It
     provides a picture of lower-class family, in-
     cluding child-rearing, courtship, and marriage.

Tumin, Melvin, with Feldman, Arnold. Social Class
     and Social Change in Puerto Rico. Princeton,
     N.J.: Princeton University Press, 1961. 549 pp.
          A study of the Social Science Research
     Center, College of Social Sciences, University

of Puerto Rico. Based on 999 interviews with
family heads who form a roughly representative
sample of the Puerto Rican population. This
study analyzes the class structure and concludes that the single most effective reducer
of past inequalities has been free public education. The study asks what men are as a result of their relative positions and what they
become when they change position.

Unannotated Bibliography

Collazo-Collazo, Jenaro, et al. Development of a
    Level-of-Living Scale for Puerto Rican Rural
    Families. Bulletin 156. Río Piedras: Agri-
    cultural Experiment Station, University of
    Puerto Rico (October, 1960). 27 pp.

Diffie, Bailey K., and Diffie, Justine Whitfield.
    Porto Rico: A Broken Pledge. New York: The
    Vanguard Press, 1931. 252 pp.

Extension of Social Security to Puerto Rico and the
    Virgin Islands. Report to the Committee on
    Ways and Means. Washington, D.C.: U.S. Govern-
    ment Printing Office, February 6, 1960.

Garver, Earl S., and Fincher, Ernest B. Puerto Rico:
    Unsolved Problem. Elgin, Ill.: Elgin Press,
    1945. 110 pp. Illus., maps.

Hanson, Alice C., and Perez, Manuel A. Incomes and
    Expenditures of Wage Earners in Puerto Rico.
    Government of Puerto Rico, Department of Labor,
    in cooperation with U.S. Bureau of Labor Statis-
    tics, Bulletin No. 1 (May 1, 1947). 152 pp.
    Illus.

Helsinger, Justus G. Serving Rural Puerto Rico:
    A History of Eight Years of Service by the
    Mennonite Church. Scottdale, Pa.: Mennonite
    Publishing House, 1952. 232 pp. Illus.

Howell, Brandon. "Patterns of Rural Settlement in
        Puerto Rico." Río Piedras: University of
        Puerto Rico, 1945. In a mimeographed collec-
        tion of papers for an Economic Planning Seminar.

Lewis, Gordon K. Puerto Rico: Freedom and Power
        in the Caribbean. New York: MR Press, 1963.
        626 pp.

Mellado, Ramon A. Culture and Education in Puerto
        Rico. Bureau of Publications, Puerto Rico
        Teachers Association. Educational monograph
        No. 1, 1948.

Packard, Walter E. "The Land Authority and Demo-
        cratic Processes in Puerto Rico," Inter-
        American Affairs, II, No. 1 (Summer, 1948),
        49-101.

A Summary in Fact and Figures: 1. Progress in
        Puerto Rico. 2. Puerto Rico Migration. New
        York: Migration Division, Department of Labor,
        Commonwealth of Puerto Rico (January, 1959).
        21 pp.

Tugwell, Rexford Guy. The Stricken Land. Garden
        City, New York: Doubleday and Co., 1947.
        703 pp.

Vazquez-Calcerrada, P. B. Castaner: A Study of a
        Planned Rural Community in Puerto Rico. Río
        Piedras; Agricultural Experiment Station,
        University of Puerto Rico, 1947.

White, Trumbull. Puerto Rico and Its People. New
        York: Frederick A. Stokes Co., 1938. 383 pp.

ABOUT THE AUTHORS

James R. Bourne's personal knowledge of Puerto Rico goes back to 1929 when he became manager of two large fruit canneries there. In 1933 he left this position to serve as Administrator of the Puerto Rico Emergency Relief Administration, which gave work and relief to approximately 200,000 people. For the next three years he directed a program aimed at developing agricultural and industrial diversification to make Puerto Ricans more self-supporting--a program credited with planting the seed which later developed into the famous "Operation Bootstrap." From 1943 to 1945, as Chief of the Caribbean Section of the Foreign Economic Administration, he was responsible for supplying and obtaining supplies from that area. Mr. Bourne is a graduate of Yale.

His wife, Dorothy Dulles Bourne, from 1930 to 1934 was Supervisor of Social Work for the Insular Department of Education in Puerto Rico, where she developed and supervised a program of training social workers in rural vocational schools. She founded and served as the first Director of the School of Social Work at the University of Puerto Rico and taught there. For the Puerto Rico Emergency Relief Administration from 1935 to 1936, she headed the Social Service Department, which dealt with child welfare, medical social work, community projects, and maternal health. She also served on committees in Puerto Rico concerned with workers' education, consumers' cooperatives, nutrition and budget service, and care of crippled children. Between 1949 and 1962 she taught sociology at Bard College, becoming Dean and Professor of Sociology in 1956. Mrs. Bourne is a graduate of Smith College.

In 1963 the Bournes returned to Puerto Rico to conduct research for the present study.